Feminist Heidegger

SUNY series in Contemporary Continental Philosophy

Dennis J. Schmidt, editor

Feminist Heidegger
Sex, Gender, and the Politics of Birth

JILL DROUILLARD

Published by State University of New York Press, Albany

© 2025 State University of New York

All rights reserved

Printed in the United States of America

No part of this book may be used or reproduced in any manner whatsoever without written permission. No part of this book may be stored in a retrieval system or transmitted in any form or by any means including electronic, electrostatic, magnetic tape, mechanical, photocopying, recording, or otherwise without the prior permission in writing of the publisher.

Links to third-party websites are provided as a convenience and for informational purposes only. They do not constitute an endorsement or an approval of any of the products, services, or opinions of the organization, companies, or individuals. SUNY Press bears no responsibility for the accuracy, legality, or content of a URL, the external website, or for that of subsequent websites.

EU GPSR Authorised Representative:
Logos Europe, 9 rue Nicolas Poussin, 17000, La Rochelle, France
contact@logoseurope.eu

For information, contact State University of New York Press, Albany, NY
www.sunypress.edu

Library of Congress Cataloging-in-Publication Data

Name: Drouillard, Jill, 1983– author.
Title: Feminist Heidegger : sex, gender, and the politics of birth / Jill Drouillard.
Description: Albany : State University of New York Press, [2025] | Series: SUNY series in contemporary continental philosophy | Includes bibliographical references and index.
Identifiers: LCCN 2024038249 | ISBN 9798855801484 (hardcover : alk. paper) | ISBN 9798855801491 (ebook) | ISBN 9798855801477 (pbk. : alk. paper)
Subjects: LCSH: Heidegger, Martin, 1889–1976. | Woman (Philosophy) | Feminist theory.
Classification: LCC B3279.H49 D76 2025 | DDC 193—dc23/eng/20241106
LC record available at https://lccn.loc.gov/2024038249

For Jasper

Contents

Acknowledgments   xi

Abbreviations: Selected Works by Martin Heidegger   xv

Introduction   1
    Feminist Heidegger: Sex, Gender, and the Politics of Birth   1
    The Challenge of Embracing a Collective Identity that
        Preserves Differences   7
    Feminist Standpoint Epistemology and *My* Reading of Heidegger   10
    Rethinking the Body and Birth of Finite Dasein   14

Part I
Heidegger's Sex/Gender Neutrality and the Politics of Birth

Chapter 1
"You're Already off the Clock": Temporalizing Laboring Dasein   23
    A Phenomenology of Laboring Dasein: Primordial Time
        versus Shared Time   24
    Authentic Temporality as a *Poiēsis* of Birth   33

Chapter 2
Problem: What Is Woman? The Hermeneutics of Sex/Gender Facticity   41
    Problem: What Is Woman?   41
    Ontology: The Hermeneutics of Facticity and Ontological
        Sex Inequality   42

The Metaphysical Foundations of Logic and the Primacy of
Sexual Difference 46
    Transcendence, World-Forming, and Care 46
    The Privileging of Sexual Difference and Biology 49
    Implications of Heidegger's Sexed/Gendered Bodies
        (*Körper/Leib*) 56

CHAPTER 3
Queering *Gestell*: Partial Enframing, Racial Breeding, and Assisted
Reproductive Technology 59
    Framing 60
    Reproductive Enframing 64
    Coda: Race as Technology in Reproductive Enframing 68
        Race as Technology 68
        The (Re)Production of Race in France 75
        Rethinking Race and Reproductive Enframing with
            Heidegger 80

CHAPTER 4
Bodyreading Grumet and Heidegger: "Setting Up" Feminist
Pedagogy and "Reproducing" the Curriculum 83
    Hermes, Messenger and Caregiver 84
        Bitter Milk and Standing Reserve Classrooms 87
    Setting Up Feminist Pedagogy 91

Part II
Heidegger's Grounding of Sex/Gender
and the Politics of Birth

CHAPTER 5
A Feminist Reading of the *Black Notebooks*: The Eternal Feminine,
Peasant Women, and "Being a People" 99
    The Historicity of Beyng and the Eternal Feminine 100
    The Blood and Soil of Peasant Women 105
    Sexual Tension in Trakl's Poetic Work: (Pro)Creating a People 110

CHAPTER 6
Bridging Heidegger after the *Black Notebooks*: Of Worlds,
Not Words 125
    Worldless Jews, Genos, and Polemos 126

Borderlands, Multiplicitous Selves, and Playful World-Traveling 129
    Anzaldúa's Bridge and Anaximander's Apeiron 135
Zurn's Trans Poetics of Dust 139
    The Creative Impotence of the University and Making
        Sense at the Margins 139
    The "In-Between" and Border Consciousness of Dust 143

NOTES 147

BIBLIOGRAPHY 181

INDEX 193

Acknowledgments

This book was born at a time when I was warned of the tension between maternal and intellectual labor. Robyn Ferrell once wrote that to write while the baby was asleep was a fantasy, and that message really stuck with me.¹ I like to think of this book as a product of maternal and intellectual labor, and not just because I birthed a child and a dissertation in the same year, but because *I wrote with my body*, a body Heidegger's work is so often said to neglect. The tension between production and reproduction is prevalent throughout the history of philosophy, and despite strides in gender equality, it remains a struggle for those who birth within academia. Those of us who are privileged enough to mitigate this tension know that we could not have done it alone.

Thank you, James, for coparenting with me—we made and continue to shape someone incredible. Thanks to my parents for their constant support, as I reckon with traditions passed down to me. Thanks to Anne O'Byrne, whose inspiring work and continued encouragement helped me better understand how meaning emerges within such generational inheritance. I am grateful to my dissertation supervisor Jean-Michel Besnier and to the Sorbonne for providing me with a research grant. Thanks to my "academic father," John Rose, for mentoring me throughout my undergraduate studies and beyond, and for passing down his knowledge of Heidegger. I am also indebted to Jennifer Merchant for her unwavering mentorship and confidence in me.

So many small moments and motivational jolts have helped me see this project through. Thanks to the following women of the Heidegger Circle for sharing their wisdom, laughter, and wine: Dana S. Belu, Róisín Lally, Kate Davies, Becca Longtin, Babette Babich, Trish Glazebrook, Jessica Elkayam, and Leslie MacAvoy. Trish read an early version of chapter 1 and encouraged me to pursue it. Thanks to Trish and Susanne Dawn Claxton for including an earlier version of chapter 2 in their edited volume *Heidegger, Dasein, and Gender: Thinking the Unthought* (Lanham, MD: Rowman and Littlefield, 2024). Thanks to Matthew Kruger-Ross for being "my biggest cheerleader" and to Joel Michael Reynolds for saying "Why not?" when I doubted whether I could publish this.

Thanks to Gregory Fried, Camisha Russell, John Rose, Josh Dohmen, and Kevin Aho for reading draft portions of this work and for offering helpful comments. Thanks to Camille Froidevaux-Metterie and Hélène L'Heuillet for being on my dissertation committee. Thanks to Richard Polt and Gregory Fried for their meticulous guidelines and instructions for citing Heidegger. And thanks to Richard for his amazing penmanship that appears on the front cover. I selected quotes from Heidegger's work that pertain to "the woman question," and he graciously accepted to lend his hand. Thanks to Scott Campbell for inviting me to participate in a symposium for *Gatherings: The Heidegger Circle Annual*, a space that allowed me to share Heidegger's early thoughts on being a sexed or gendered human being. Thanks to the Heidegger Circle, at whose meetings I shared initial musings of some of this work. Thanks to Casey Rentmeester for his ongoing words of encouragement and for, along with Jeff Warren, editing and including my previous work in a volume on *Heidegger and Music*. Thanks to Gail Weiss and Alan D. Shrift for editing and including a section of chapter 3 in a Society for Phenomenology and Existential Philosophy (SPEP) edition of the *Journal of Speculative Philosophy* 36, no. 3 (2022): 194–205, https://doi.org/10.5325/jspecphil.36.2.0194. Portions of that text are reprinted here with permission from Penn State University Press. Thanks to Jeffrey Gower for confirming a translation question regarding GA 63.

Thanks to *philo*SOPHIA: a society for continental feminism for continuously offering a space to share my work. Perry Zurn presented portions of the chapter "Dust" from his forthcoming book, *How We Make Each Other: Trans Poetics in and at the Edge of the University*, at the 2022 meeting. "Dust" inspired the last section of chapter 6. Thank you, Perry, for entrusting me with an early draft of your work.

Merci mille fois à Edouard pour son soutien, et merci aux amis du Bistro de la ferme. Thanks to Layla and Jason for their support and friendship. Thanks to Luisa Benton for making her employees feel valued. Thanks to the Mississippi University for Women for providing me with travel funding to present my research at various conferences. Thanks to the "Works in Progress" group at Mississippi State University for inviting me to discuss an initial draft of my introduction and to the University of Mississippi for inviting me to present a larger overview of this work. Thanks to Steven for his lively conversations and for buoying me up as a "rock star." Thanks to Andy Amato and folks at the North Texas Philosophical Association for inviting me to present aspects of this research. Thanks to Clare Hemmings for supervising my master's thesis on Heidegger and for uttering a gem I'll never forget—"Heidegger is not your daddy." Thanks to Judy Beris for giving me the women's studies books from her office after retiring, a gesture of intellectual inheritance I'll always remember. And finally, thanks to Dennis Schmidt for seeing promise in my work and to Michael Rinella for making my experience with SUNY Press a positive one.

Abbreviations

Selected Works by Martin Heidegger

BDT	"Building Dwelling Thinking"
GA 2	*Being and Time*
GA 26	*The Metaphysical Foundations of Logic*
GA 29/30	*The Fundamental Concepts of Metaphysics: World, Finitude, Solitude*
GA 40	*Introduction to Metaphysics*
GA 63	*Ontology—The Hermeneutics of Facticity*
GA 65	*Contributions to Philosophy (Of the Event)*
GA 89	*Zollikon Seminars: Protocols—Conversations—Letters*
GA 94	*Ponderings II–VI: Black Notebooks 1931–1938*
GA 95	*Ponderings VII–XI: Black Notebooks 1938–1939*
GA 96	*Ponderings XII–XV: Black Notebooks 1939–1941*
QCT	"The Question Concerning Technology"
OEG	"On the Essence of Ground"
OWA	"The Origin of the Work of Art"

Note: Heidegger's work will be cited in the Notes and in the Bibliography according to a citation guide created by Gregory Fried and Richard Polt.

Introduction

Feminist Heidegger: Sex, Gender, and the Politics of Birth

"Feminist Heidegger" seems like a contradiction in terms. Heidegger himself was no feminist. Furthermore, feminist scholars, whose agenda is necessarily political in their fight for sex/gender equality have distanced themselves from the self-proclaimed political naivete of a man who was a member of the National Socialist Party. And yet, Heidegger generates important resources for feminist thinking. His philosophy offers tools for analyzing the historical contingency of our being, including attributes such as sex/gender, and his story serves as a cautionary tale for the dangerous political thinking that occurs when totalized categories of identity privilege any one people. From the moment in 1923 when he posed the question "What is woman?" in his Freiburg lecture, through his analysis of being with others in *Being and Time* (1927), all the way to his reflections on world and embodiment in the *Zollikon Seminars* (1959 to 1969), and even including the notorious *Black Notebooks* (1931 to 1970), he provides insights for grappling with what has been known as "the woman question."

Historically, this question raises concerns regarding the biological, sociological, economic, and political status of women in relation to men, while contemporary debates question gender roles and the very logic of this binary. Whereas "man" has represented a taken-for-granted neutral standard, "woman" has symbolized the mark of sexual difference.[1] "Woman" has occupied a special place in our social imaginary because replies to "the woman question" disclose our very relation to being. Or as I'll demonstrate, questions of sexual difference are intimately tied to questions of ontological difference.[2]

But what do we mean by sex/gender? I take sex and gender to be collapsible terms in their historical contingency such that, as Judith Butler notes, "sex is always already gender."³ What this means is that definitions of *both* sex and gender change over time, according to ontological, ethical, and political motivations. Prior to Butler, many feminist theorists such as Gayle Rubin defined sex as an agglomeration of fixed biological traits such as genitalia, hormones, and chromosomes, with gender being a creation of social arrangements based on such perceived biological difference. Rubin's sex/gender system is "a set of arrangements by which the biological raw material of human sex and procreation is shaped by human, social intervention."⁴ For Butler, there is nothing "raw" about sex in terms of its existing in a true and natural state. By undergirding the social construction of sex/gender, Butler confronts the heteronormative context in which these terms are conferred meaning, while directly confronting the monolithic understanding of "woman" that such a system engenders. By speaking of sex/gender, I really want to highlight the temporal constitution of these terms. Perceptions of sex/gender are constantly shifting but our fascination with sex, that is always already gender, is immemorial.

I am less concerned with defining sex/gender and more interested in the motivations that ground these definitions. For Heidegger, each era is governed by a certain historical awareness and epistemological framework from which it ascertains being; likewise, each era has its own framework regarding "the woman question." These chapters represent my attempt to think this question alongside Heidegger's thought. And while Heidegger may not have admitted it, ontologies are politically motivated, and for that reason, I follow Paisley Currah's assertion that "sex means what a particular state actor says it means."⁵ Currah examines sex/state rather than sex/gender to highlight the juridical-political narratives in force when deciding legal recognition of sex/gender, with "sex" being the term most often used in such policies and decisions (even though sex and gender are often used interchangeably in legal documents). While I write "sex/gender," I find Currah's introduction of "state" useful for thinking sex/gender facticity in that it highlights the politics at play in forming ontologies, in deciding "what is."⁶

This book was written during a certain historical moment that saw a revival in the metaphysical/ontological question of woman, particularly as it pertains to the question of birth. Birth is not only a biological event, or a material coming-to-be in the world, but an epistemological passing down, and a political establishing of world order. When someone is born, they inherit the world of their ancestors, are conferred or denied certain statuses in relation to others, and learn to do as *they* (*das Man*) do.⁷ Historically, the pronouncement of one's sex/gender at birth could decide the fate of a monarchy or could secure the economic and social success of a family. Since 2011, with the invention of noninvasive prenatal testing (NIPT), we can know the sex/gender of our anticipated progeny in as little as nine weeks of gestation and disseminate such information under the fanfare of a gender reveal or use such data to opt for a sex selective abortion. The desire to know the sex/gender of one's child has historically been guided by economic, social, and religious factors, yet the very assignment of such markers take place within specific historic contexts and social arrangements. Our historical moment has seen important shifts in how we read and regulate sex/gender classification.

Since 2003, certain countries have allowed a third gender or nonbinary legal category, many countries have forgone previous sterilization or medical requirements for changing one's sex/gender identity, and new and emerging reproductive technology has permitted familial planning outside of heteronormative contexts; still, others have passed stifling legislation that limits legal gender recognition and/or procreative freedom.

Transness, as Jules Gill-Peterson documents, is nothing new, but the *hypervisibility* of trans bodies exploded in the 2010s with a particular focus being placed on trans women.[8] Increased visibility brings both progress and pushback. These are not mere *ontic* concerns, for who is allowed to procreate, who is allowed to create potential cases of Dasein, that being for whom its very being is an issue, is regulated under a certain technological framework. Heidegger briefly mentions birth as a complement to death in 1927 (GA 2) to highlight how we are thrown into a particular historical situation, where our possibilities for existence are realized in anticipation of our future death (Being-toward-death), but he raises the very act of procreation to an ontological level in the 1930s when he describes "racial breeding" as the quintessence of machinational thinking, an insight I will further analyze in chapter 3.[9]

Whenever people start asking the question "What is woman?" whether that is Heidegger in 1923, Beauvoir in 1949, or Tennessee lawmakers in 2023, the question comes out of a unique moment driven by specific ontological, political, and moral concerns regarding who *we are* and what *we should be*. The question of sexual difference, again with woman historically symbolizing the mark of such difference, is a question of ontological significance in that the type of *beings* we are allowed to be in terms of our sex/gender facticity regulates "what is" or *being*. "Man" has been the narrator of history (*his story*), and if Beauvoir is correct in her analysis that woman is defined in relation to man, then any upset in "the woman question" shakes the very foundation on which man rests. While the man/woman relation is unequal, it is still a reciprocal one in that man is only able *to be* in relation to what *woman is*. Furthermore, if Dasein is that being for whom its very being is an issue, and if such reckoning with being is always understood in a world with others (*Mitsein*), then certain ways of understanding being are necessarily foreclosed if there are others with whom we are not allowed to be. And there are others with whom we cannot be in the sense that societal constraints forbid such modes of existing or birthing politics don't allow certain others to exist at all. Replies to questions of sexual difference and ontological difference are historically specific, and such contingency is always interrogated via certain political and ethical motivations, motivations that regulate what type of beings can exist in the world.

This book examines such motivations in two separate parts. Part 1, "Heidegger's Sex/Gender Neutrality and the Politics of Birth," provides a generous reading of Heidegger's work where I see him providing important insights for examining the fluidity of sex/gender and for thinking how certain aspects of sexed/gendered experience coordinate our conditions of birth. I interrogate how the medical community and our technological era of *Gestell*[10] regulates how we come into the world and how it limits our potential for authentic temporality (chapter 1); how Heidegger's critique of Judeo-Christian origin stories of birth provides useful resources for thinking the historical contingency of sex/gender (chapter 2); how ideologies of sex/gender and race are a form of technology that determine who is allowed to give birth and who is allowed to be born into the world (chapter 3); and how traditional learning models pass down the "law of the father," a form of patriarchal pedagogy that forces us to forget the situation of our birth and the relational and empathic body knowledge that it fosters (chapter 4). Part 2, "Heidegger's Grounding of Sex/Gender and the Politics of Birth," examines another side of Heidegger, one that not only provides a totalized reply to the woman question but uses tropes of the feminine to advance a Nazi political agenda. Here, I evaluate how Heidegger makes use of such tropes to espouse a politics that privileges German identity and that advocates for the birthing of a particular form of "people" (chapter 5) before reading Heidegger against himself in a way that allows us to rethink sex/gender fluidity and that permits us to speak of collective communities and the passing down of identity without leading to potentially fascist thinking (chapter 6).

Yet, why Heidegger? If we are concerned with the politics and ethics of "the woman question," why turn to a man whose politics were appalling?

Why turn to a philosopher who prioritized ontology over ethics?[11] It is Heidegger's failings that make him a perfect cautionary tale. Heidegger initially asks the question "What is woman?" as a way of suspending any definite response regarding the nature of our "being there" or Dasein. Heidegger interrogates Dasein and our being-in-the-world in his search to recover the question of being ("what is"), a question that for him has been long forgotten. In his 1923 Freiburg lecture (GA 63), Heidegger notes his reason for choosing Dasein instead of "man" as the subject of his existential analytic, as "man" assumes certain predicates of existence that are already founded on Judeo-Christian origin stories of sexual difference. For Heidegger, to speak of "man" is to already define him in relation to "woman" (and to God). If we are interested in "what is," in being, we must turn to the being for whom its very being is an issue, but we must not assume to already know the sexed/gendered predicates of this being. Dasein, he suggests, is neutral.

Most feminist interpretations of Heidegger begin with his 1928 Marburg course (GA 26), where Heidegger explicitly states the sex or gender neutrality of Dasein (depending on the translation of *Geschlecht*).[12] Feminist scholars have demonstrated how such positions of neutrality are just masked masculine perspectives, particular men making universal claims. Yet, Heidegger's work resists such universalism and emphasizes the importance of our historical situation. Heidegger's suspension of "the woman question" offers important resources for feminists to think the fluidity of sex/gender, to think the historical construction of these categories. More important, however, is what happens when Heidegger no longer suspends this question, when he totalizes her, and manipulates tropes of her to advance his politics—he turns fascist.

By providing a particular feminist reading of Heidegger that makes a distinction between the Heidegger that suspends "the woman question" and the Heidegger that totalizes her, I do not mean to make a facile claim that his grounding of "woman" is *the* reason for his Nazism, though tracing the (nonlinear) trajectory of his thought on "the woman question" offers insights into the extent of his fascist thinking. There are *many* Heideggers, and this is just one reading, *my reading* during a certain historical time. I am not trying to provide a correct reading of Heidegger, and I think an attempt to do so (as if one lived in an historical vacuum) would belie an important aspect of Heidegger's hermeneutic project. For example, Meyer Shapiro tries to prove Heidegger's aesthetic project wrong by tracing the genealogy of a pair of shoes that Heidegger attributes to a peasant woman.[13] Shapiro is right in proving that the shoes belonged to van Gogh himself and that contrary to being the product of a harsh rural life, they were purchased in an industrialized urban area. But it doesn't matter if the peasant shoes actually belonged to a peasant. Shapiro shows that they clearly did not. What matters here is the type of historical awareness that allows Heidegger to even consider such a possibility, a point to which I'll return in chapter 5, as I discuss the importance of the peasant woman in Heidegger's politics, and by extension, his ontology. In short, I can only understand how being manifests itself through a specific temporal awareness, and so my reading of Heidegger demonstrates how being manifests itself during my time. That I am able to think sex/gender alongside Heidegger's thought in this way points to the historical time in which I live and says something significant about the way that being/beings show themselves at this moment in history.

When I speak of "early" Heidegger, I am referring to his writings of the 1920s, and I reference "later" Heidegger to discuss his work from the 1930s onward. This shift in thinking between the 1920s and the 1930s is referred to as the *Kehre*, a turning point in Heidegger's thought where language, especially poetry, and technology take a more pronounced role in his philosophy. It is difficult to speak of a consistency in Heidegger's posthumous publications like the *Gesamtausgabe* or *Black Notebooks* because of certain omissions and questionable assertions (Kisiel, Wolin).[14] Heidegger's *Black Notebooks*, his personal journals that reveal an unmistakable anti-Semitism, begin in 1931, and Heidegger joined the Nazi Party in 1933. While these historical facts situate him within a certain political terrain, I do not mean to insinuate that his early works were free of fascist thinking, for several scholars such as Emmanuel Faye and Victor Farías argue that his entire corpus is informed, and thus tainted, by his appalling politics.[15] It is undisputed that Heidegger's politics were reprehensible, but as I'll demonstrate in the sections that follow, it is important to examine Heidegger's philosophy, not despite his political past but because of it.

Here, I will map out what makes my reading of Heidegger a feminist reading, explain the social and historical location from which I am reading Heidegger, and provide a breakdown of how each chapter, in some way, responds to the question "What is woman?" While all chapters respond to this query, particularly as it pertains to our conditions of birth, this book does not unfold in a linear progression, and thus, each chapter can stand on its own.[16] However, chapter 5 bleeds into chapter 6, and readers may notice a change in tone as these two texts grapple with Heidegger's politics in the *Black Notebooks*. Though markedly different in subject matter, I'm reminded of Pearl Cleage's *Mad at Miles: A Black Woman's Guide to Truth*, in which Cleage vents her frustration at beloved jazz musician Miles Davis's betrayal and abuse of Black women. Cleage states, "[Davis] is guilty of self-confessed violent crimes against women such that we should break his albums, burn his tapes and scratch up his CDs until he acknowledges and apologizes and rethinks his position on The Woman Question."[17] It is this outrage and reckoning with what we should do with the work of someone, once revered, in light of self-confessed atrocities that resonates here.

I was introduced to Heidegger as a frosh in college, sprawled out in the commons room reading "The Question Concerning Technology" for a class titled The Problems of Being Human. As a seventeen-year-old product of the Internet Age, living on my own for the first time while bearing the usual existential coming-of-age angst, I wanted to know about this "problem" of being. I had a charismatic teacher and mentor who taught Heidegger in several of his classes, who never failed to elicit moments of wonder (*thaumazein*) and who compelled me to pursue philosophy. Though, not much was said back then about Heidegger's politics. The extent of his *active* involvement with the Nazi Party was brushed aside, and the fact that Hannah Arendt, his former Jewish student turned lover and author of a major opus on totalitarianism defended him until the end of her days was thought reason enough to believe his supposed political naivete. Several years later, having read his *Black Notebooks*, I am a conflicted reader of Heidegger, vacillating between betrayal and wonder, but I nevertheless believe there are important feminist resources to rescue from both his philosophy and his biography.[18]

Cleage asks whether we should burn the tapes of Davis, upon discovering his abuse, and philosophers have asked whether we should cancel Heidegger's works from the canon; yet, burning books, even metaphorically, cannot be an appropriate response to fascism. Feminists must engage with Heidegger, not just despite his past, but because of it.

The Challenge of Embracing a Collective Identity that Preserves Differences

First, an outright rejection of Heidegger's thought will not prevent the propagation of his ideas, given his significant influence on French thinkers, among others, who have shaped contemporary feminist thought and the twentieth- and twenty-first-century philosophical canon. Second, Heidegger serves well as a cautionary tale in that his resistance to grounding being ultimately fails because of his inability to properly think the ethical and political implications of ontological projects, especially as discussions of "what is" inform our lived experiences of identity and difference. *Or* he understood perfectly well the connection between ontology and ethics and used his ontological project in support of German identity politics, in which case we must read Heidegger against himself. We must interrogate where he went wrong, how such promising paths that resisted universalism nonetheless converged to a point of endorsing German superiority.

French poststructuralist/postmodern philosophers such as Derrida, Irigaray, Kristeva, Foucault, Deleuze, Guattari, and Cixous have been especially influential to contemporary feminist thought, though as Patricia Huntington highlights, "The Anglo-feminist alliance with French philosophy bypasses one important precursor to [such] thought: Martin Heidegger's existential phenomenology."[19] Huntington fills the gap of this lacuna by demonstrating the Heideggerian inheritance of some of these thinkers. She also examines the masculinist ethos that drives his politics and suggests this stems from "lacking a sufficiently dialectical view of agency," or an ethics of recognition.[20]

In trying to reconcile his fruitful philosophy with his reprehensible politics, Gregory Fried suggests that Heidegger's failure to respect ethics as a praxis caused his "unhinged *phronesis*" or unsound judgment in dealing with public affairs.[21] What is paramount for Fried is that an engagement with Heidegger's *polemos*,[22] the myriad conflicts and tensions that arise in his work and in the very quest for being, offers important insights for how communities reckon with identity and difference. Essentially, analyzing Heidegger, both the conflicts in his philosophical thinking and the tension in his political life reveal the very "Being of our politics." Fried states, "The continuing fascination with Heidegger's philosophy and politics points to the unresolved problem of how human beings can or will cope with the tension between an exclusive belonging to a particular group (identity) and a universalizing respect for diversity and otherness (recognition of difference)."[23] Heidegger's philosophy, especially as it trickles into his political thought, offers opportunities for thinking this tension between identity and difference. Heidegger, whose historical ontology questions the universalization of truths and combats epistemological essentialism, belonged to a political party founded on a conviction that there was an essence to what it meant to be German. Though Heidegger would go on to strongly critique National Socialism, as I'll elaborate in chapter 5, his eventual distancing from this party was not in response to its unjust or unequal treatment of human beings; rather, he lamented the *equalization* of the German people and its promotion of mediocrity, as "only a few" are capable of understanding the truth of being. How can a thinker who celebrates the diversity of *becoming* fall prey to an identity politics that universalizes the truth of being in a way that assumes only a few superior Germans can ascertain it? A dialogue of identity and difference and how our view of "what is" becomes grounded or essentialized in the face of historical contingency is a running thread throughout these chapters, particularly with respect to questions of sexual difference.

Heidegger serves well as a cautionary tale in that his ambiguity of language, particularly prevalent in his later works, and abstraction from materiality, what Gunter Anders calls his "pseudo-concreteness,"[24] led him to deplorable politics. In providing a feminist reading of Heidegger, there is no abstraction of the personal from the political, the intellectual from the material, or the ontological from the ethical. On the one hand, Heidegger rejects a Cartesian mind/body split and emphasizes the embeddedness of our being-in-the-word. On the other hand, he is notorious for his onto-somatic denial, or lack of attention paid to the body.[25] Throughout this book, I hope to show that ontological questions and our understanding of "what is" are always political insofar as such questions motivate how we act at a certain historical moment. Such questions are always linked to materiality insofar as these actions have consequences on real lived bodies. The experiences of these bodies are always sexed or gendered insofar as the predicates of sex and gender remain significant in intersubjective understandings of "what is." That is, largely, as a community whose shared understanding hinges on intersubjectivity, medical (chapter 1), legal (chapter 3), pedagogical (chapter 4), and political (chapters 5 and 6) desires continue to be informed and reinforced by perceived notions of sex/gender and the conditions of our birth. This is not to say that sex and gender are the primary markers of identity, and important intersectional work in race, disability studies, decolonial studies, and trans philosophy has demonstrated the harm of such a claim, but sex/gender does have a particular relation to being insofar as understandings of both are deeply tied to origin stories (of which I'll say more in the following section).

Thus, a feminist engagement with Heidegger is essential in two important ways: first, his influence on the philosophical canon, particularly on those French thinkers who have been foundational for contemporary feminist theory, leads to an indirect engagement with his work. Engaging with the source of these ideas will give feminists a better understanding of how his thinking could lead to a form of liberation for some, that is, a Heideggerian inheritance leads Derrida to think outside the margins,[26] and in turn, permits Spivak to think the "subaltern,"[27] yet led to a reprehensible politics for Heidegger. Second, if Heidegger's thought continues to be relevant because of an unresolved tension between identity and difference, his thought is significant for treating questions of difference with respect to sex and gender, especially as these markers of identity remain influential for defining "what is."

Feminist Standpoint Epistemology and *My* Reading of Heidegger

This reading of Heidegger is feminist in that it shares the following key claims of standpoint theory or standpoint epistemology put forth by Sandra Harding: (1) contrary to the empiricist "view from nowhere," standpoint researchers are embodied and visible, that is, the thought *of an age* is from *an age*; (2) forces that shape objects of knowledge also shape knowers. Even "nature" as "an object of knowledge" is socially situated; (3) communities, not individuals, produce knowledge; (4) the subjects and agents of knowledge for feminist standpoint theory are multiple, heterogeneous, and contradictory or incoherent, not unitary, homogeneous, and coherent as they are for empiricists—we need, as Patricia Hill Collins asserts, "dialogues across differences";[28] and (5) insofar as history and science have been created from the perspective of dominant groups, it is essential to listen to the voices of the marginalized.[29] In following these claims, Harding's goal is strong objectivity. That is, she believes that situated knowledges—those ways of knowing that take into account one's social position—are *less* partial and more capable of producing truth than supposed value-neutral claims. Though not a feminist, Heidegger would agree with some of these assertions, especially as they highlight history's role in the formation of truth. While he is not interested in truth in terms of strong objectivity, his ontological project does aim at a closer approximation of the truth as *alētheia*, a simultaneous revealing/concealing that resists the calculative thinking of our technological age.[30]

Whereas Harding targets modern science as the perspective of a dominant group of white Western bourgeois men, Heidegger targets modern science and its tradition of a metaphysics of presence, though both targeted groups are guilty of attempting to define "what is" outside of historical contexts. That is, they approach objects of nature as static entities whose truth can be revealed through an ahistorical process of calculative thinking. For both Harding and Heidegger, science itself is not the problem but rather its modern epistemological underpinnings that purport to reveal physical reality from a social and historical view from nowhere, what Donna Haraway calls "the God trick."[31] Likewise, Trish Glazebrook clarifies that, for Heidegger, in critiquing science, he was first and foremost critiquing science as modern physics, as a mathematical projection of nature, a projection that led to our current state of Enframing (*Gestell*) whereby everything is viewed as resources to be optimized, stockpiled, and used for future utility. Glazebrook states, "His objection is not so much to science as to scientism, that is, the preclusion of other ways of thinking by the representational thinking of the sciences, and the marginalization, displacement, and devaluation of other methodologies and bodies of knowledge by the scientific standard of objectivity that has become epistemologically dominant in modernity."[32] This rejection of representational thinking that purports to know the essential truth of physical reality, to the detriment of other methodologies, had contributed to Heidegger's pseudoconcreteness, or his inability to properly think the material conditions of our lived bodies. Heidegger recognizes the complexity of the body, yet in refusing to reduce it to mere extension, and risk falling prey to scientism, he declares in *Being and Time* (GA 2) that he will "not treat it here."[33] In part, this book fills in Heidegger's lacuna by focusing on the lived experiences of our sexed/gendered bodies and how they are legally, medically, pedagogically, and politically able to exist in the world.

However, an important question arises: If Heidegger's pseudoconcreteness is due to antiscientism, a refusal to objectify the body as an ahistorical presence before us, do feminists (like myself) risk the same pseudoconcreteness in refusing to limit the body of woman to mere representational thinking to be measured by calculative thinking? That is, by refusing to reduce woman to mere biology, do we risk antiscientism that could be misconstrued as being antiscience? This is certainly the charge of gender critical feminists who ask, "Can't you see that women are defined by the materiality of their reproductive difference? Aren't women *real*?" Women certainly are real, but the bodies of women should not be reduced to mere objective matter, let alone to a static unchanging matter. While Heidegger was unable to "treat the body" in GA 2, thirty-seven years later in the *Zollikon Seminars*, he analyzes the complexity of the body by undergirding the Husserlian distinction between the lived body (*Leib*) and the corporeal body (*Körper*), the former of which has been neglected in previous philosophical attempts to treat our bodily nature. While *Körper* stops at the skin, and is thus limited to mere extension, the body as *Leib* interacts with space, time, and world. I will return to a discussion of this distinction in chapters 1 and 2, but feminists are able to escape claims of being "antiscience" by not only following the rules of strong objectivity set forth by Harding, but by also analyzing the bodies of women as *Körper* (corporeal) and *Leib* (lived). It is not that biology does not matter at all, but that it is not the only thing that matters. Furthermore, as recent work in the new feminist materialist tradition has shown, our bodily nature is not mere passive matter.[34]

There is, of course, a difference between an essence of "woman" and particular "women." Intersectional feminists have shown how speaking of women as a universal group has often meant speaking about white, middle-class, heterosexual women. How to speak of women while recognizing the differences among them? Certain conservatives who take a "commonsense" or "naturalist attitude"[35] may inquire, "We want to talk about women, but how can we, if we can't say who she *is*?" Heidegger says, "Being is the most said and at the same time a keeping silent," and "Being is the most worn-out and at the same time the origin."[36] Woman, like being, is a question of origin. Sexual difference is tied up with ontological difference, and not just because we must interrogate a relation of what is particular to what is universal (that is, the relation between women/woman and beings/being), but because historically, the very question "what is woman?" is tied to an inquiry of "what is being?" The very notion of sexual difference arises for the first time in Heidegger's 1923 lecture where he analyzes *man's* emergence in Genesis. The "commonsense view" of responding to "the woman question" relies on this same origin story of reproductive difference, origin stories that Heidegger cautions us against in both his 1923 lecture and "The Origin of the Work of Art." This latter work advises "that which dwells near its origin abandons the site," suggesting the impossibility of finding being via a search for its inaugural emergence.[37] Woman and being are without ground. Yet, even if we locate an origin of "woman" or "being" in our adherence to certain scientific or religious doctrines, there is nothing about this original "is" that "ought to be," or that ought to remain unphased by historical evolutions.

On the one hand, because of his refusal to define our being-in-the-world in terms of Judeo-Christian origin stories of the flesh, Heidegger is able to suspend the question "what is woman?" he is able to think about our existence apart from an original sexual difference. However, by evading the question of bodily existence in his earlier works, he misses an important opportunity to explore how and why sexual difference *matters* so much in our accounts of being. That is, a neutralization of sex/gender may undergird possibilities for sex/gender fluidity that is desirable to feminists, but it may also prevent a framework through which we are able to analyze the real physical harm done to such bodies because of their sex/gender.

Heidegger knew we couldn't stay in a suspended state of questioning being forever; he knew that eventually we have to "ground the ground." What I mean by "ground the ground" is that ultimately, we have to provide a resolution to the conflict of meaning, or *polemos*, that characterizes all sense-making. We want to acknowledge possibility and potentiality that is inherent in beings, though we must, to some extent, place such potential in stasis in order to speak of any particular being in concrete terms (that is, we must be able to say *x is*). While Butler mentions "free-floating" categories of gender, she recognizes that feminists cannot erase the category "woman," nor did she say it was a desirable project. Politically, we must speak about *woman* to, for example, stop the rape of *women*. This is where the harsh reality of identity politics comes into play. We need to be able to talk about *woman* as a symbolic set of meanings without universalizing who *women are*. As Butler suggests, "woman" must remain open-ended, even if concretized as a political strategy. How can we speak of collective identities, without dissolving differences among them? How can we belong to any given group, with a sense of pride, without that pride turning into a hubris that leads to supremacist thinking? As I will argue, this is what happened in Heidegger's case; his discriminatory preferencing of "a people" led to genocidal politics.

The necessity to "ground the ground," or to not stay in a suspended state of nothingness (or pure potentiality for being) is elucidated in Heidegger's notion of the *Augenblick*, that moment of vision when I am held out to nothingness. In this instant, I am (theoretically) stripped of certain fixed ways of existing according to cultural convention. I am in a position where I can make *owned* and *resolute* decisions regarding how I want to live. Here, I must *choose* in order *to be*. To not choose a certain way of existing is to live in a nonsensical world. More importantly, the world to which I must return after this *Augenblick* is one of a shared community, where living only makes sense in reference to shared understandings of meaning (intersubjective experience). In this instant, we are stripped in a *theoretical* way and not in any *embodied* way, because try as I may to explore different possibilities before me, certain *material* potentialities of existence will always be foreclosed due to historical circumstances passed down to me.

In this book, I am interested in the sexed/gendered circumstances passed down to us. I believe in a certain historical contingency of sex/gender facticity, and I will argue for a certain fluidity of these terms, yet such terms are always understood intersubjectively, in a world with others. How to think "what is woman?" in a way that doesn't universalize her being, while still collectively thinking about woman in a way that provides the potential for political transformation? These are not new questions to feminism. Heidegger's story can, however, be used as a cautionary tale in replying to them. In GA 63 (1923), he suspends the "woman question" providing us the opportunity to think fluidity. However, in works such as the *Black Notebooks* (1931 to 1970), "Language in the Poem: A Discussion on Georg Trakl's Poetic Work" (1953), and "Building Dwelling Thinking" (1951) he manipulates tropes of the feminine, tied to a rootedness in the soil, to speak of *one dwelling space* and *one historical destiny* in a way that not only forecloses possibilities for thinking "the woman question" but that actively participates in harmful exclusionary politics. In realizing that he had to "ground the ground," Heidegger made an owned decision to join the National Socialist Party and to espouse a rhetoric founded on the superiority of the German people. Identifying with a community is not in and of itself a pathway to Nazism, as it is possible to participate in identity politics without turning genocidal. This is what I hope to demonstrate in the last chapter by turning to Latina feminist scholarship and Perry Zurn's trans poetics. *We* can speak as a *we* without upholding an "us versus them" mentality that leads to privileging any one group.

Rethinking the Body and Birth of Finite Dasein

Heidegger's focus on the lived body has become increasingly important for work in the phenomenology of medicine (Aho, Carel, Svenaeus),[38] but apart from a few scholars (Young, Rodemeyer, Belu),[39] an account of lived temporality *during* birth, that oft-overlooked existential condition, particularly how such time is experienced by the laboring subject remains undertheorized. Heidegger's emphasis on death and finitude, associated with transcendence, at the expense of birth and natality, associated with immanence, accounts for such a dearth of scholarship.

In attempting to mine new theoretical resources for feminist methodologies, Harding asks, "Why is risking death said to represent the distinctively human act but giving birth is regarded as merely natural?"[40] That is, why is the Western canon so preoccupied with death as an important philosophical issue that's worthy of scrutiny? Why does death tell us something profound about the human condition, while birth is mere biological production? Luce Irigaray, Anne O'Byrne, Alison Stone, Leslie MacAvoy, Lisa Guenther, and other feminist scholars have asked Heidegger a similar question, as his privileging of finitude neglects or diminishes the ontological significance of birth for both our understanding of existence and for the possibility of living authentically.[41] Adriana Cavarero asserts that Western metaphysics' obsession with death stems from the fact that we are born from a woman's body.[42] Karen Warren and Deborah Orr demonstrate that such disregard for a woman's body and its negation of ontological significance can be traced back to a "logic of domination" that begins with Parmenides's distinction between "what is" and "what is not." "Woman" is relegated to the realm of "is not" insofar as she is associated with the body and an inferior form of knowledge.[43] Or, as Carol Bigwood demonstrates, thanks to Aristotle's science of reproduction and the inessential role that woman's body as mere passive matter plays in the procreative process, "mother doesn't matter."[44]

In turning to the ontological significance of birth to correct the Western canon's obsession with death, I do not mean to conflate a "woman's body," or "the feminine," with the act of birthing. Such conflation is already present throughout the history of Western philosophy and has led to the subordinate position of women or of those bodies that embody the feminine. For example, in Plato's *Symposium*, the procreation of bodies is a lesser form of "giving birth to beauty" than a procreation of the intellect, the latter of which is propagated by men.[45] Reproduction, particularly contemporary debates regarding assisted reproductive technology, has been a prominent topic of feminist bioethics because of the focus on women's bodies as laboring subjects. Such laboring bodies have also been conceived as products of exchange (Rubin, Rawlinson, Belu).[46] Labor as an act of re*production*, as exchange, holds particular significance for Black bodies whose "womanhood became defined solely through their forced reproduction of enslaved, unfree offspring."[47] This association of "woman" with "reproduction" is already there, so while I do not wish to reify this relation, I find it necessary to provide ample space teasing apart its significance in defining "what is." Thus, I raise questions such as, "Who is legally allowed to reproduce?" "How does the clock time of the medical community interfere with the lived temporality of the laboring subject?" "In reproducing the curriculum, how does our public project of educating children ignore the intimate act of nurturing them?" And, "How does Heidegger betray his initial rejection of sexual difference, when he advances a politico-poetic agenda that culminates in one generation [*Geschlecht*], founded on a 'twofoldness' of sex?" For, as I'll demonstrate in chapter 5, Heidegger will advocate for one historical destiny of the German people that is founded on two sexes.

Insofar as Heidegger's key philosophical project centers on the notion of ontological difference, and insofar as sexual difference has been historically significant in undergirding this difference, a questioning of reproduction and its role in defining "what is" is essential to this project. I challenge the position that birth is a one-off natural event, in contrast to the futurity of death that is taken up continuously. While Heidegger analyzes Dasein as it stretches along from birth to death, birth as an ongoing project is only considered in terms of our being born *to die*. Yet, Irigaray describes a uterine longing to return to our site of origin and assesses that it is this desire for the beginning that forces us to establish solid meaning in a world of flux. She searches for a way to move beyond a world of "solid" thinking, based on a phallocentric language and turns to an experience of female temporality that explores "becoming" rather than a static presence of being (Irigaray, Ziarek).[48]

While standpoint theory centers in on the primacy of one's social location in producing knowledge, Heidegger highlights the centrality of time for interpreting "what is." This is made especially salient in *Being and Time*. Furthermore, in GA 63, he states, "The being-there as our own Dasein is what it is precisely and only in its *temporally particular 'there,'* its being *'there' for a while*. The today ontologically: *the present of those initial givens which are closest to us*, every-one, being-with-each-other—'our time.'"[49] If time is that Archimedean point through which any attempt at ontology remains possible, then one's social position must likewise hold ontological significance, as time can never be analyzed outside of such a position. *My time* is *our time* to the extent that each of us negotiates temporality within the confines of intersubjective understandings of existence. For example, scholars have shown how Blackness affects narrative time and historical time (Goffe 2022), how gender nonconforming bodies experience ruptures of time and a sense of being "out of sync" (Halberstam 2005), and how disabled people are "written out of the future" and forced to "bend the clock" (Kafer 2013).[50] Not to take into account the social position of one's experience of time would be to represent temporality as stemming from a static view from nowhere. Such would entail a projection of nature as devoid of motion and would be guilty of the scientism that Heidegger critiques. It is in this spirit that I provide a feminist reading of Heidegger from *my time* and social position.

I am reading Heidegger as a white cisgender bisexual woman from a lower socioeconomic background. These social positions influence how I read Heidegger and why I choose to focus on certain aspects of his philosophy rather than others. For example, in chapter 1, my socioeconomic status matters for my interpretation of authentic temporality during labor insofar as my experience with Medicaid limited the choices that I was able to make. In chapter 3, I examine how trans bodies are excluded from the recent French revised bioethics legislation that extends assisted reproductive technology (ART) to "all women," and in chapter 6, I use Zurn's trans poetics to think of Heidegger's bridge (in "Building Dwelling Thinking") as the apeiron of sexed/gendered existence. In Jacob Hale's "Suggested Rules for Non-Transsexuals Writing about Transsexuals, Transsexuality, Transsexualism, or Trans__," he suggests that we "interrogate [our] own subject position" and the way that this position affects how we see and what we say.[51] Taking these rules into account, I find it necessary to state the cisgender viewpoint from which I am writing, but not without complication.

Megan Burke cautions against using cis as an identity category because such identification may further risk the inferiorization of trans bodies.[52] Following Robin Dembroff,[53] she highlights how cisgenderism is used as a commonsense identity marker, as if cis as a given is perfectly understood to be the norm. She suggests focusing on cis sense, the intersubjective way that institutions confer normative identities onto us. Burke is not questioning the political and ontological strategy of identifying as cis as a means of highlighting one's privilege. Rather, it is important to undergird that in identifying as cis, one is *negotiating an imposition of meaning*, rather than declaring something essentialist about themselves. It is in this spirit that I identify as cisgender, in that the privilege I have navigating my being-in-the-world, in part stems from as Burke says, never having my body or existence mistaken as "nonsense."

Dasein, and more specifically its sex/gender, only makes sense within a shared community of already existing signifiers and social structures. And yet, as Kevin Aho asserts, treating *das Man* as the source of Dasein's intelligibility is only partially correct, as it "fails to come to grips with the ultimate source of intelligibility, 'temporality' [*Zeitlichkeit*], a source more original than the social relations of *das Man*."[54] In other words, the sense (*Sinn*) of the being of Dasein is temporality.[55] Thus, Dasein is only able to render something like sex/gender intelligible due to an *originary temporality* that Heidegger analyzes through our "'thrown projection,' by the *existential* structures of the Past (*Vergangenheit*) and the Future (*Zukunft*)."[56] Heidegger characterizes our existence as one of *thrownness* in that we are born in a world as not-yet-determined beings, where we understand our potential possibilities of existence through a reckoning with the traditions passed down to us (past) and a projection into a future where we know our days are numbered (Being-toward-death). For the most part, Dasein is inauthentically absorbed in the world and does not experience time in any originary sense where notions of past/present/future collide; rather, Dasein understands time as a linear succession of nows, as a forward trajectory of this triad. Yet, my projection onto such potentialities of existence is only possible because they *matter* to me, they show up as I navigate my world, in what Heidegger calls, a mode of circumspective *concern* (my negotiation with objects) and *solicitude* (my negotiation with others), because the being of Dasein is *care*.[57]

Care is a neutral temporal structure of affective receptiveness that discloses our relation to ourselves and our world (with others). It is on the basis of care that I experience entities in the world and make sense of my "thrown projection," though as Heidegger highlights, "The primordial unity of the structure of care lies in temporality."[58] Yet, most of the time, what matters to me is what matters to them (*das Man*), and I experience time as a mathematical projection of clock time or the world time of *das Man*. Authentic temporality, or originary temporality, experienced as a unity of past/present/future is only possible during certain moments (*Augenblick*). For Heidegger, an *Augenblick* may occur in an affective state such as anxiety whereby I am held out to *nothing*; in this mood, I am seized by a certain meaninglessness, and there is a suspension of concern/solicitude as things do not yet *really matter* because I have not yet freely chosen them.[59] This moment of nothingness is pure potentiality for being, a moment of freedom where I can choose to be authentic, where I am able to make owned decisions regarding my way of being, instead of just falling into the *doxa* of the they.

Dasein exists as its possibilities, but such possibilities are only realized based on the structure of care that lies in originary temporality. It then follows that my possibilities regarding sex/gender are likewise indebted to such a primordial source of time. Care is a neutral temporal structure, but I would argue that how it becomes enacted and how we understand what matters to us is contingent on the historical era in which we dwell. Heidegger says, "temporality temporalizes," meaning it's constantly evolving, constantly resisting any attempts at grounding. In chapter 1, I reckon with my (in)ability to have an authentic experience with temporality during labor, an ecstatic moment thought possible by certain feminist scholars; in chapter 2, I briefly mention the transcendental structure of temporality and its importance for neutral Dasein; and in chapter 6, I refer to Ortega who likens Anzaldúa's

Coatlicue states to Heidegger's disclosive mood of anxiety in that they both involve a breakdown in meaning that invites news possibilities of existence. Beyond these engagements, I will not provide a more exhaustive treatment of temporality insofar as I am in dialogue with *many* Heideggers, thinking across several different texts. Heidegger never finished *Being and Time* and he later abandons his focus on originary temporality, choosing to center on dwelling, technology, and language. Heidegger's thought does maintain an engagement with "origins" or "beginnings," as evidenced in his *Beiträge* (GA 65, 1936 to 1938) but always in a way that thinks about generative possibilities.[60] In GA 2, what I find most essential in terms of thinking time alongside sex/gender facticity is how "temporality temporalizes," how it self-generates in a way that renders any linguistic attempts at characterizing it unstable. This insight explains Heidegger's foray into poetry, a space that allows our already acquired signifiers to signify something else. Yet, while Heidegger may have abused the polyvalence of language to satisfy his own reprehensible political ends, Zurn's trans poetics resists sex/gender facticity as any grounded metaphysics of presence (chapter 6). *My* time is *our* time at a certain *historical* time, but never really *is*.

Overall, this book represents a trajectory of thoughts as I grapple with the significance of Heidegger's "woman question" as it pertains to today's society. This orientation is not linear, nor are these thoughts to be set in stone. In Susan Brison's *Aftermath*, she quotes Ursula K. Le Guin to help readers understand the nonlinear and changing nature of her thought process: "It doesn't seem right or wise to revise an old text severely, as if trying to obliterate it, hiding the evidence that one had to go there to get here. It is rather in the feminist mode to let one's changes of mind, and the processes of change, stand as evidence."[61] As I reread these chapters together, I'm tempted to change certain ideas and modify certain claims, but I like evidence of a trajectory of thought, that I had to go there to get here. This is *my* reading of Heidegger from *my* time, which is *our* time, but it is limited. This is, in part, the point—to avoid universal claims of sexed/gendered truths.

Part I

Heidegger's Sex/Gender Neutrality and the Politics of Birth

Chapter 1

"You're Already off the Clock"

Temporalizing Laboring Dasein

"You're already off the clock" is a phrase I've been mulling over, since the birth of my son; it was uttered by a member of the medical staff, when my delivery wasn't going as planned. Whose clock was I supposed to be on, and what are the implications of my having gone "off" it? In trying to make sense of this phrase, I provide a phenomenological account of my time reckoning during childbirth to ask, what sort of temporalities are experienced by laboring Dasein, and how may the tension between clock time and lived time affect the possibility of having an authentic birthing experience?

I speak of laboring Dasein to more accurately reflect the intersubjective quality of our being-in-the-world, and while laboring Dasein is not synonymous to the laboring subject, the former includes the latter. As John Haugeland notes, "being-in-the-world is a single entity with two interdependent structural aspects: self and world are like two sides of one coin, the actual 'metal' of which is the whole of concrete being-amidst."[1] As a composite of self/world, Dasein is that being for whom being is an issue, an issue that is always approached via a certain understanding of temporality. According to Heidegger, each era is governed by a particular historical awareness in relation to being, and correspondingly, in relation to temporality. Our current era follows a technological ideology that Heidegger refers to as enframing (*Gestell*) whereby we view the world as an amalgam of resources called standing reserve (*Bestand*), ready to be calculated, exploited, and put on reserve for future utility.[2] While not all laboring subjects, or laboring Dasein, experience time in the same manner, we may all be up against some form of clock in a technological childbearing age that Dana S. Belu refers to as "reproductive enframing."[3]

A Phenomenology of Laboring Dasein: Primordial Time versus Shared Time

I felt the antagonism of intersubjective time as soon as I entered the hospital. I experienced this estrangement as a loss and a questioning of autonomy, not autonomy in the sense of self-freedom but as a temporospatial fracturing, a splitting of the nondichotomous temporal consciousness I was experiencing.

I knew I wasn't in the "active" phase of labor, and I told the nurse I wanted to walk around. I had "body knowledge" that I was in the early stage of labor, but in the hospital, perception won over sensation. The progress of my labor could not be known until there was visible confirmation on the state of my contractions. The nurse hooked me up to a machine and showed me a digital image, akin to those recording earthquakes, pronouncing the latency of my labor. Yes, she said, it appears you are not in the active phase. This tangible proof, provided by the machine, told the truth. Checking how far I was dilated acted as further confirmation. What the nurse *saw* on the monitors and *felt* with her fingers was more valid than what I sensed, because my sensations could not be objectified. Corine Pelluchon asserts, "It is important to understand why the privilege accorded to vision and to touch is inseparable from a philosophy that not only establishes a division between the constituting subject and the constituted object—the conscience and the world—but also conceives the latter as that which resists our will or cedes to our power."[4] According to such a philosophy, the ego tends toward an object, or other human being who becomes objectified, and perceives it within the boundaries of an accessible space that can be manipulated. Vision thus invites the hand to exercise its grasp on things.[5] I felt this grasp from the medical community (nurses, doctors, technology), as I tried to negotiate the terms of my birth.

Prior to going into labor, I felt intersubjective temporal pressure, as one of my doctors asked if I would like to schedule my birth, suggesting a "planned" delivery may be more beneficial than a "spontaneous" birth. I would like to highlight why I specify "one of my doctors," because the context in which I was receiving medical treatment limited some of the choices I was able to make. While living in the United States, teaching during the day and bartending at night, I was on Medicaid.[6] I had to choose among a short list of medical clinics within this insurance network, and though I could choose a primary obstetrics and gynecology (OB-GYN) physician, I saw whoever was available during appointment times. Because I was receiving "free" care, I already felt that I was in a vulnerable position. Socioeconomic concerns are not the only factors that influence how pregnant subjects experience phenomena, as a myriad of other contingencies, including but not limited to, age, gender, race, sexuality, and religion, affect our being-in-the-world—a world whose outlook on self will always be determined as an intersubjective experience with others. While I recognize the diversity of birthing experiences, and I challenge attempts by the medical community to regulate labor according to a universal shared clock time, this chapter will limit its phenomenological analysis to my lived experience with labor.[7]

The doctor suggesting a scheduled induction tried to make the offer enticing by telling me a planned labor would allow those I wanted present for the birth to be there. He would also be in Mexico around my due date, so if I wanted him to deliver the baby, it would be best to mark my calendar. I actually preferred the other doctor. His bragging about delivering nearly 100 babies the month before didn't sit well with me. I kept imagining H. R. Gieger's "The Birth Machine," and this made me feel like a helpless automaton. Is my birth the same, just one more body on the birthing factory line?

Like Belu, I am concerned with how medical technology may *challenge forth* children under the rubric of reproductive enframing. However, whereas Belu appears skeptical of any technological interventions being freely chosen, I worry about the personal and political consequences of her chalking up such decisions to the dupery of "ideological choice talk." I would like to believe that laboring Dasein can make owned choices and that laboring subjects can find their voices amid the talk (*Rede*) of the medical community. That laboring Dasein can be "off the clock" points to the impossibility of regulating all pregnant subjects according to a universal clock, but where does Dasein go once derailed from this intelligible intersubjectivity? I use intelligible here in the same way that language is intelligible in its use of universal signifiers. Words make sense because we speak the same language; likewise, a clock makes sense when we are all in the same time zone (numerically speaking, the time is universal). Like speaking a different language, experiencing disparate temporalities makes intersubjective communication unintelligible. As one voice, having "gone off" the anticipated timeline, I offer my own temporal experiences with labor.

I told my doctor I didn't want to be induced. I feared the procedure of induction would increase the risk for further medical intervention, frequently in the form of a caesarean. In the US, one-third of births are via caesarean, a statistic that should concern us. He proudly told me he could perform caesareans quickly, though his expediency with a knife further deterred me from wanting him to deliver my child.

Once my water broke, it was again suggested that my labor be induced. Since I was in the early stages of childbirth when this happened, the nurse wanted to give me a drug called Cytotec to incite labor. *My body felt it wasn't time.* Yet, such body knowledge couldn't be made visible in the form of objective data. It is this supposed ability of mathematical projections to properly announce the truth of its object that Heidegger highlights in his critique of science. That mathematical properties of *Körper* (material body) can speak the truth of *Leib* (lived body) is doubtful. The drug Cytotec also carried a specific significance to me, because after suffering a missed miscarriage the year before, it was the drug I took to expel the fetal tissue.[8] Mention of Cytotec took me out of the moment toward a painful memory of the past. The doctor said I could wait twelve hours to "let things happen." I did, and then twelve hours later, the nurse informed me I had to be induced, because I was "already off the clock." This phrase really stuck with me, because I was waiting for my "ecstatic moment," unaware that I was supposed to be on some sort of clock. Was my authentic primordial experiencing of time eclipsed by an inauthentic shared public time, reinforced through constant medical intervention? Whose clock was I on? What sort of time is this clock keeping?

In order to understand how one can go off this clock, we must first try to analyze the type of time that it represents. Throughout the history of philosophy, time has been dissociated from space, privileging the former as masculine and active and disparaging the latter as feminine and passive. Time is viewed as an individual transcendent construct and is associated with the mind, whereas space is seen as an intersubjective immediate constitution and is linked to the body. Lanei Rodemeyer challenges the space-time divide and its correlating active/passive dichotomy by highlighting the passive and intersubjective quality of temporality, attributes usually ascribed to spatiality. Drawing from Susan Bordo's "slender body," Rodemeyer examines the intersubjective quality of time by analyzing the way a person with an eating disorder may "subdue" their body.[9] On the one hand, the fact that our bodies need to be subdued points to an active dimension of our flesh that is usually discredited in passive accounts of corporeality. On the other hand, we cannot pretend an independent active temporal structure, when public media images, what Rodemeyer refers to as the "appresentation of societal images of the feminine," have such a strong influence on our conception of self.

Appresentation is a Husserlian term that describes how that which is not currently present influences our sense of perception; whereas a presentation is present in the "now," an appresentation is not directly present, but is copresent as a possibility that affects my current experience. For Rodemeyer, a passive element of temporality becomes salient, as these appresentations of societal images "become even more powerful than the actual presentation of my own body."[10] In searching for passive accounts of time, she does not wish to reverse the dominant script of time being active and the body being passive; rather, she questions the integrity of such divides and undergirds the intersubjective dimension of time and space. Though she challenges the tenability of any rigid distinction between time/mind and space/body, she does illustrate how intersubjective interpretations of the body can lead to a splitting of an individual temporal consciousness. Rodemeyer asserts,

> This splitting occurs when an intersubjective constitution is antagonistic to the subject in some way and yet is appropriated, and intensified, by the subject. In an effort at survival, the two modes of constitution, temporal consciousness and body-consciousness, split from one another and oppose one another. Neither temporal constitution is the "true" subject in the sense of "pure" subject, as all constitution involves intersubjectivity to some extent. But we can say that one form of constitution is more dangerous to the subject than the other, because it leads to the subject's turning against her own body, and in some sense, her self.[11]

Thus, even though all temporospatial constitutions involve intersubjectivity, there is still a self that shares a world with others (Dasein as *Mitsein*). This being-with-others affects my perception of self and may negatively influence the choices I am able to make regarding my body. I would like to think about how such a splitting of individual temporal consciousness occurs while the pregnant subject is in labor. Laboring Dasein includes the pregnant subject, and an essential feature of Dasein is its "mineness" (*Jemeinigkeit*). Heidegger asserts, "Because Dasein has *in each case mineness* [*Jemeinigkeit*], one must always use a *personal* pronoun when one addresses it: 'I am,' 'you are.' Furthermore, in each case Dasein is mine to be in one way or another. Dasein has always made some sort of decision as to the way in which it is in each case [*je meines*] [emphasis made by Heidegger]."[12] While "I am" as Dasein, and while there is a "personal pronoun" behind the choices "I" make, such decisions are not always freely chosen by me, but are rather passed down from the *they* (*das Man*), a term we can understand as public opinion and social convention. Heidegger will distinguish between authentic and inauthentic choices, categorizing the former as those that are resolute in their being owned by the individual.

Rodemeyer suggests pregnant Dasein is capable of experiencing authentic or primordial time, a form of temporality that is a prerequisite for such owned or resolute choices. Authentic time is experienced as an ecstatic moment when past, present, and future collide.[13] She states, "[pregnant Dasein] recognizes her temporality as communicated to her through the Other. This Other within her—an Other that is not entirely other—forces her out of an individualized presence into the otherness of past and future of intersubjectivity."[14] Laboring Dasein thus "throws" the other into the world, while being able to reflect on their own thrownness, experiences the present as a self/other interaction, and is able to anticipate the future of both. This coalescing of past, present, and future offers an ecstatic moment of time, a moment often eclipsed by inauthentic shared time that is usually experienced as a flowing succession of a series of "nows." Heidegger states, "Thus, for the ordinary understanding of time, time shows itself as a sequence of 'nows' which are constantly 'present-at-hand,' simultaneously passing away and coming along. Time is understood as a succession, as a 'flowing stream' of 'nows,' as the 'course of time.'"[15] This "now-time" is described as a "world time" and is made physically manifest in our usage of clocks. This is a shared time, a simultaneous temporality present-at-hand. Everyone in the maternity ward can look at their watches and agree that it is x amount of time. There can be a communal temporal understanding that it is, say, 1:00 a.m. However, such measurements of time say nothing about temporality and its primordial structure; in parceling out spatial stretches of time, are we really just talking about common space? For laboring Dasein and nurses who inhabit the same room, they can perceive the same clock and agree on its measurement, but outside of their shared numerical perception, how can we think their temporality is shared? Heidegger asserts,

> What is ontologically decisive lies rather in the specific kind of *making present* which makes measurement possible. Dating in terms of what is "spatially" present-at-hand is so far from a spatializing of time that this supposed spatialization signifies nothing else than that an entity which is present-at-hand for everyone

in every "now" is made present in its own presence. Measuring time is essentially such that it is necessary to say "now"; but in obtaining the measurement, we, as it were, forget what has been measured as such, so that nothing is to be found except a number and a stretch.[16]

Essentially, in trying to understand time, we objectify it and make it present-at-hand, yet as soon as *it* becomes present it is no longer time, but always already space. And yet, temporality is the very reason for such a clock, as there is something about my existential structure that makes me reckon with the fact that "my days are numbered." I exist between the past of my thrownness and a future that is experienced as a being-toward-death.[17] From this latter futural projection springs the need for a clock to ensure that I "have enough time" or that I "do not lose time." Yet, these clocks say nothing of authentic temporality as they treat past, present, and future as separate entities (and as disparate spatial occurrences).

Though an ecstatic moment of time occurs as a collision of past, present, and future, Heidegger nonetheless privileges the futural dimension of this triad. He states, "The 'now' is not pregnant with the 'not-yet-now,' but the present arises from the future in the primordial ecstatical unity of the temporalizing of temporality."[18] The future receives special consideration here, because it is only through a realization of my finitude felt via a being-toward-death that I experience the "passing of time." For Heidegger, in the individualized moment of vision (*Augenblick*) where I confront my death, I experience time authentically outside of a public shared time ruled by clocks. In this moment of vision, I am able to make owned choices about my life apart from the chatter of the they (*das Man*). Yet, why must authenticity be realized as an individual project? Furthermore, why must such choices be made upon a reflection of death?

To be clear, an ontological experience of being-toward-death is not a futural projection I can consciously take up. I cannot wish to understand being, close my eyes, reflect on death, and experience this ontological event. According to Heidegger, being-toward-death is felt in a mood of anxiety whereby I am held out to the "nothing." In this disclosive affective state of anxiety, I am not anxious about something, but rather nothing at all. I realize my own finitude in this moment, though the "nothing" I experience cannot be chalked up to my mere demise (my death) but rather the angst of there being nothing at all. This realization that I am born on the basis of a nullity (nothingness) opens me up to different possibilities of existence. There is thus a freedom in this futural projection of being-toward-death.

My question for Heidegger is, "why cannot this moment of being be understood when I am held out to something, namely, the coming-to-presence of a being?" Why cannot an ecstatic moment occur at this initial moment of thrownness (where the baby is literally thrown from the body of an Other)?[19] Can we be held out to this moment of a new coming-to-be, felt as an understanding of, not finitude, but *infinitude*? If we can marvel at nothingness and the facticity that "there is," why can't we be astounded at the reality of there being anything at all? Is not a generational understanding of time, or rather an embodied passing down of time necessary for being at all? As Anne O'Byrne remarks, "We are natal, generational beings. That is to say, we are generated by our parents; we become a generation in the company of our contemporaries; we are capable of generating, in turn; we eventually pass away. Thus, the concept of generation amounts to an early, Lucretian hint at our infinitude."[20] Heidegger searches for an experience of authentic temporality in order to understand being, hence the eponymous *Being and Time*, yet O'Byrne questions whether such time must only be linked to an understanding of temporality as finite; furthermore, O'Byrne finds disclosive moments of being not only in our being-toward-death, but also in our being-toward-birth. Leslie MacAvoy, likewise, turns to a phenomenology of birth, asserting, "both my birth and my death are mine and mine alone."[21] Alison Stone references O'Byrne's notion of a syncopated temporality to explain how infantile amnesia causes us to forget the significant event of our birth. Nevertheless, these forgotten moments play out in the future via transference where our pasts are carried forward and manifested in our personalities and behavior. For Stone, birth is that "taken-for-granted anchor to which my life history is tethered."[22] If the moment of my birth, the moment I am separated from my birthing parent, is experienced as primordial time, then the event of labor would hold ontological significance, and as Rodemeyer muses, "would be an interesting twist in the history of philosophy."[23]

Considering childbirth as an experience of the *Augenblick*, a moment of vision where an authentic experience of time is possible, Rodemeyer refers to Iris Marion Young and remarks, "part of such an ecstasis is its seemingly lack of temporal quality. Authentic temporality appears to go 'beyond' time into a 'moment' of timelessness."[24] Prior to being told I was "off the clock," time, in any measured sense of the term, was of no consequence to me. Time, especially as a linear progression, was something forced from the outside. In feeling pangs of discomfort as my labor progressed, I worked with my body (that was also another body) in a rhythm that felt right to me. It was the medical gaze that made me conscious of a particular plan that needed to be followed.

That it was 1 am meant nothing to me, but for the medical staff it meant I had x amount of hours left to deliver the baby to make space in the delivery room for the next laboring subject. This antagonistic intersubjectivity is highlighted in the shared public time of the they (*das Man*), as they set cultural norms and standards that our bodies both resist and accommodate. Haugeland, who translates *das Man* as the *anyone* states, "The total assemblage of norms for a conforming community largely determines the behavioral dispositions of each nondeviant member; in effect, it defines what it is to be a 'normal' member of the community. Heidegger calls this assemblage the *anyone*."[25] The conformity of *das Man* is made salient by its experiencing time as both "shared" and "public" and yet it is something that I never really have. Heidegger asserts, "The only time one knows is the public time which has been levelled off and which belongs to everyone—and that means, to nobody."[26] Everyone can read the same number on the clock, but that shared perception is not felt by anyone as an actual temporal moment, as it is already spatial for Heidegger. And yet, to be a "normal" member of the community, or in this case a "nondeviant" patient, there is the expectation to conform and follow the rules of a universal clock. Is it impossible to have an ecstatic moment or authentic moment of temporality while under the medical gaze?

From the very beginning of my labor, the "two in one conundrum" had to be made intelligible by treating mother and child as separate entities. This is first objectified, as fetal heart monitors are aptly placed to detect the heartbeats of both mother and child. To be clear, I am not denigrating the usefulness of medical technology, though feminist scholars have questioned the necessity of continuous fetal monitoring;[27] rather, I am recounting and illuminating procedures that were particularly salient to me. I am highlighting technological interference that turned my lived experience with time into an objectifiable clock time.

Because my labor took thirty-six hours, there were two separate nurses responsible for my care. Both nurses took radically different approaches, and I can most justly describe their presence as incarnations of good cop versus bad cop. One nurse let me eat when I was hungry, the other did not. One made me stay in bed, the other encouraged me to walk around and bounce on a ball. One told me that pelvic probing was unnecessary, and the other prodded me frequently and tried to "remove a lip" that caused the baby to remain stuck under my pelvic area. Though the "good cop" who refrained from touching me told me that such probing could actually cause inflammation to my pelvic area, making it harder for the baby to come out, I didn't stop the "bad cop" from touching me, because she scared me by insisting that if she didn't "coax" the baby to come out, he could get stressed, his heart could stop beating, and I would need an emergency C-section.

The "good cop" seemed to be interested in my needs, while the "bad cop" just wanted the baby to come out. One nurse made me feel like a subject, while the other made me feel like an object. I know that subjects must necessarily be objectified to be treated as patients; however, as work in the phenomenology of medicine has demonstrated, taking into account both the corporeal (*Körper*) and lived experiences (*Leib*) of embodiment allows for more nuanced and positive experiences of objectification.[28] The "good cop" saw me as more than a body (*Körper*) and empathized with other ways of my being (*Leib*) that could not be made readily present to her. In *Zollikon Seminars*, Heidegger uses the Husserlian distinction between *Körper* and *Leib* to highlight how the latter *says* something about our being, where to *say* (*Sagen*) means to *show* (*Zeigen*), as in to show something ontologically significant.[29] Whereas my lived time *says* something about my being, clock time does not really *show* anything about what "is," even though this form of time can be visually represented and demarcated.

I don't think any moment *says* something more about my time reckoning during labor and the tension between primordial and shared time than the moment I was crowning. At this point, there were more than two nurses in the room, and one held up a mirror and insisted that I look at what was happening. I said I didn't want to see several times, but she insisted that I didn't want to miss it. Part of me was scared to look, as I didn't want to see anything that would upset me and cause me to stop pushing. I was exhausted. The nurse persisted in saying that I should look and continued to hold the mirror. This could accurately be called the "mirror stage" of my labor. Lacan coined the term *mirror stage* to capture the decisive moment when a child becomes individualized; the infant sees themself in the mirror and objectifies themself as existing as a separate entity in the world. While my son didn't become self-individualized in this moment, for me it was the ultimate moment of medicalized clock time. It was visual confirmation from the medical community that had insisted on perception over sensation from the start. From that instant, it was only clock time. The baby was born and any confusion of the "two in one" that offered moments of vision

(*Augenblick*), of authentic temporality, had passed. There was no longer any ambiguity regarding subject and object, a prerequisite for clock time.

The intersubjective antagonism of the medical community risks a temporospatial fracturing of the laboring subject. I found myself teetering and negotiating between an understanding of lived time and clock time, primordial time and shared time, with technological interventions exacerbating the disparateness of the two. In order to ask whether an authentic experience of time is possible in an age of reproductive enframing, I turn to a discussion of Belu's notion of a "*poiēsis* of birth."

Authentic Temporality as a *Poiēsis* of Birth?

Belu describes the oppressive condition of our present technologies of childbearing as "reproductive enframing" and attempts to offer a way of birthing that resists treating mother and child as mere resources, a labor she describes as a "*poiēsis* of birth."[30] A *poiēsis* of birth is thus the bringing-into-being of a child without challenging them forth via technological domination. While Belu does not liken a *poiēsis* of birth to an experience of authentic temporality, I believe the type of "bringing forth" that she describes is akin to the form of primordial time that Rodemeyer examines in her phenomenological analysis of pregnant Dasein. That is, at the moment when a being presences via *poiēsis*, there is a moment (*Augenblick*) when past, present, and future coalesce.

Belu's book is the most comprehensive and exhaustive study of the link between Heidegger's philosophy and reproductive technology to date. It offers important insights regarding the pregnant subject's unique experience as part of the standing reserve; however, there is an oversimplified privileging of natural over technological childbirth from the start, a privileging that haunts the rest of the text. Also, Belu is concerned with how women figure among the standing reserve and expresses a fear that reproductive technology may usher in what she calls a "motherless age." Thus, insofar as her focus is on maternal ontologies, I will speak about mothers rather than laboring subjects as I engage with her work.

Belu begins, "Sexual reproduction and natural (or drug-free) births are increasingly marginalized by high-tech alternatives. Surgical births such as cesarean sections and elective cesarean sections are becoming ever more popular, even fashionable. The latter, especially, bypasses the experience of labor because it extracts the baby without any active input from the mother. But *a baby delivered is not a baby born*."[31] "A baby delivered is not a baby born" insinuates that a "baby born" is better (read: more authentic) than a baby delivered. Also, prior to this phrase, Belu directly states that a woman who has a caesarean section does not have any "active input." While a woman's body may be rendered passive to a certain extent during such a procedure, it is hardly the case that no active temporal consciousness remains. I understand that Belu means "active input" in a bodily sense, in terms of pushing, breathing, and birthing in a way that demonstrates *empathic* attention, but insofar as space and time can hardly be so neatly dichotomized, I think exploring this "active temporal input" *says* (*Sagen* as *Zeigen*) something ontologically significant.

On the one hand, for those women who do not choose elective caesareans, which is the case for most caesareans, this emergency procedure already produces a great deal of shame and guilt for women who would have preferred vaginal delivery. The phrase, "but a baby delivered is not a baby born," further mommy shames and risks alienating women who could not have chosen otherwise. Many women who must undergo caesareans report feelings of shame and guilt, and a great majority express fear.[32] Such affective states, experienced during an active time of reckoning during labor, are ontologically disclosive.

Heidegger asserts that our state-of-mind (*Befindlichkeit*), disclosed by certain moods and feelings, offer us a particular openness or attunement to being. As Sandra Lee Bartky states, "A mood makes manifest 'how one is and how one is faring'; boredom, joy, and above all dread are ontologically disclosive in ways that a passionless pure beholding can never be. These and other states of mind constitute a primordial disclosure of self and world whereby 'we can encounter something that matters to us.'"[33] Bartky then goes on to assert that insofar as women are differently situated in social relations, women will have their proper affective states, most notably of shame and guilt. We previously noted that an ecstatic moment of authentic temporality occurs, for Heidegger, in a mood of anxiety whereby we are held out to the nothing. I challenged Heidegger on this point and wondered why such a moment of vision could not occur when being held out to something, namely, a new coming-into-being. Rather than focus on finitude and being-toward-death, why not explore the ontological significance of infinitude and being-toward-birth? While the woman obtaining a caesarean section may appear passive in the bodily sense, like the woman who delivers "naturally" or "vaginally," she reckons with time in a manner that makes her capable of experiencing, as Rodemeyer states, "the ultimate

Augenblick." No matter your mode of delivery, you are held out to the possibility of a new coming-to-be, and perhaps in experiencing heightened moods of fear, shame, and guilt, the woman who undergoes a caesarean may privilege an *Augenblick*. I do not have the space here to fully unravel a phenomenology of caesarean births, though I find it essential to warn of the danger of distinguishing between active/vaginal and passive/caesarean, a dichotomy that reinforces the kind of binary thinking Rodemeyer questions in her analysis of intersubjective temporospatiality.

I just discussed women who had emergency caesareans, but what about women who *chose* caesareans as an elective procedure, could they be described as having no "active input"? Belu seems to imply that a woman cannot give such informed consent and that women who believe they can actively choose a position of passivity are motivated by "ideological choice talk," which is guilty of "instrumental thinking"; such thinking propelled by a "means to an end" rationale hides technological thinking as a mode of enframing (*Gestell*). She states, "With respect to reproductive enframing, instrumental reason can be seen to explain the development of IVF and ARTs for the sake of increasing women's reproductive freedom or for consolidating patriarchal control of women's reproduction by means of ideological choice-talk."[34] She later continues to critique the notion of informed consent, noting that while liberal feminists view such acquiescence through a *"technophilic lens"* as a means of respecting women's individual rights, radical feminists assert, "full informed consent is not possible considering the [patriarchal] social context within which the medical profession operates."[35] She seems to agree with this radical feminist position as she goes on to assert, "Thus, all reproductive technologies dominate and harm women and informed consent can be seen as a means of legalizing and of thereby neutralizing this patriarchal and capitalist oppression."[36] Viewing consent as a "derivative or degenerative form of empathy," she notes, written contracts (informed consent) should not substitute affective bonds (empathy). I agree with her point that empathy is vital for any patient relation, and I also agree with her remark that empathy risks being covered up by the overuse of reproductive technology. As I described in my phenomenological account of labor, there is a tendency to (over)use technological interventions in ways that negatively objectify the patient. However, there is something unsettling when caesarean births and other forms of medicalized births are automatically discounted as being capable of a *"poiēsis* of birth."

Belu seems to suggest that all technological births are necessarily devoid of empathy and are forms of what she calls "reproductive enframing," where women's bodies are viewed as resources prone to medical optimization. She explores what an unenframed birth would look like, birth as a coming into life that is not forced, specifically not challenged forth through technology. Here, she is not just talking about instruments of technology but any form of technological thinking, that is, any sort of mind-set that approaches labor as something that needs to be controlled and dominated. For example, even the "Lamaze woman" falls under the rubric of reproductive enframing. In attempting to self-master control of her body, she objectifies herself and self-transforms into a docile body that tries to suppress the pains of labor via breathing techniques. Such a collapse of subject/object distinction is a key characteristic of *Gestell* where control, discipline, and optimization are enforced.

Elsewhere, Belu critiques the setting up of a false dilemma between technological birth and its supposed natural alternative, noting "both types of childbirth, technical and natural, reflect the ontological norms that Heidegger associates with modernity: order, control, and efficiency."[37] Here, she recognizes that technophobia and its refusal of technology is not an adequate response to birthing in our modern era, as the option between natural and technological birth only gives one the illusion of choice. All births fall under the rubric of reproductive enframing whether they engage with technological devices or not. For Heidegger, it is not the technological apparatuses themselves that pose a danger to humanity, but rather the ideology that gave birth to them, an ideology that views control and efficiency as ends desirable in themselves.[38] Her assessment of the "Lamaze woman" demonstrates how such ideology affects our approach to childbirth whether we opt for a medicalized birth or not.

And yet, in her new book, there is an instance where thinking outside of such ideology is possible; she presents water birth as a form of labor that lies outside of reproductive enframing. Her suggestion that water birth may offer a *poīesis* of birth didn't sit well with me, because as someone on Medicaid at the time of my pregnancy, one thing was made explicitly clear—*I did not have the option of a water birth*—nor do 42 percent of laboring subjects (or 30 percent to 65 percent depending on race).[39]

Using Sara Ruddick's notion of "the work of conscience," she says in water birth, the mother enters into a relationship with her baby based on "empathy," one that doesn't turn herself or her baby into mere resource.[40] Whereas Ruddick asks whether an authentic form of educating children is possible, in opposition to an inauthentic pedagogy built on domination, Belu uses this authentic/inauthentic differentiation to think about two distinct modes of solicitude set forth by Heidegger, "leaping-in" (authentic care) versus "leaping-ahead" (inauthentic care). Although "leaping-in" involves a relation of care based on domination and control, a "leaping ahead" entails promoting a work of conscience where the other encourages "self care." Belu states,

> In childbirth, especially in water birth, we see *physis* as *poiēsis*, albeit in an ambiguous way. Quite literally the baby emerges into unconcealment. She arises and brings herself forth into the world. [. . .] Immersed in a big tub of water at home or in the sea, the woman is free to move around. [. . .] The woman is not challenged-forth nor does she challenge herself forth through technology or the need to perform. [. . .] The midwife encourages the woman's labor without intrusion or domination.[41]

So, whereas during a medicalized birth, doctors "leap-in" (inauthentic care), during a water birth, the pregnant subject and midwife "leap-ahead" (authentic care). Belu says in water birth, we see *physis* (nature) as *poiēsis*, because something comes into being via *physis* when something emerges into existence from out of itself, rather than being coaxed into being from outside influences, that is, technological interference. While Belu states that water birth is not the only way to experience a "*poiēsis* of birth," we are left wondering what other "nonmedicalized" options are available. While she asks us to engage in a "work of conscience," where we reflect on the conditions of our giving birth, that choice is only dubbed "authentic" if it is followed by an opting for a nonmedicalized birth. It appears that a woman who performs a "work of conscience" and chooses a medicalized birth is guilty of false consciousness. This is very problematic because it devalues and undermines the experiences of the laboring subject, indicating that her "work of conscience" didn't provide her the right form of clarity.

Furthermore, Belu speaks about the undertaking of a water birth at home or in the sea in the presence of a midwife, yet she doesn't take into consideration the social context in which this is possible. Previously, in her critique of the Lamaze woman, she notes that such women are of a certain demographic, namely, affluent white women attempting to empower themselves in light of the patriarchy. Can a similar point be raised with respect to those women choosing water births? They are largely affluent white women. When roughly 42 percent of women in the US are covered by Medicaid, who can afford a private midwife to "leap ahead"? And, if a water birth is performed at home, a midwife should be present, as poor women delivering at home without one have a higher risk of mother mortality, and the risk is even greater for Black women. Water births are not possible under Medicaid, so this means roughly half of women in the United States must, out of necessity, be duped by "ideological choice talk." Again, Belu does not say that water births are the only authentic means of birthing, but if medicalized births are off the table, what else is left besides an alternative "natural" birth, where we are left with the same false distinction between the natural and the technological, a gulf further divided according to socioeconomic concerns?

Antoine Pageau-St-Hilaire raised the concern that my issue with water birth is less about the experience it offers women and more about the confines of a deplorable health-care system.[42] While he is correct that there is a larger issue with the institution of the American health-care system rather than with water birth itself, I am concerned with the actual *lived* experiences that pregnant subjects are able to have. One of Heidegger's failings stems from the fact that he favors ontology over ethics; despite examining Dasein as being-in-the-world, he is unable to see how the act of defining "what is" prescribes normative conditions for how we "should" exist in said world. An ontology of birth that favors water birth is making an ethical claim. If women *ought* to choose water births because such form of labor offers a privileged experience of being, but women do not exist in a world where this is possible, how does such privileging devalue the birthing experiences of laboring subjects? Certainly, just because something "is" does not mean it "ought" to be that way, but the point is, mapping out an ontology of birth necessarily makes value judgments about the practical conditions of birth. The fact that water birth is not an option for women on Medicaid does speak to the deficiencies of the American health-care system, but even if it were permitted, the issue remains as to whether one should privilege "natural" versus "technological" childbirth, and who are the authorities who draw the line?

Given my apprehension regarding water birth being exemplary of an unenframed birth, does this mean that all births must necessarily fall under the rubric of reproductive enframing? If so, is laboring Dasein capable of experiencing the ultimate *Augenblick* as that ecstatic moment in time where past, present, and future collide? Or do the external influences of technology privilege a futural time founded on utility and efficiency? While I am reluctant to classify water birth as a "*poiēsis* of birth" that favors an authentic form of temporality, I cannot provide a clear alternative. I find attempts by the medical community to regulate all laboring subjects according to the same clock problematic, but so too is favoring one form of birthing over another.

The key issue with seeking a *poiēsis* of birth or an authentic experience of time during labor is that it is not something that I can take up consciously. I cannot will a disclosive moment of my being-toward-death; I cannot wish to understand being, close my eyes, reflect on death, and experience this ontological event. Nor can I consciously project myself into a future where "I" and "other" become separated during the event of labor. It is in a moment of anxiety, but not of an *intentional* something of which I am anxious, that discloses my being-toward-death. I cannot plan being held out to the anxiety of nothingness (as an ontological event) any more than I can plan the circumstances of my labor (as an ontological event). What Heidegger refers to as the "call of conscience" seizes us, without our conscious enforcement.[43] This "call of conscience" discloses our basis of freedom and our ability to be authentic, but it is not something I can beckon by my volition alone. Thus, I am at a loss for properly planning conditions that would be conducive for a *poiēsis* of birth, as that moment of vision (*Augenblick*) cannot be premeditated.

Chapter 2

Problem: What Is Woman?

The Hermeneutics of Sex/Gender Facticity

Problem: What Is Woman?

What does Martin Heidegger say about sex or gender? According to most accounts, including Derrida's influential essay "*Geschlecht*: Sexual Difference, Ontological Difference,"[1] Heidegger makes a marginal reference to sex in a 1928 Marburg Lecture later translated as "The Metaphysical Foundations of Logic" (GA 26).[2] However, an earlier allusion to sexual difference appears in a 1923 Freiburg Lecture, translated as "Ontology—The Hermeneutics of Facticity" (GA 63), where he explains why he uses the term *Dasein* instead of *man* in his existential analytic.[3] *Man* carries *his* own historical baggage, representing a living being endowed with reason, as well as a pregiven understanding of what it means to be a person. This latter definition has its roots in a Judeo-Christian tradition where *man* is created in the image of God as the firstborn of many "brethren." In a perplexing move, Heidegger then cites biblical passages to highlight the sexed emergence of man in Genesis as he poses the question, "Problem: What is woman?"[4] This chapter untangles what it means for Heidegger to ask such a question, particularly as he leaves it unanswered and seemingly negligible in his pursuit of a hermeneutics of facticity.

An initial version of this chapter is set for publication as "Problem: What Is Woman? The Hermeneutics of Sex/Gender Facticity," *Heidegger, Dasein, and Gender: Thinking the Unthought*, ed. Trish Glazebrook and Susanne Dawn Claxton (Lanham, MD: Rowman & Littlefield, 2024).

Heidegger states, "Hermeneutics is itself not a philosophy. It wishes only to place an object which has hitherto fallen into forgetfulness before today's philosophers for their 'well-disposed consideration.'"[5] I place the object of sex/gender[6] facticity before today's philosophers, situating the "Problem: What is woman?" within the context of Heidegger's larger ontological project, namely, to rediscover the question of being or to rethink the phenomenological relations that constitute "what is," that allows for being. Captured in the eponymous title *Ontology—The Hermeneutics of Facticity* is the insight that the study of being (ontology) can only be carried out as an interpretive nonobjectifying process (hermeneutics) of our existence at a particular time in history (facticity). What does it mean to exist as a certain sex or gender during a particular time? How are sex and gender related to the question of being and the ontological difference? How are we defining sex and gender and to which term does Heidegger refer? Throughout this chapter, I will examine a few instances where Heidegger reckons with the sex/gender question. By posing the inquiry, "Problem: What is woman?" within the parameters of Heidegger's philosophy, I suggest that sex and gender must be fluid categories insofar as such properties describe the "whatness" of our existence rather than the "how" of our world-forming. That is, such attributes only show up (as owned) after a time reckoning and authentic enactment of our neutral temporal structure of care. I also suggest that Heidegger privileges sex/gender facticity in undergirding such neutrality as he contests Judeo-Christian origin stories of the flesh (GA 63) as well as evolutionary theories and the *Lebensphilosophie* of his time (GA 26). Finally, I conclude by demonstrating how Heidegger's distinction between *Körper* and *Leib* further upholds sex and gender fluidity.

Ontology:
The Hermeneutics of Facticity and Ontological Sex Inequality

If we are to remain true to Heidegger's project of historical ontology, neither sex nor gender can be grasped as essentialist concepts that defy the influence of history. That is, what it means to exist as or to be a sex or gender changes over time. In the rare instances where Heidegger evokes concepts of sex or gender, such terms appear to be linked to a question of generation/*genos*/genesis. In GA 63, when Heidegger explains his choice of the term *Dasein* over *man*, he refers to the book of Genesis and quotes the following two passages:

For a *man* ought not to cover his head, since he is the image and glory of God [*emphasis mine*].—Paul, 1 Cor. 11:7

For those who he foreknew, he also predestined to be conformed to the image of his *Son*, in order that he might be the firstborn among many *brethren* [*emphasis mine*].[7]—Cf. 2 Cor. 3:18 and Rom. 8:29

Without further examination regarding the significance of these quotes, he very abruptly remarks, "Problem: What is *woman?*" (*emphasis mine*). This question, "Problem: Was ist die Frau?"[8] is never answered but merely interjected. Yet, three thoughts necessarily flow from its inquiry. First, the concept of man, with its Judeo-Christian roots, necessarily excludes woman from having a direct relation to being (if being is God), since only man was made in his likeness. Second, man, in not having to cover his head, is already established within a hierarchy of sexual difference and such differences are predicated prior to an interpretative investigation of facticity.[9] Third, the problem of woman introduces a problem of the flesh that makes of man (spirit)/woman (flesh) a dialectical relation, and Heidegger accuses dialectics of committing the same error as static juxtapositions. Of dialectic he asserts, "It steps into an already constructed context, though there really is no context here [. . .] Every category is an existential and *is* this as such, not merely in relation to other categories and on the basis of this relation."[10] His disdain for dialectics and its inability to properly adhere to historical ontology is further evidenced in the Appendix XI *On Paul* that is directly related to the section that raises the question, "Problem: What is woman?" In further demonstrating a dialectical relation on which Judeo-Christian origin stories of sexual difference rely, the Appendix elucidates, "Flesh-*spirit* [. . .] to be in them, a *how* as a "what," objective heavenly, the *what* as the how of a history coming to an end. Explanation of facticity: of the unredeemed, and being redeemed: [. . .] [sons of God] (Rom. 8:14). Death-life, sin-righteousness, slavery-sonship [. . .]. 'History of salvation' unclear!"[11] Heidegger thus asserts that dialectic turns the "how" of facticity (as an historical process) into an objective "what" (a stasis) in relation to other categories. Also, apparent in this text is what side of the dialectic woman would fall on: flesh, unredeemed, death, slavery.

Though Heidegger does not explicitly explain why he poses the problem of woman, I will argue that the issue of *Frau* as woman is tied to a question of generation, as interpreted by St. Augustine who Heidegger declares a few pages earlier as the philosopher who provides "the first hermeneutics in grand style."[12] In reckoning with the ontological inequality between the sexes, St. Augustine declares that man was created for the contemplative life (of the spirit), whereas woman finds her origins in corporeality (of the flesh) and procreative purpose (even though man and woman are equal in the eyes of God).[13] That is, she was created for Adam to have a descendent; she was created for her sex. Woman's particular relation to sexual fecundity is why she must cover her head and man "ought not." From her inception, woman is born with a specific form of guilt, accorded because of her bodily intention. Such predetermined guilt runs contrary to Heidegger's notion of Dasein's primordial "being guilty," that is being born on the basis of a nullity, on groundlessness.[14] As Dasein, we are "thrown" into the world without a plan, without a blueprint, and so, woman could not be created for her flesh any more than man could be designed for the contemplative (read rational) life. While Arendt does not directly refer to Heidegger's mention of Genesis in GA 63, she highlights Augustine's thought in describing the plurality of human action, noting "To Augustine, the creation story offers a welcome opportunity to stress the species character of animal life as distinguished from the singularity of human existence," a species being Heidegger will go on to critique.[15] Aware of "man's" historical baggage as already being predetermined as not only a rational animal but as a person whose hierarchy is predetermined through an ontological sex inequality, Heidegger prefers to use the term *Dasein* in his existential analytic.[16]

In part, such a reading agrees with Kevin Aho who argues that Dasein cannot be a "man" or "woman" with fixed properties, as Dasein is not a static entity but rather a dynamic way of being.[17] Additionally, he contends that such a dynamism of sexed or gendered practices can only be intelligible on the basis of temporality, for time is that reference point by which any being(s) can be understood at all. My temporal structure is so that I understand myself as a past "thrownness," taking up a history that has been passed down to me, a present series of nows, and a future projection in which I anticipate the possibilities of what I can be. Yet, describing myself *in time* tells me *what* I am but not *how* I came to be so. This is because I exist *in time* inauthentically, experiencing the passage of time as a series of "now" moments. The *how* of my existence only makes sense in terms of care (*Sorge*), the fact that something can matter to me at all; yet "the primordial unity of the structure of care lies in temporality."[18] Care is a temporal receptiveness that allows sex or gender to have any significance, and that allows such predicates to be of concern to me.

I will return to a discussion of care in the next section, but I want to highlight a point that Aho raises with respect to those thinkers (Dreyfus, Guignon, Haugeland, Brandom) who view the they/the Anyone (*Das Man*), rather than temporality, as the source of Dasein's intelligibility. For such thinkers, our disclosive nexus of social relations (*Das Man*) is responsible for an understanding of being, so insofar as such institutions are patriarchal and founded on social hierarchies, Dasein must necessarily be gendered. I agree with this *to some extent*. To borrow a term from Haugeland, insofar as we are "cases of Dasein,"[19] the *whatness* of my case, my mineness (*Jemeinigkeit*) that is also part of a larger shared community, is already gendered, for as Trish Glazebrook notes, "This world is *very much informed* by gender."[20] Yet, this does not explain the *how* of my world-forming, the neutral disclosive structures of *how* this is possible.

Returning to Aho's question for such thinkers, he states, "The question we come to is this: Is Heidegger's project shortsighted because it fails to grasp the fact that the disclosive clearing we rely on to interpret things *as such* is ordered in terms of social hierarchies? This criticism is particularly sharp if we maintain—as many Heidegger commentators do—that the origin or source of intelligibility is *Das Man*."[21] Is Heidegger that shortsighted with respect to social hierarchies? Heidegger's question, "Problem: What is woman?" was raised to highlight an unequal sex difference that was predetermined prior to an investigative interpretation of facticity. "Man" and his dialectical relation to "woman" is loaded with preestablished significance, hence Heidegger's preference for the term *Dasein*, which signifies a neutral "being there" prior to intelligibility. However, such reference to sex inequality is not meant to laud Heidegger as a feminist, for I think he was shortsighted insofar as the "ontic entanglements" he found worthy of pursuing in his quest for being neglect issues of significance to the "second sex."[22] Furthermore, Heidegger's critique of origin stories founded on sexual difference does not mean that Heidegger was an advocate for equality. Reckoning with social hierarchies may be subtle in this 1923 lecture, but Heidegger explicitly deals with the significance of rank as it correlates to his ontological project in the *Black Notebooks*. I will return to such hierarchies and what *Geschlecht* may mean for Heidegger's politics in chapter 5.

In this section, I've demonstrated that Heidegger's first reference to sex/gender facticity that occurs in GA 63 dismisses Judeo-Christian origin stories of sexual difference in that such differences are assumed prior to a proper ontological investigation. Such distinctions may describe the "whatness" of an already biased world, but they do not explain the "how" of such world-forming. It is this "how" and the neutral temporal structures that disclose it that interests Heidegger. The "how" of these structures is further examined in *The Metaphysical Foundations of Logic* (GA 26), the key text that scholars usually analyze in trying to understand Heidegger's position on sex and gender neutrality.

The Metaphysical Foundations of Logic and the Primacy of Sexual Difference

Transcendence, World-forming, and Care

Heidegger will go on to further examine the neutrality of this not-yet-determined Dasein in GA 26, where he understands Dasein as the condition of its possibilities. The problem of being is necessarily a problem of freedom insofar as Dasein exists as an openness to other ways of existing.[23] Here, Dasein is analyzed as prior to its factual concretion, prior to its predetermined predicates. Heidegger asserts that any understanding of being, where being is not yet determined, involves a primordial transcendence.[24] The issue becomes, how can Dasein, as "being there" at a certain time and always already in a world, a world arguably characterized by sex and gender, transcend said world? Heidegger asserts, "Dasein is thrown, factical, thoroughly amidst nature through its bodiliness, and transcendence lies in the fact that these beings, among which Dasein is and to which Dasein belongs, are surpassed by Dasein. In other words, as transcending, Dasein is beyond nature, although, as factical, it remains environed by nature. As transcending, i.e., as free, Dasein is something alien to nature [. . .] That towards which the subject transcends is what we call world."[25] In defining transcendence as such, Heidegger does not wish to make a subject/object distinction in the way of Descartes. That is, we cannot transcend the world as disinterested observers, using reason to declare objective facts about our environment. Dasein can transcend nature while remaining factically environed by it, because nature, as it appears to us, is not pregiven in advance; it is *given* to the extent that we are thrown into a physical environment, but it is not *pregiven* in terms of having an absolute essence; nature can mean different things, therefore making up a different type of world. That is, how nature appears to us depends on a mix of phenomenological perception and environment, with such perception depending on the "there" of our being, the situated knowledges and attunement (*Stimmung*) from which we approach our surroundings.

To be clear, as being-in-the-world, we are both in a "concrete" world *and* a "phenomenological" one. In transcending world (phenomenologically) in a "moment of vision" (*Augenblick*), we are able to suspend any *grounding* of meaning. In this instance, there is a "potency of essence" or a certain adjournment in the enaction of care because I am not, at this moment, engaged in a mode of circumspective concern or solicitude; I am not interacting with other entities in my "concrete" world/environment in a mode of average everydayness, as such entities are now under theoretical examination. During this *Augenblick*, I am in the process of examining the different phenomenological relations that confer meaning to my relations with things (concern) and others (solicitude). And yet, during this *Augenblick*, I factically exist in this environment, in a body, alongside other beings.

The difficulty teasing apart the relation between phenomenological world and concrete world is enmeshed with the problem of ontological difference (and sexual difference) in that these relations do not lay bare before me for objective calculations. Insofar as Dasein is always "chained to a body" this relation cannot be clearly distinguished, as we'll see in the next section when exploring the body as *Körper* and *Leib*. Being is always understood via a certain worldview of beings, neither of which (beings/being) can be understood apart from a certain historical awareness. Dasein does not transcend over and above a world (as subject/object), but *toward* it. Care, as a temporal neutral structure, propels Dasein to transcend world (to be free for possibilities), a world constantly evolving as "temporality temporalizes."

Transcendence is tied to Heidegger's definition of understanding as projection. Dasein understands itself as a projection onto its possibilities of existence, a projection made possible by our underlying structure of care that lies in temporality.[26] Projection necessarily implies an understanding of our already being in a world insofar as we must be able to imagine the world that we are in as existing other than it is. Dasein is always in a world, but that world may change insofar as self, others, and nature are not static entities. There is always an interplay of relations involving phenomenological perception, attunement, environment, and language that allows us to say "what is."

As Heidegger states in "On the Essence of Ground" (OEG), as transcending, Dasein is "world-forming."[27] The transcendence that is required for any *understanding* of being is different from intentionality, as the latter implies a conscious being-toward an object. As transcending, as being in the process of world-forming, Dasein moves beyond a simple cognizance of entities into an authentic engagement with, or into an authentic enactment of, its neutral structure of care. As world-forming, Dasein comes to understand its mode of being. It is on the basis of care that entities can matter (either negatively or positively) for Dasein and that they can become possible within the purview of what Heidegger calls a mode of circumspective concern or solicitude.[28]

As Heidegger makes clear in *Being and Time* (GA 2), things appear to us in the world because of our care for them, that is, they matter to us. My ability to be factically dispersed, into one world among others, into one sex/gender among others, depends on how I engage with my existential structure of care (negatively or positively). Heidegger calls that being who does not yet own its choices or understand its world positively as mythic or primitive Dasein. Primitive Dasein lets itself be governed by nature (via an inauthentic concern for its environment) and fails to enact its structure of care in a way that allows for "world-forming."[29] Primitive Dasein may describe the "what" of its environment but does not engage with "how" such surroundings, coupled with phenomenological perception, come to form a potential "world." It is this "how" of sex/gender facticity that interests Heidegger and not the "what."

In keeping with Heidegger's project of historical ontology, sex and gender must be fluid categories, as they are possibilities that may be differently owned. Yes, we are (quite literally) thrown into the world as sexed/gendered bodies, but to say that I was assigned female at birth and to remark that I was forced to wear a bow on my head to indicate my girlhood is to describe the "what" of my existence and not the "how" in terms of this being possible and how it could be otherwise. It is important to highlight that Heidegger turns to an existential analysis of Dasein, that being for whom its being is an issue, as a *preparatory* step in his project of fundamental ontology to address the problem of being (the *how*). The *whatness* of my being, how I/others show up in the world is disclosive, but only ontologically so, insofar as the *how* of such an emergence is revealed, that is, insofar as an understanding of care and temporality as a neutral structure is broached. As such, the not-yet-determinedness of Dasein, what Heidegger will go on to describe as a neutrality, may make sense, but what is curious about Heidegger's discussion of transcendence and its insistence on a not-yet-determined ground is the primacy that sexual difference is accorded in undergirding such neutrality.

He asserts. "Selfhood is the presupposition for the possibility of being an 'I,' the latter only ever being disclosed in the 'you.' Never, however, is selfhood relative to a 'you' but rather—because it first makes all this possible—is neutral with respect to being an 'I' and being a 'you' and *above all with respect to such things as sexuality* [emphasis mine]."[30] Selfhood, at other times described as *jemeinigkeit* (in each case mine), is my way of being that is not totally separate from others and from the world but is nevertheless my possibility, my projection onto an array of diverse projects that matter to me.[31] Such selfhood is described as neutral, insofar as such not-yet-determinedness implies potential, but why does Heidegger find it necessary to mention such neutrality with respect to sexuality? As Derrida inquires, why the "*à plus forte raison*," why the "above all," as if we risked mixing the question of sexual difference with the question of being?[32] In accentuating this "above all," is Heidegger simply reiterating that at which he hinted in GA 63, that we must abandon Judeo-Christian origin stories of the flesh that are founded on unequal sexual difference if we are to raise the question of being anew? To understand why Heidegger highlights the sexual neutrality of Dasein, we must unpack certain principles he sets forth in GA 26.

THE PRIVILEGING OF SEXUAL DIFFERENCE AND BIOLOGY

In his first principle, he reiterates that neutral Dasein and not man is under analysis. Then, he reinforces the sexual neutrality of Dasein as he states, "This neutrality also indicates that Dasein is neither of the two sexes. But here sexlessness is not the indifference of an empty void, the weak negativity of an indifferent ontic nothing. In its neutrality Dasein is not the indifferent nobody and everybody, but the primordial positivity and potency of the essence."[33] This reference to primordial positivity and potency of the essence is in line with Dasein's constitution as a condition of its possibilities, as both terms speak of the potential of Dasein to be, of its freedom; such freedom consists of its prerogative to establish a ground, the freedom to define "what is." But, in describing the "how" in which one establishes a ground, why must Heidegger declare Dasein's *sexual* neutrality above all other attributes? In surmising the need for such clarification, Derrida posits, "Perhaps he was then responding to more or less explicit, naïve or sophisticated, questions on the part of his hearers, readers, students, or colleagues, still held, aware or not, within anthropological space. What about the sexual life of your Dasein? They might have still asked."[34] Glazebrook responds to this supposition that Heidegger may have been replying to the query of a student, asserting, "[In GA 26], he argues presumably in response to a question that could have come from Helene Weiss, that Dasein is a gender-neutral term. It is in the part of Heidegger's lecture constructed from the notes of Weiss that his comments on the neutrality of the term *Dasein*, in particular, on its gender-neutrality, appear."[35] While Glazebrook suggests that his specification of neutrality may be in response to Weiss, she also puts forth a further clarification that, contrary to Derrida's supposition that "*keines von beiden Geschlechtern ist*" indicates that Dasein is neither of the two *sexes*, it actually asserts that Dasein is neither of the two *genders*. Derrida does notice the polyvalence that the term *Geschlecht* will later take on, stating that in thirty years' time, it could stand for sex, gender, family stock, race, lineage, generation.[36] Does *Geschlecht* mean sex or gender for Heidegger?

While Weiss could have inquired about gender, Heidegger appears to discuss *Geschlecht* in terms of generation, as a fecundity founded on sexual difference. From a contemporary viewpoint, to designate something as "neither of the two genders" seems to ignore the fact that to posit the existence of (only) two genders does nothing more than to reify an already supposed binary sexed system. As Judith Butler inquires, if gender has nothing to do with sexual difference, why suppose there are only two genders? From here, Butler puts forth a social constructionist view that sex is always already gender.[37] In *Phenomenal Gender: What Transgender Experience Discloses*, Ephraim Das Janssen, who draws from Heidegger's phenomenology to characterize the experience of gender, holds a similar view, asserting, "My fulfillment of the role 'man' in my culture is thus dependent on my assumption of this culture's particular, historical conception of 'masculinity' at this time. And what of biological sex? In this regard, biology is to a great extent a function of *Mitsein* as well, since scientific endeavors are shaped by cultural needs and presuppositions."[38] If sex is always already gender, then it doesn't matter much if *Geschlecht* is meant to connote one term over the other. The term *gender* as we know it, wasn't used in the language, or *Rede*, of Heidegger's time, though both early and later Heidegger reference *Geschlecht* in binary terms. Early Heidegger (1928) states, "Dasein is neither of the *two*," and later Heidegger (1959), despite addressing the versatility of the term *Geschlecht* asserts, "At the same time, the word [*Geschlecht*] always refers to the twofoldness of the sexes."[39] In this section, I am interested in how early Heidegger understands this binary and why sex/gender neutrality in particular is investigated in attempting to reveal the underlying neutral structure of care/temporality.

Why does Heidegger specify "neither of the two"? Could it be to reiterate his argument against a Judeo-Christian ground founded on sexual inequality? Could Heidegger specify sexual neutrality as a way to dismiss Freudian accounts of psychosexual development? Or is it possible that Heidegger posits Dasein as neither of the two sexes to separate himself from biologists and practitioners of *Lebensphilosophie*, a philosophy of life?

In the fourth principle of GA 26, Heidegger makes clear that the analysis of Dasein is prior to all prophesying and heralding worldviews, and he directly sets his analysis apart from any *Lebensphilosophie*.[40] Such philosophies of life were highly influenced by the evolutionary ideas of Darwin for whom the proliferation and future of the species rely on sexual selection. For Darwin, sexual difference is the ground on which all other attributes of difference are possible. Heidegger appears in conversation with evolutionary biologists in his ninth principle when he discusses Dasein's neutrality in terms of its being-with, for Dasein is always a being-with others; yet, such neutral being-with "is not explained solely on the basis of the supposedly more primordial species-being of sexually differentiated bodily creatures."[41] Does Heidegger notice a proximity to Darwin or to theories of evolution from which he must distance himself? As Heath Massey demonstrates, despite Heidegger's brief discussion of and subsequent dismissal of Henri Bergson, Heidegger is much more indebted to the author of *Creative Evolution*'s philosophy of temporality than he lets on.[42] I am not going to dwell on the issue of temporality specifically, rather I mention Heidegger's engagement with Bergson to suggest that he was more influenced by evolutionary theories than he acknowledges.

In *The Descent of Man, and Selection in Relation to Sex*, Darwin examines sexual selection and sexual difference and how on the basis of two sexes additional differential attributes become possible.[43] One year after GA 26 (1928) in *The Fundamental Concepts of Metaphysics: World, Finitude, Solitude* (GA 29/30, 1929), Heidegger clearly disagrees with biologists and evolutionary theorists who fail to distinguish between the relational structure of the animal and that of the human environment. Heidegger states, "The worker bees know the flowers that they seek, their color and scent, but they don't know the stamens of these flowers *as* stamens . . . they don't know something like the goal of the stamen and petal. Over against this the world of man is rich, greater in its sphere, wider-reaching in its penetration."[44] The animal is restricted in its openness to being. The bee, for example, is receptive to the things in its environment (*Umwelt*) and has its own way of navigating such environs, but that environment will never *matter* enough to constitute a world. The bee does not have an authentic capacity for care that is required to understand being. As Zimmerman states, "Just as Dasein opens up a temporal-historical clearing which makes it possible for entities to manifest themselves in such a way that Dasein can interact with them, so too the organism opens up a sphere which reveals things in ways that enable it to interact with them in specific ways. Despite this structural analogy, Heidegger maintained that the animal's perceptual 'capacity' (*Fähigkeit*) for perceiving is different from the human's 'potentiality for being' (*Seinkönnen*)."[45] The human's "potentiality for being" is markedly different because of their self-awareness of things *as* things. But also, the human has a capacity for language and a particular relation to death. The human organism is aware of their death, not as a perishing, but as an ontological disclosure of finitude, a finitude that informs its language and process of world-forming. Noting that the essence of finitude is "unveiled in *transcendence as freedom for ground*," Heidegger elaborates, "Clarifying the *essence of finitude* in Dasein from out of the constitution of its being must precede all 'self-evident' assumptions concerning the finite 'nature' of the human being, all description of properties that first ensue from finitude, and *above all* any hasty 'explanation' of the ontic provenance of such properties [emphasis mine]."[46] Heidegger thus warns that we must approach the essence of finitude differently than the mortality of the human being, and *above all* without reference to any ontic properties of death. Could it be that this "above all" reference is linked to the previously discussed "above all" with reference to sex? That is, is Heidegger alluding to the close association of sex and death in evolutionary theory and the link between sexual selection and species survival?[47] Is the "neither of the two sexes" clarification meant as a further contestation of Darwin or of other biologists?

In GA 2, Heidegger states, "The existential analytic of Dasein comes *before* any psychology or anthropology, and certainly before any biology."[48] Why the *certainly* before any biology as if to privilege biology over other mentioned disciplines? Heidegger is writing in an intellectual milieu that finds itself in dialogue with two opposing movements: mechanism versus vitalism. Mechanism is a biological approach that views an organism in terms of its material parts functioning like a machine, whereas vitalism supposes some form of immaterial force that sparks or drives life. Heidegger is clearly against mechanistic approaches as he questions the "primordial totality of Dasein's structural *whole*."[49] He also separates himself from vitalism by explicitly calling out Bergson, who coined the term, accusing him of moving in the direction of a "philosophical anthropology."[50] He then returns to a critique of biology as he introduces the term *Umwelt* in his analysis of Dasein's being-in-the-world in general. Heidegger states, "Nowadays there is much talk about 'man's' having an environment [Umwelt]'; but this says nothing ontologically as long as this 'having' is left indefinite. In its very possibility this 'having' is founded upon the existential state of Being-in [. . .] Although this state of Being is one of which use has made in biology, especially since K. von Baer, one must not conclude that its philosophical use implies 'biologism.' "[51]

The term *Umwelt* was coined by biologist Jacob von Uexküll and is meant to convey the *relational* structure between an animal and its environment. Heidegger appears inspired by Uexküll's work as Dasein ("being there") is always "there" in a world, a world experienced by a mode of circumspective concern in which it navigates its environment. Though, Heidegger doesn't directly reference Uexküll after introducing *Umwelt*, he mentions Karl Ernst von Baer. Brett Buchanan traces Heidegger's engagement with biologists and highlights that Baer's name reappears in GA 29/30 where Heidegger more thoroughly explores Dasein's relation to animals, plants, and material substances. Heidegger asserts, "It is true that one scientist of the grand style, Karl Ernst von Baer, was able to see something essential in the first half of the last [nineteenth] century, even though it remains concealed within modern philosophical and theological perspectives."[52] Heidegger does not say what this "something essential" is, but Baer was considered the founding father of embryology, and Buchanan suspects that it's Baer's emphasis on epigenetic development and the way that an organism unfolds as a *whole* that was of interest to Heidegger. Buchanan paints a picture in which Heidegger is inspired by certain biologists but never fully satisfied. Darwin was too mechanistic; Hans Driesch conceived of the organism in holistic terms but ascribed to a form of neovitalism where some immaterial force, irrespective of its environment, drives its development; F. J. J. Buytendjk considers the intimate nature with which we interact with our environments but nevertheless speaks of the organism and the environment as separate entities, not as a unity. Uexküll seems to capture the interrelatedness of organism/environment in his conception of *Umwelt*, but Heidegger is unhappy with his inability to distinguish Dasein from other animals.

For Heidegger, biologists cannot address the "having" of an environment or the "how" of our being-in-the-world, despite what he calls their "objective fertility."[53] When Heidegger states that Dasein is "neither of the two," he seems to be in dialogue with biologists who locate sexual difference as the origin of a species. Yet, while his earlier works show him distinguishing himself from biological notions of sexual difference (whatness), while seeking neutral structures prior to sex/gender facticity (how), his later works such as "Language in the Poem: A Discussion on George Trakl's Poetic Work" (1959) and "The Origin of the Work of Art" (1950) demonstrate his playing with the language of sexual generation in a way that supports a certain politics of the state, a point to which I will return in chapter 5.

In further clarifying the essence of finitude (OEG), Heidegger leaves an interesting footnote that specifies, "The leap [*Sprung*] into the origin [*Ursprung*]! (Da-sein) origin—freedom—temporality; finitude of Dasein not identical with the finitude of the human being, to be grasped otherwise: character of origin!"[54] The origin (*Ursprung*) that Heidegger refers to is different than the origin (*Entstehung*) that Darwin refers to, as *Ursprung* is later defined in "The Origin of the Work of Art" (OWA) as "to originate something by a leap, to bring something into being from out of its essential source in a founding leap."[55] Such a founding leap runs contrary to Darwin's slow-paced theory of evolution informed by natural selection. Quoting Darwin, François Jacob notes, "For natural selection can act only by taking advantage of slight successive variations; she can never take a leap but must advance by the shortest and slowest steps."[56] Yet, the founding leap that Heidegger is after is not a question of the finitude of the human being (as a species being) but of Dasein, and this leap implies a projection, a transcendence, of which the animal is not capable. And yet, while Heidegger's OWA examines the origin of the artwork, rather than that of our species, we can hardly ignore the sexed dimensions of earth/world and how the evolutionary interplay of these terms is responsible for the artwork, a work who, like the child, is "the bringing forth of a being such as never was before and will never come to be again."[57]

David Krell suggests that the introduction of "earth" and its relation to origin (*Ursprung*) to Heidegger's already established "world," comes from the poetic influence of one of the most ancient Homeric Hymns, "To Earth, Mother of All" in which Gaia has the "power to give mortal men life. Or take it."[58] However, it appears unlikely that Heidegger believes in any goddess origin, as he concludes OWA with a warning from Hölderlin, "That which dwells near the origin abandons the site," thus cautioning against searches for a solid ground.[59] In the same way that Dasein is "neither of the two sexes," the origin of the artwork is "neither earth nor world," as it is not a question of neither/nor but rather of both/and. Yet, even though this both/and rejects a unitary origin, escaping any philosophy of "the One," it nevertheless hints at an origin grounded on a binary difference, leading us to ask, as Derrida did, "What if sexual difference were already marked in the opening up of the question of the sense of being and of the ontological difference?"[60]

Insofar as sex is conceived in terms of a binary, such distinction appears to be thinking of sex as a reproductive difference, or sex as a binary reflects the history of the times in which nonbinary and genderqueer were not yet part of the vernacular, and subsequently, not yet thinkable. I do not mean to reify such a binary by speaking of "neither of the two sexes," rather I am working with the language of Heidegger's philosophy to interpret the significance that sex/gender may have had for him.

In the sixth principle of GA 26, Heidegger asserts, "Dasein harbors the intrinsic possibility for being factically dispersed into bodiliness and thus into sexuality. The metaphysical neutrality of the human being, inmost isolated as Dasein, is not an empty abstraction from the ontic, a neither-nor; it is rather the authentic concreteness of the origin, the not-yet of factical dispersion [*Zerstreutheit*]."[61] The not-yet of this dispersion is Dasein's potential, its conditions of possibility, though this "not yet" implies a "both/and" that is prior to "neither of the two sexes." For example, the artwork is both earth/world at its origin, yet while "set up" as an artwork, earth recedes, and we are left with an "historical truth" that is a world that is experienced at a particular time. Dasein as the not-yet of two sexes implies that it is both at its origin, yet one upon dispersion (one sex); sexual difference is the process of "how" Dasein becomes factically dispersed into the "what" of its sex. This process is further described in the sixth principle as Heidegger explains that dispersion is an affair of "multiplication (not 'multiplicity') which is present in every factically individuated Dasein as such."[62] The distinction between multiplication and multiplicity is key here, for multiplicity implies that a plethora of attributes are already found in Dasein that then becomes factically dispersed, whereas multiplication signifies the *process* of such dispersed multiplicity (the how and not the what).

In this section, I've further demonstrated the fluidity of sex and gender by drawing from Heidegger's concept of neutral Dasein set forth in GA 26. Here, he describes the process by which one becomes a sexually differentiated being. I also suggest that by declaring, "Dasein is neither of the two sexes," Heidegger is trying to separate himself from biologists and evolutionary theories of the time, theories for which sex and death were essential concerns. Though I do not wish to reify sex and gender as binary categories, and I've tried not to offer determinate definitions of either attribute, I believe Heidegger comments on the duality of the sexes insofar as he is thinking of sex in terms of reproductive difference, in terms of generation. Heidegger is thus contesting evolutionary theories for whom the actions of Dasein would be essentially motivated by sex and death.

Implications of Heidegger's Sexed/Gendered Bodies (*Körper/Leib*)

The process by which Heidegger describes the formation of sexed/gendered bodies could have significant impacts on the field of ontology, a philosophy whose goal at defining "what is" has been criticized for its (potentially harmful) exclusionary practices. For example, if I state that a woman is *x*, I necessarily exclude all persons who do not fit the unequivocal criteria required for membership of *x*. What is insightful about Heidegger's historical ontology is that he is not interested in the "what" of identity but the "how," the process by which, for example, one *becomes* sexed. Heidegger's remark that Dasein is "neither of the two sexes" can be read alongside contemporary thinkers of the feminist new materialist tradition such as Elizabeth Grosz (2011) and Stephen Seely (2016), both of whom draw from Gibert Simondon (2017).[63] For example, Heidegger's emphasis on our "freedom for ground" shares parallels with Grosz's analysis of Bergson's notion of freedom. Grosz asserts, "Indetermination is the 'true principle' of life, the condition for the open-ended action of living beings, the ways in which living bodies are mobilized for action that cannot be specified in advance."[64] Such indetermination sounds a lot like Heidegger's not-yet determinedness of neutral Dasein. What's more, Grosz will further elaborate on this freedom and posit sexual difference as the "indeterminable difference, the difference between two beings who do not yet exist, who are in the process of becoming."[65] Such a statement echoes the "both/and" of Heidegger's "neither of the two sexes" as a process of becoming.

Such a process is possible due to Dasein's primordial constitution as transcendence, its possibility of understanding itself as a subject in its world, a subjectivity that is fundamentally characterized as sexed. But does this mean that there is a part of Dasein that is immaterial in its transcendence? Heidegger states, "Dasein harbors the intrinsic possibility for being factically dispersed into bodiliness and thus into sexuality."[66] Does this presume a consciousness or life force, unfettered by a body, thus risking a form of Cartesianism or vitalism? We are tempted to think so, but this would be a mistake, for "bodiliness" has two separate meanings for Heidegger, *Körper* and *Leib*. Body is not just mere physical matter (*Körper*) but a way of interacting with the world (*Leib*). To say that neutral Dasein is prior to a factical dispersion into bodiliness does not insinuate that Dasein is prior to physical matter. As Heidegger highlighted in the Davos debate with Cassirer, Dasein is "chained to a body" in a milieu that is always historical and contingent.[67] Thus, if Dasein is always already in a material body, three possible thoughts follow from his assertion that Dasein is neither of the two sexes: (1) sex does not refer to biological matter here, insofar as Dasein is always chained to a body, as physical matter, prior to dispersion; (2) sex does refer to a biological category but such matter is historically contingent and not given; and/or (3) sex is not just physical matter but an interaction of said matter with the world, what certain theorists would describe as gender.

Heidegger's clarification of bodiliness pulls from all three, ultimately insinuating that sex does have to do with physical matter, but such matter is historically contingent and dependent on one's interaction with the environment (the way one chooses to set up a world). It is this interaction between one's body and the environment, the "how" of world-forming, that constitutes Dasein's spatiality and establishes how neutral Dasein is disseminated in space as a sexed body. Heidegger recognized the difficulty in explaining this process and has been denounced by several French philosophers for his lack of attention paid to the body.[68] Whereas he skirts the issue in GA 2,[69] in the *Zollikon Seminars*, he tackles the problem of the body as a problem of method, noting it is difficult to distinguish *psyche* from *soma* insofar as we can't objectify ourselves for measurable analysis. The problem of the body, of which sex is a privileged attribute for Heidegger, is tied to the same problem of the ontological difference, namely, how to describe Being without turning it into a being (to be measured), something that every utterance of "Being is . . ." necessarily accomplishes.

In clarifying this problem, Heidegger reproaches his French critiques who scorn him for his neglect of the body, asserting that they fail to understand the complexity of the matter insofar as their language only has one understanding of body, *corps*. In distinguishing *Körper* from *Leib*, the former is only concerned with ontic entanglements (corporeal limits), whereas the latter is ontologically significant. For example, my eyes are made of physical matter (*Körper*), but they also "body forth" in their receiving and perceiving of an entity that matters to me (*Leib*). This "bodying forth" (*Leiben*) is historically contingent, as Heidegger states, "the limit of my bodying forth changes constantly through the change in the reach of my sojourn."[70] Sojourn indicates a being here for a while at a particular time.

Derrida appears to miss this notion of "bodying forth," as he tries to unpack the following assertion from Heidegger: "Dasein in general hides, shelters in itself the internal possibility of a factual dispersion or dissemination (*faktische Zerstreuung*) in its own body (*Leiblichkeit*) and thereby in sexuality (*und amit in die Geschlechtlichkeit*)."[71] Here, Derrida understands body (*Leiblichkeit*) as *flesh*, asserting that *flesh* draws Dasein into its dispersion.[72] Yet, body as *Leiblichkeit* does not refer to corporeal limits (*flesh*) but rather to the way in which our spatial encounters make sense, the receiving and perceiving of things of my concern. Thus, my body as matter exists for neutral Dasein, but such matter is not *understood* as sexed or gendered prior to the process of "world-forming."

The question remains as to whether sex/gender are privileged attributes in the process of such "world-forming," in establishing ground. That is, in undergirding Dasein's sexual neutrality, in stating that Dasein is "above all" neither of the two sexes, is he merely responding to a student's inquiry, contesting religious origin stories founded on sexual difference, or setting himself apart from the biology of his time? In denouncing the relevance of sex, is he implicitly privileging such a trait? Whether or not sexed/gendered traits are privileged attributes that describe the whatness of my being remains open-ended. However, if we pose the question, "Problem: What is woman?" within the parameters of Heidegger's larger ontological project, we must conclude that the properties of sex and gender are fluid and not already determinate characteristics of Dasein, as they only show up after an authentic engagement with and enactment of care prior to world-forming. To say that Dasein is sexed or gendered describes the "whatness" of my being, but it says nothing of the neutral temporal structures that make such attributes possible (the "how"). Heidegger's historical ontology could prove useful for future feminist work that questions static properties of sex and gender. While Heidegger may not have been able to think outside of sexed/gendered binaries, his language of neutral temporal structures, his contestation of evolutionary fatalism founded on sex and death, and his distinction between *Körper* and *Leib*, offer tools for exploring the fluidity of sex and gender.

Chapter 3

Queering *Gestell*

Partial Enframing, Racial Breeding,
and Assisted Reproductive Technology

In 2013, France legalized "same-sex"[1] marriage, a promulgation that incited a larger question of whether access to marriage necessitated the right to filiation, or the right to have children. The question became: now that queer couples are able to marry, should they be granted access to reproductive technology that would allow them the ability to have children? Despite numerous delays and protests by groups such as the *Manif pour tous*, in 2021, a bill touted as "*La PMA pour toutes*" was passed that extended access to assisted reproductive technology (ART) to "all women," technologies heretofore reserved for heterosexual couples.[2] Yet "all women" refers to single women and lesbian couples, excluding trans bodies from such access. Through its revised bioethics legislation, France not only raises "the woman question" but frames the query in such a way that only a totalized response can be given.

In this chapter, I think Judith Butler's epistemological problem of "framing" alongside Dana S. Belu's notion of "reproductive enframing" to analyze how French law dictates who is considered the appropriate reproductive citizen. Then, I turn to a discussion of Belu's notion of "partial enframing" to queer, or upset, our current technological ideology that Heidegger refers to as *Gestell* or enframing. I also examine how race is (re)produced through France's ART legislation to highlight how Heidegger's example of racial breeding as quintessential of machinational thinking makes race itself a technology of ontological significance. Essentially, as "partially enframed" we may not be able to think outside of technological ideology, though we may be able to queer normative frames of reproduction, permitting a reorientation of the way that we perceive reproductive technology; that is, we may not be able to escape our tendency to wield sex/gender and race to certain ends, but we can order them about in different and unexpected ways.

Framing[3]

Judith Butler is concerned with the epistemological problem of framing, the process by which we come to apprehend knowledge and to discern the types of lives we consider worth living. Butler is primarily interested in the frames of war, including the nationalist discourse that delineates boundaries between "us" and "them." However, in the introduction to *Frames of War*, she notes that the knowledge-practice of framing may extend to issues regarding reproductive freedom as well.

Manon Beury wrote a personal tribune to *Libération* recounting how the "*PMA pour toutes*" bill fails to take into consideration the existence of trans women.[4] Beury explains that she is in a relationship with a trans woman who had previously frozen her sperm; however, the bill forbids her from using her partner's gametes for IVF. Despite the fact that her partner's sperm is readily available, the law requires her to use an anonymous donor. Beury could search for a country willing to use her partner's genetic material for IVF, but even then, her partner would not be legally recognized as a biological parent in France, since a birth certificate requires one mother and one father.

Beury's case undergirds the rigidity of a system that must maintain a sharp association between sexual difference and filiation. Beury's partner is allowed to be a woman, but only if she is willing to accept that women do not have sperm. The inability of the revised bioethics legislation to neatly uphold a distinction of the sexes based on generation is further evidenced by the fact that trans men are also excluded from the bill. One could easily say, "Well, the bill is called 'ART for all women,' and trans men have fought hard to be recognized as men," but this misses the point that lines of sex, gender, and generation are not necessarily congruent. In asking to legally be recognized as a man, a trans man must dissociate himself from his uterus, because "man" and "uterus" are already regulated in such a way as to be a contradiction in terms.

The framing of French reproductive policy can, in part, be attributed to its Catholic heritage and privileging of carnal procreation. Yet, France's secular politics (*laïcité*) uphold a separation of church and state and are founded on principles of universalism. *Laïcité* insists that French citizens are united based on the universal idea of "Frenchness." According to such universalism, particular individuals may not receive "special" treatment. For example, no students are allowed to wear ostentatious religious symbols in public school. Though this all-inclusive ban may seem "just" on the face of it, it explicitly targets certain religions (for example, Muslims who veil) viewed as incompatible with a particular understanding of French culture (one informed by its Catholic heritage). A similar train of reasoning was previously used to bar nonheterosexual couples from gaining access to ART, as prior to the extension, unless there was a concern of genetic inheritance, medical infertility was the only grounds on which ART could be accessed. Single women or lesbians do not typically request ART on the grounds of infertility and thus were demanding to be treated as "special cases," and such cases are in conflict with universalism.

Universalism gives the illusion of a uniform body, when it really reinforces the type of "us" against "them" rhetoric that Butler explores in her notion of framing. This "us versus them" opposition is most stringently upheld in anthropological claims of sexual difference. Such difference has been highlighted by philosopher and public intellectual Sylviane Agacinski who asserts that the parenting model (mother/father) mirrors our biological foundation (female/male), while also noting that such a model is not quantitative (1 + 1), but qualitative (male + female).[5] Thus, nonheterosexual couples do not possess the right *qualia* to reproduce.

I find it especially important to queer *Gestell* within a French context, because Agacinski has called on Heidegger's philosophy of technology to critique the ART extension and to prevent the legalization of surrogacy. Agacinski, philosopher and wife of former prime minister Lionel Jospin,[6] spoke at the National Assembly, accompanied by an antisurrogacy group called CoRP, a play on the French word for body (*corps*) and an acronym for *collectif pour le respect de la personne*. Agacinski used her platform to warn French citizens against what Heidegger called *Machenschaft* (machination), our calculative way of thinking that he would later refer to as *Gestell*. She recounted how ART turns women's bodies into standing reserve (*Bestand*) to be stockpiled and optimized for future use. She called on French people to resist neoliberalism and cited California as a type of transhumanist haven where the surrogacy industry flourished. This is not the first time that Agacinski has cited Heidegger's thought to advance her anti-ART and antisurrogacy agenda. At a conference titled "Heidegger, *une pensée brûlante* (Heidegger, an incendiary thinking),"[7] a meeting called after the publication of the French translation of the *Black Notebooks*, Agacinski located Heidegger's politics between a struggle against the communism of the USSR and the ultraliberalism of America. She would then go on to extend Heidegger's antiliberal views to argue against the calculative thinking of assisted reproductive technology. I am not contesting that such a danger lies in the potential of reproductive technology; rather, what is politically perilous is the "us versus them" rhetoric that Agacinski uses to separate an enlightened France from a liberal America. In her book *Corps en Miettes* (Body into Pieces), she states, "*Non, la France n'est pas en retard, elle est en avance sur la protection, la loi, de la dignité des personnes et de leur corps* (No, France is not behind. It is ahead on the protection, the law, and the dignity of persons and their bodies)."[8] Agacinski uses California as a paradigm of calculative thinking and a site of women's oppression, all the while advancing a political project that would prevent queer persons from reproducing in the French Republic.

While Agacinski supports same-sex marriage, she rejects the claim that marriage opens access to filiation, clarifying that to accept this claim would be to confuse "sexual difference" with the "difference of sexualities," where the former has always been defined in relation to procreation.[9] For Agacinski, sex is a question of biological generation and sexuality is a matter of desire. Agacinski, like others who opposed the ART extension, feared it would upset normative claims of sexual difference and lead to a fatherless society.

Butler adds insight to this fear as she asserts, "In France, the notion of a 'framework of orientation'—called 'le repère'—is understood to be uniquely transmitted by the father [. . . . .] To the extent that heterosexual marriage maintains its monopoly on reproduction, it does so precisely through privileging the biological father as the representative of national culture."[10] "Le repère" is the "knowing orientation" by which someone may find their way home, like a landmark that directs you to the right location. In the word *repère* is the French word for *father*, *père*. Despite claims of *laïcité*, the "law of the father" and France's Catholic heritage still remain influential to a bioethics legislation that can most justly be categorized as paternal. This play on the words *père* and *repère* can be seen in French protest signs against the "*PMA pour toutes*" extension that declare, "un enfant a besoin d'amour, mais aussi de rePÈRES" (a child needs love, but also knowing orientations/fathers). The father is the "framework of orientation" according to which we find ourselves in the world.

In Sara Ahmed's *Queer Phenomenology*, she examines how objects appear to us according to the manner in which we orientate ourselves, acknowledging that our bodies take shape and tend toward objects that are reachable and attainable. She asserts, "Phenomenology can offer a resource for queer studies insofar as it emphasizes the importance of lived experience, the intentionality of consciousness, the significance of nearness or what is ready-to-hand, and the role of repeated and habitual actions in shaping bodies and worlds."[11] Phenomenology aims at describing different possibilities of experiencing our existence, highlighting that our orientation toward objects, our intentionality, greatly informs such experience. An important question is what makes the objects that appear to us "reachable" and "attainable?" According to Heidegger, things appear to us and come to matter based on our neutral temporal structure of care.[12] Yet, how things come to matter is not apolitical. For as Ahmed states, the role of repeated and habitual actions shapes our bodies and how they are able to navigate space. The continuous regulation of one's reproductive freedom and the explicit exclusion from such a procreative possibility greatly contributes to how one experiences their being in the world; such actions thwart possibilities by making certain modes of orientation unattainable and out of reach.

Until recently, only heterosexual couples were permitted access to ART, because the ideology behind such technology was to aid the heterosexual couple in their project to form a family. The basis of this ideology rests on the biological fact that a meeting of egg and sperm is necessary for procreation, yet such a meeting is not without its own historical construction.[13] Likewise, ART has its own historical baggage that informs the way we orient ourselves toward it. While a meeting of egg and sperm is necessary for procreation, we cannot claim, from this fact, that all families must be headed by equal parts egg- and sperm-making individuals. This would be to deny the reality of familial construction. ART bypasses the need for carnal procreation, yet by only allowing heterosexual couples access to it, France was able to preserve the illusion that ART was somehow an extension of the heteronormative family, merely aiding its formation.

Thus, until the recent bioethics extension, France explicitly defined the heterosexual couple as paradigmatic of productive reproduction. Further, while the new legislation extends ART to single women and lesbian couples, it continues to define such citizens based on certain qualifying criteria of sexual difference. While lesbians may be regulated in such a way as to promote traditional family values, through a process that Lisa Duggan has called "homonormativity,"[14] the trans body escapes intelligibility, representing a crisis of meaning that T. Benjamin Singer refers to as the "transgender sublime."[15] According to French legislation, lesbians and single women are women with uteruses who seek access to sperm banks (with the understanding that sperm is created by men), thus preserving the integrity of heterosexual reproduction. That is, a biological sex/gender congruency is upheld. A trans woman, however, may represent a "crisis of meaning" by being a woman who produces sperm. According to the frames of reproduction, woman and sperm are on opposite sides of the binary system and must be excluded from the legislation.

In this section, I've applied Butler's notion of "framing" to analyze how French society understands and defines the productive reproductive citizen. I've specifically shown how trans persons lie outside the frames of who is considered the worthy reproductive subject. I now turn to a discussion of how the ideology behind assisted reproductive technology can be queered to orientate us toward new modes of reproductive enframing.

Reproductive Enframing

In *Heidegger, Reproductive Technology, and the Motherless Age*, Dana S. Belu is critical of assisted reproductive technology for revealing a particular form of technological domination that she refers to as reproductive enframing. Through a phenomenological analysis of different ways that women become pregnant (that is, IVF, surrogacy) and experience labor (that is, scheduled c-section, induction), Belu demonstrates how women's bodies are viewed as resources prone to medical optimization under our technological ideology of *Gestell*. Belu concludes her work by trying to find a way outside of reproductive enframing, a way to birth that evades laboring techniques of domination and control. Here, I am not interested in assessing Belu's way outside of *Gestell*, something I do not view as possible; rather, I find her notion of "partial enframing" helpful for queering the ideology of technological domination from the inside.

According to Heidegger, each era is defined by a certain historical structure of truth as a revealing/concealing, and the essence of our modern technological age is enframing.[16] Heidegger is not interested in technological instruments as such, but rather the technological mode of thought that informs the way we navigate the world as an amalgam of resources, ready to be exploited and stockpiled for their ultimate utility (that is, standing reserve [*Bestand*]). Belu is concerned with what she deems "reproductive enframing," how women's bodies and reproductive parts are viewed as efficient resources to maximize laboring results.[17] Belu's critique of ART is in part motivated by radical feminist arguments against liberal feminism, as she questions whether women can truly choose such technology within a patriarchal framework of domination. While it is true that we should question the choices we are able to make, given that the objects we tend toward, that matter to us, appear after repeated and habitual practices of framing, new modes of orientation do remain possible.

Belu's work is successful for providing a detailed account of the way ART may potentially abuse women's bodies. On the one hand, she is right to critique a technological ideology that from its inception categorized the father as the knowing orientation. For example, while surrogacy is illegal in France, its legality in the United States was initially solidified by the signature of the father; that is, despite the use of women's bodies, the husband's signature validated the contract. However, many of the abuses that Belu puts forth occur within a heteronormative framework, and so rather than focusing on how ART may be better wielded to open possibilities, she only centers on its capacity to reify existing gender norms.

Belu states, under the mode of *Gestell*, "techne (fabrication) no longer partly completes what nature cannot bring to a finish . . . rather, IVF produces what nature stubbornly refuses to conceive."[18] Whereas natural entities contain both matter and form, with a little added push from the artisan to bring its form to completion, in the case of IVF, the fertility doctor coerces nature to form an embryo. For Belu, babies born from IVF are not natural, yet she says we have to hide the aspect of their technological birth and trick ourselves into thinking they are so. Such an assertion reifies carnal procreation as the only "natural" alternative, but is it possible to reorientate ourselves and ask, "Could IVF be considered 'natural' insofar as there is something about our genetic material that allows it to be other than what it is?" The fertility doctor cannot turn just any old thing into an embryo, rather they work with genetic material that is "naturally" predisposed to other forms of becoming.[19]

Belu is also concerned that IVF technologies reinforce a patriarchal mentality that privileges genetically related offspring. Yet, here, she is already analyzing IVF within a very heteronormative framework. For example, for many queer persons the desire for genetically related children is not due to a biological imperative that demands a resemblance of offspring, but the fear that they may have less of a legal claim to nongenetically related children.

Belu says, "IVF technologies may produce a baby, but they do not restore fertility."[20] Once again, the narrative is already being recounted in heteronormative terms, as access to IVF is not always motivated by infertility, as previously mentioned when discussing the faulty secular politics that forbade it to nonheterosexual couples and single women in France.

Viewing IVF, and other modes of reproductive technology, as motivated by a logic of domination that falls under the rubric of *Gestell*, Belu searches for a way outside of reproductive enframing, a *poiēsis* of birth. A *poiēsis* of birth occurs when the child is able to come forth in their presencing without being coaxed forth via techniques of domination. The scope of this chapter is not to provide a critical analysis of her way outside of enframing, but rather to highlight the fact that such thinking is possible due to her notion of "partial enframing." I find this notion of "partial enframing" helpful, not as a means to evade reproductive enframing, but to queer it from the inside. The term *queer* does not just refer to nonheteronormative forms of sexuality/identity but is used as an action to upset the usual frameworks of orientation. Belu is just in critiquing the ways that ART may be harmful to women who feel pressured to seek it within a heterosexual patriarchal society, but she neglects the way that ART may open up new possibilities of existence that may lead us to critique this very society.

Belu coins the term *partial enframing* after confronting a paradox of *Gestell*, the problem being that if we are "totally enframed," we should not be able to think of a way outside our domination. As Belu notes, "our essence is compromised and no theory of enframing is conceivable."[21] However, if we are partially enframed, then the essence of technology is compromised. I agree with this assessment, yet I question whether the liberatory aspect of this paradox lies in our finding a way outside of enframing. We are partially enframed in that we are able to become conscious of our techne-centered way of thinking; however, consciousness of our enframed state does not mean we can escape such a logic of thought. Even feminism is a knowledge-practice claimed by technology.

In "The Question Concerning Technology" (QCT), Heidegger makes clear that the danger of *Gestell* does not lie in technological instruments but rather the thought that gave birth to them. Thus, even if we forbid the use of IVF or other forms of ART, the ontological desire that bore its emergence would remain.[22] Though Heidegger is critical of technology, he does mention the possibility of a "saving power" inherent in its essence, a power that can be harnessed if we view technology like art.[23] What this means is further explored in his "The Origin of the Work of Art" (OWA), as he describes the truth of the artwork, clarifying that art preserves the truth of our historical situation.[24] I take this to mean that art reveals the ontological contingency of our historical situation, that what we accept as true ("what is") changes over time. Robyn Ferrell plays with such ontological contingency and asks whether ART can be viewed as art in its capacity to bring forth more possibilities of existence.[25] While it may have been true that ART was originally created to solidify a heterosexual familial bond, we are now able to think beyond these frames. We cannot escape our technological ideology; we cannot escape the calculating mode of our mentality, but we can use such calculations to different ends, to more possible ends. On the one hand, the option of ART may reinforce the message that heterosexual white women must breed at all costs, but on the other hand, ART offers the possibility to upset traditional frameworks of orientation by offering queer bodies reproductive potential.

Queer bodies that enter fertility clinics are, according to Rachel Epstein, "space invaders," the term that Nirmal Purwal uses to describe gendered, racialized, and minority bodies who are out of place.[26] These bodies invade spaces that have hitherto been defined in terms of male power, a power that values white heterosexual affluent bodies, bodies that Shannon Winnubst would define as "phallicized whiteness."[27] A queering of such spaces, an upsetting of who they have been traditionally geared toward forces us to reorient ourselves. In the case of the fertility clinic, when such spaces are open to queer bodies, neatly congruent scripts of a sexed/gendered/fertile body no longer serve as the point of orientation. To use Heidegger's example, the hammer fails, the equipment breaks down, and a problem becomes glaringly obvious.[28] Yet in this situation of crisis a new context of meaning arises, an occasion to interrogate the "how" of an equipment's working. Heidegger's ontological project was never interested in the "what" of something appearing but rather the "how" of its emergence. In queering, we ask anew, not "what is" reproductive technology, but "how" does reproductive technology as part of a technical ideology create "what is" during a certain historical time?

It seems to me that French bioethics legislation in foreclosing access to ART is more embedded in techniques of domination than IVF, a procedure that allows different possible means of existence. IVF may allow nontraditional models of parenting to presence, rather than concealing them by means of certain social and legal regulations. Rather than thinking outside of *Gestell*, I suggest queering *Gestell* and Belu's notion of "partial enframing." We cannot help but respond to the world via a calculating ideology, but we may be able to use such a logic of thought to calculate better modes of existing. Can we use ART to queer the frameworks of orientation on which our current parenting model rests? By analyzing the epistemological problem of reproductive "framing" in conjunction with the ontological issue of reproductive "enframing," I believe we can. That is, by queering ART, by using it in ways for which it was not originally intended, we open a space for new ways of understanding reproduction. Such a manipulating of our technological "know-how" (episteme) is reminiscent of Foucault's notion of the "tactical polyvalence of discourse," the ability to reorient the meaning of discursive productions (reproductions?) as a form of resistance.[29]

Coda: Race as Technology in Reproductive Enframing

Insofar as we are "partially enframed," can we use the calculating ideology that is part and parcel of our enframed state to wield different and potentially better possibilities of existence? I suggested that since we cannot escape our desire for mastery, we can queer *Gestell* from the inside by using instruments of technology outside of their intended purposes. Rather than view assisted reproductive technology as something that reinforces the view that (typically white) women should breed at all costs with the goal of preserving the heteronormative family, we may view its utility as upsetting such heteronormativity by allowing queer persons procreative potential. Though what am I concealing in this revelation of nonheteronormativity? Or how may an emphasis on the instrumentality of queer progress be utilized in a way that obscures how race informs our situation of reproductive enframing? Before turning to a discussion of how race is both produced and reproduced within the context of France's bioethics legislation that extends access to ART, we must first look at how race itself is a form of technology.

Race as Technology

In *The Assisted Reproduction of Race*, Camisha Russell uses Heidegger's ontology of technology to demonstrate how race and racial identity function within assisted reproductive technology and to emphasize how ART is far from racially neutral. To emphasize the ideological danger of technology, Heidegger asserts that to speak of technology in terms of its instrumental nature is "correct" but not "true."[30] For Heidegger, truth emerges as an aletheiac unfolding, a simultaneous revealing and concealing;[31] where there is presence, there is absence. What is "true" about the essence of technology as enframing is that it challenges us "to reveal the actual, in the mode of ordering, as standing reserve [*Bestand*]."[32] Thus, any understanding of "what is" outside of this calculating ideology, "what is" outside of an ordering and stockpiling for future utility is concealed. In highlighting technology as ideology, apparatuses themselves are not the primary issue but the very desire for mastery, and in the case of ART, the desire for control of human reproduction that is paramount. According to Russell, race, as a technology, organizes nature in a way that is reflective of this desire. She asserts, "Seen as technological, particularly in a Heideggerian sense, race can be recognized as a fundamental part of the prism of heritability that shapes our view of the world."[33] That is, race as ideology categorizes and orders what we perceive to be "true" about our world. While Heidegger does not reference race in QCT, preferring to use the hydroelectric plant as paradigmatic of technology, in his earlier years from 1936 to1940, he spoke of technology as machination (*Machenschaft*), using racial breeding as a quintessential example of the technological worldview.[34] What is the significance of referencing racial breeding as the ultimate example of machination or *Gestell*? In examining our relationship to the essence of technology, we discover "what is"—we discover our relationship to being and how we respond to the call of being as revealers.

Heidegger is using the example of racial breeding to critique the National Socialist Party and their claims of superiority founded on biology or blood ties. However, it is important to note that it is not the superiority of the German people in and of itself that is called into question, for Heidegger believes such status is merited due to their privileged relationship as revealers of being during that particular moment in history.[35] Such revelation is concealed, however, by focusing on techniques of breeding said superiority. Heidegger asserts, "*The new politics is an intrinsic essential component of 'technology*' [. . . .] In itself, this politics is the machinational organization of the people to the highest possible 'performance,' whereby even people are grasped with regard to the basic biological determination in an essentially 'technological'—machinational way, i.e., in terms of breeding."[36] This passage is akin to Heidegger's discussion of the human being becoming a part of the standing reserve in QCT.[37] Heidegger is right to note that there is something grossly wrong with humans being ordered as things and with people being bred according to discriminating ideas of racial superiority. What Heidegger fails to see, however, is the very relationship of being to the generation of beings. Heidegger views biological reproduction as an ontic concern that conceals more pressing ontological matters; however, how beings, for whom being is an issue, reproduce is very much related to questioning "what is."

Tina Chanter critiques Heidegger for focusing specifically on the equipmental nature of objects, treating our involvement with the world as if it were purely "task oriented." She states, "If one problem with Heidegger's account of Dasein's multifarious relations with the world is that it always seems to have decided in advance in favor of ontology and against the ontic level of experience, another problem is that it is geared almost exclusively to the world of work."[38] This world of work neglects aspects such as "sexuality" and "eroticism" and severely limits any analysis of the body and its spatial encounters outside of understandings governed by language such as "in-order-to" and "for-the-sake-of-which."[39] In only focusing on our involvements that are "task oriented," is Chanter critiquing Heidegger for only thinking in terms of utility, a type of thinking that he seeks to evade in his discussion of technology? I would say that Heidegger focuses too much on how *things* become intelligible, on how *things* come to matter, without giving proper consideration to why *how we reproduce* matters so much. For Heidegger, a hammer merits discussion, because an aspect of its being is concealed through its presence as "ready-to-hand," as something functioning within an already intelligible environment. We only see the hammer as "hammer" when it breaks down. The hammer lays bare before us, unintelligible outside of its utility and *productivity*. If this example is in any way disclosive of our being-in-the-world, if it says anything about how things come to matter to us, then surely any upset in our very *reproductivity* must be significant. Heidegger focuses on the world of productive labor but not the world of reproductive labor. Yet he does grant reproduction an ontological status when he once again discusses the machination of racial breeding in *Nietzsche, Volume 3*. Here, he states,

> The breeding of human beings is not a taming in the sense of a suppression and hobbling of sensuality; rather, breeding is the accumulation and purification of energies in the univocity of the strictly controllable "automatism" of every activity. Only where the absolute subjectivity of will to power comes to be the truth of beings as a whole is the principle of a program of racial breeding possible; possible, that is, not merely on the basis of naturally evolving races, but in terms of the self-conscious thought of race. That is to say, the principle is metaphysically necessary. Just as Nietzsche's thought of will to power was ontological rather than biological, even more was his racial thought metaphysical rather than biological in meaning.[40]

For Heidegger, breeding in and of itself is an ontic concern, as our births are mere biological facts, in contrast to the revelatory condition of our death. While Heidegger notes that Dasein is that being which stretches along between *birth* and *death*, and while I must necessarily reckon with the past of my thrownness, birth as an antecedent event (even though it is something that I take up again and again) is never ontologically privileged in the way that the futural projection of my death is.[41] Yet when such breeding is controlled through racial ideology, ours births become ontologically disclosive. This appears to be the case because our desire for mastery, our "will to power" is no longer projected on objects in the world but on ourselves as Dasein, as revealers of being. We, ourselves, figure among the standing reserve. Race, in and of itself, does not appear to be questioned, as Heidegger suggests that races are "naturally evolving." What is distressing to Heidegger is that the "natural" racial order is upset, as race becomes a "self-conscious" thought.

Racial breeding is thus artificial breeding; that is, race *is* assisted reproductive technology. The natural biological fact of breeding, a breeding that Heidegger sees as necessarily tied to a "natural evolution of races," becomes technologized and is thus rendered artificial. And again, such racial breeding is the quintessential example of the technological worldview. If, for Heidegger, it is necessary to question our relation to the essence of technology in order to reveal the essence of truth, of being, and if such a technological worldview is most saliently revealed by assisted reproductive technology (which racial breeding is), then the very nature of reproduction is worth questioning.

Despite rejecting a Cartesian subject/world distinction, Heidegger seems to imply that there is something biologically natural about the evolution of our bodies, untainted by historical influence and its correlating environment. Yet this would be a gross misapplication of his hermeneutics of facticity. We are not subjects standing over and against objects, for as Dasein, we are always in a world with objects and others, and such objects and others should mutually enforce who we are. Though this is perhaps what is so distressing about the ideological framework of *Gestell*, as it forgets such mutuality of being-in-the-world and consciously makes such a subject/object distinction for the purpose of being able to calculate and challenge forth all utility. Yet, why is racial breeding, or the reproduction of human beings according to race, the quintessential example of this technological worldview? Outside of using more sophisticated technological instruments, racial breeding is not unique to our era, or even the eras leading up to

Gestell. For while *Gestell* is categorized by a total optimization of utility, such ideology did not occur overnight but began centuries ago when Aristotle (and Plato) defined being in terms of *ousia* instead of *physis*.[42] That is, an understanding of being became conceived in terms of "presence" as a unified thing that is here for observation, rather than as an essential unfolding that lets itself come forth in its presence.

Though critical of Aristotle for dissimulating a deeper understanding of being with his language of *ousia*, he nevertheless privileges Aristotle's four causes and laments that beings no longer come forth via such "coresponsibility," a coresponsibility that allows for beings to emerge by way of *physis*.[43] In our era of modern technology, the mutuality of these four causes (material cause, formal cause, final cause, and efficient cause) is erased by an essentializing of the efficient cause. For example, a chalice comes to be through the coresponsibility of the silver (material cause), the shape the silver vessel takes (formal cause), the end goal of the chalice, that is, a sacrificial rite (final cause), and the silversmith who gathers these other causes together to co-constitute it (efficient cause). Under our current mind-set, however, under the rubric of enframing, the silversmith sets the standard for all causality. Can we extend the idea of these four causes to thinking about the emergence of human beings? If we return to Heidegger's quintessential example of racial breeding, could it be said that persons no longer naturally evolve via the coresponsibility of these four causes, but rather human beings, with their self-conscious understanding of race, set the standard as the efficient cause? They create racialized bodies via racialized ideology. But, did a pre-*ousia* era of breeding ever exist? Was there ever a time when the reproduction of human bodies was not, in some way, ordered? Heidegger turns to the ancient Greeks to gauge a better understanding of our relation to being, to think *physis* as a revealing/concealing, but as Lorraine Markotic illustrates, "In relation to paternity, the ancient Greeks sought certainty, created standing-reserve, and enacted Enframing—precisely what Heidegger ascribes to modernity."[44] How humans reproduce and with whom has long been regulated according to different kinship systems. In fact, it's hard to think of any origin story that doesn't describe our birth as being ordered about in some way.

Heidegger quotes Plato's *Symposium* to elucidate what a bringing-forth in the way of *physis* would look like, what it would be to "release" something via a gathering of the four causes. He asserts,

> "Every occasion for whatever passes beyond the nonpresent and goes forward into presencing is *poiēsis*, bringing-forth." It is of utmost importance that we think bringing-forth in its full

scope and at the same time in the sense in which the Greeks thought it. Not only handicraft manufacture, not only artistic and poetical bringing into appearance and concrete imagery, is a bringing-forth, *poiēsis*. *Physis*, also, the arising of something from out of itself, is a bringing-forth, *poiēsis* [. . .] the bursting of a blossom into bloom, in itself.[45]

Thus, under *Gestell*, things are challenged forth by the efficient cause rather than allowed to "bloom in itself" as *poiēsis*. We must rethink such bringing-forth, "in the sense in which the Greeks though it." Yet isn't Plato, who Heidegger says may help us rethink such bringing-forth, also the author of *The Republic*, a text that is often cited for its early references to eugenics and selective breeding?[46] Could Plato be accused of machinational thinking in that he proposed eugenics as a way of ordering citizens according to their aptitude? While Plato's tripartite government was supposed to represent balance in that each caste functioned according to its "natural" predispositions, such a government hardly let persons "naturally" evolve, and the caste of the philosopher kings were, without a doubt, seen as superior.

On the one hand, what is particular about our modern age of enframing is not the appearance of assisted reproductive technology, for such reproduction has always been assisted via some form of ideology, but rather the instruments of technology. And yet, for Heidegger, our technological age is not merely instrumental, but ideological, for the very word *technē* is linked to *epistēmē*, insinuating a certain know-how, a certain way of revealing what is true. Isn't it true, and not merely correct, that assisted reproductive technology has always mattered and informed the way we navigate the world in a mode of circumspective concern and solicitude?[47] On the other hand, is it also true that what is particular to our modern age is the way that such reproduction is assisted via ideologies of race and its imbrication with nation and empire, for "it is usually agreed that the term 'race' was first used in something like its contemporary meaning at the end of the seventeenth century."[48] Race as a concept was (still is) largely used to differentiate the colonizer from the colonized, and racial discourse was (and still is) used to claim national sovereignty. As Sylvia Wynter asserts, " 'Race' was therefore to be, in effect, the nonsupernatural but no less extrahuman ground (in the reoccupied place of the traditional ancestors/gods, God, ground) of the answer that the secularizing West would now give to the Heideggerian question as to the who, and the what we are."[49] That is, the "who" of what we are is no longer determined by Judeo-Christian origin stories of the flesh (man/woman) but is founded on evolutionary tales regarding natural selection and the concept of race. According to Wynter, the "who" of what we are may be secularized, but the dialectic of colonizer/colonized (thus replacing man/woman) is still informed by religious dictates of good/evil and redeemed/unredeemed. That is, there remains a moral and ontological privileging of the former. Yet, it seems that for Wynter, following Quijano, race has supplanted gender as the grounding of our "who." She states,

> This seeing that if, as Quijano rightly insists, race—unlike gender (which has a biogenetically determined anatomical differential correlate onto which each culture's system of gendered oppositions can be anchored)—is a purely invented construct that has no such correlate (Quijano 2000), it was this construct that would enable the now globally expanding West to replace the earlier mortal/immortal, natural/supernatural, human/the ancestors, the gods/God distinction as the one on whose basis all human groups had millennially "grounded" their descriptive statement/prescriptive statements of what it is to be human, and to reground its secularizing own on a newly projected human/subhuman distinction instead.[50]

I agree that race "grounds" what it means to be human and, as Russell would argue, is a technology in that it orders our experience of existence; however, I disagree that gender has been replaced by the "race concept." Gender[51] and its imbrications with sexual difference (particularly the grounding of said difference) very much continues to inform the "who" of Dasein in an originary way. The role that race plays in the realm of assisted reproductive technology, coupled with Heidegger's remarks of racial breeding being the quintessential example of machination, indicates that race interacts with sex and gender in complicated ways to (re)produce and ground ethical claims of good/evil and ontological statuses of human/subhuman. Wynter does address how race interacts with sex/gender as she references Darwin and discusses Malthusian concerns of population, yet she appears to suggest that race has a more primordial status than sex/gender in grounding human experience, since race, unlike gender (that has a correlate), is an invention.

Ann Laura Stoler demonstrates how historical constructions of sexuality are always accompanied by correlating ideas of race and nation. She states, "These discourses of sexuality could tell not only the truth about individual persons, but about racial and national entities. They linked subversion to perversion, racial purity to conjugal white endogamy, and thus colonial politics to the management of sex."⁵² Such management included laws and codes that regulated with whom you could marry and with whom you could reproduce. If the management of sex via such legal regulation is intricately tied to certain racial ideologies, then one wonders how race is (re)produced through France's recent bioethics legislation. I'm going to put the language of Heidegger's philosophy aside for a moment to focus on the "ontic experiences" of choosing and regulating ART, for I think such instances hint at a larger experience of our relationship to being. If the "self-conscious thought of race" raises the act of procreation to an ontological level, then we must analyze how such a thought is (re)produced via ART.

THE (RE)PRODUCTION OF RACE IN FRANCE

In the previous sections "Framing" and "Reproductive Enframing," I demonstrated how an anthropological claim of sexual difference is essential to defining what it means to be a "productive reproductive" French citizen. Now, we must question how race fits into this narrative of what sort of beings have the right "to be" or "to exist." In her discussion of ART, Russell demonstrates how the skin color of those participating in assisted reproductive technology (that is, infertile woman, baby, surrogate) matters insofar as race serves as a proxy to kinship. This infertile woman is typically white and middle-class, and ART is seen as part of a "natural" progression to help her succeed in a task that she is seen as rightly due to perform. Recent critiques of what has been called "white feminism" point to how feminist concerns of reproductive justice are usually framed around a woman's right to choose an abortion, and while such movements challenge any natural womanly disposition to motherhood, they neglect a history of how, largely, Black women have had to fight for the right to keep their children, or to rightfully be viewed as acceptable mothers.

Dorothy Roberts recounts a history of forced sterilization of Black women, both directly and indirectly through state welfare policies or carceral solutions such as the "war on drugs."⁵³ She also highlights a plethora of stereotypes that feed into the viewpoint that Black women are unfit mothers such as those of the Welfare Queen, Jezebel, Mammy, and Matriarch.⁵⁴ Examining surrogacy arrangements in India, Russell shows how racial myths are further reproduced through assisted reproductive technology as, "Ultimately, it is white or lighter skin as physical characteristic that is valued and actively produced, since such skin confers social advantage on the end products of reproductive markets: babies."⁵⁵ Russell's statement is true within a market economy that allows the purchasers of ART to choose the characteristics of their children, whether that is through the selling of sperm, eggs, embryos, or surrogates, but such is not the case in France. This is not to say that France is more progressive, as its bioethics legislation is perhaps a quintessential example of Russell's elucidation of how race serves as a proxy to kinship.

In France, for roughly the past forty years since the regulation of assisted reproductive technology, gamete donors must be anonymous and must not be compensated. Furthermore, those seeking access to IVF with the assistance of such donations have no say regarding the type of sperm or egg they get. In the United States, we like to imagine prospective parents flipping through catalogs of possible donors, choosing potential babies based on features such as skin and eye color, but no such commercial transaction exists in France, as only doctors have the right to choose such gametes for you. Since medicine in the United States is largely administered on a market model, a neoliberal American attitude may say, but I am paying for this procedure, so I should be able to choose the product; but, in France, social security pays for IVF, so again, ART is not seen as a market transaction. The question remains, however, what are the qualifying criteria for such a selection? What leads the doctor to choose sperm x instead of sperm y? I use the example of sperm here, because while egg donation is legal in France, there is not a huge supply, since such donation must be both anonymous and noncompensatory. Not many people want to undergo such an invasive procedure to aid in the fertility of someone that they cannot know in advance, or for which they receive no remuneration.

As Laurence Brunet clarifies in an article on ethno-racial categories, such gametes are chosen based on the physical resemblance of the donor in comparison to the legal father.[56] That is, they choose a donor based on what the potential baby of the legal father would "naturally" look like. Here, choosing x sperm is seen as natural, not eugenics. Furthermore, in addition to physical resemblance, the doctors also factor in the blood type of the donor, to correspond with that of the legal father in order to further hide the *assisted* reproduction of the child. I do not highlight "assisted" to point to the "unnaturalness" of this procedure, as I agree with Russell who refers to Bruno Latour in undergirding the social construction of the very term "natural."[57] What is interesting here is how the binary between "natural" and "unnatural" is further (re)produced through such techniques of assisted reproduction. That the conceived baby *ought* to resemble the legal father is taken as a given, insinuating that to use a different skin color would be "unnatural." Russell asks, "(1) What sorts of racially inflected desires are reflected and naturalized in the uses of and rhetoric surrounding ARTs? And (2) how is the category of race itself renaturalized in this process?"[58] In the French context, these questions are difficult to mitigate because race as a category is believed to not exist. In France, there are no boxes of "White or Caucasian," "Black or African French," "Hispanic," "Asian-French," and so on to check because there is, it is said, only one human race. The strictness of not identifying people based on disparate racial categories is a response to Nazi racism. While race as a term may be omitted in good faith, attempts to not see race have further led to the marginalization of certain groups who are, in reality, oppressed based on something that looks like socially constructed notions of "race" but cannot be explored as such. As Kimberlé Crenshaw asserts, "When there's no name for a problem, you can't solve it."[59] Or, as Russell elucidates, "Race is sociopolitical rather than biological, but it is nonetheless real."[60] How to discuss the reality of race's role in the (re)production of bodies within the context of reproductive enframing, if race is not acknowledged as such?

In the United States, data is collected regarding the racial make-up of all those parties participating in ART in some form. Because of this data, we know, for example, that there is a serious shortage of Black sperm and egg donations in the US due to suspected reasons such as the stigma of infertility in Black communities, a mistrust of medical authorities within these communities, and a marketing toward a white customer base.[61] Because racial identity does not exist in France, we cannot know (quantitatively) if racial discrimination influences access to ART.

I have previously discussed the way that the ART extension, touted as ART for all women (*PMA pour toutes*), continues to define the reproductive *woman* according to lines of sex/gender congruency, yet as Jasbir Puar illustrates, "the woman question" that she views as correlating to "the homosexual question" is always tied to an understanding of race and nation. Puar inquires, "How has 'the homosexual question' come to supplement 'the woman question' of the colonial era to modulate arbitration between modernity and tradition, citizen and terrorist, homonational and queer?"[62] Puar is interested in how liberal rights discourse that celebrates "gay friendly" nations simultaneously celebrates the detention and deportation of racialized bodies that are not "properly queer." Genderqueer bodies also lie outside the frames of who is considered the appropriate (re)productive citizen. Puar states, "The homosexuals seen as being treated properly by the nation-state are not 'genderqueer.' They are rather the ones recreating gendered norms through, rather than despite, homosexual identity. Obscured by pinkwashing is how trans and gender non-conforming queers are not welcome in this new version of the proper 'homonationalist' Israeli citizen."[63] While Puar is speaking specifically about Israel here, homonationalism is not restricted to this geographical region, as trans bodies are not "being treated properly by the nation-state" of France, as evidenced by their exclusion from the ART extension. Yet, how does race figure into narratives of queer progress in France?

It must be understood that a prominent national call for queer access to assisted reproductive technology emerged after 2013, with the passage of the Taubira Act that legalized same-sex marriage. There was a general supposition that access to marriage necessitated access to claims of filiation, or the right to have children. This is largely due to the stipulations of the Napoleonic Code of 1804, which is still the living law (with amendments) in France. According to chapter V *Of the Obligations Accruing from Marriage*, "Married persons contract together, by the single act of marriage, the obligation of nourishing, supporting, and bringing up their children."[64] Opponents such as the *Manif pour tous* accused the "marriage for all" act of upending the civil code on which French society relies, claiming that by erasing the terms "husband" and "wife" for "asexual" and "undifferentiated" terms, the very notion of human identity, heretofore founded on a reproductive sexual difference, is placed into question.[65] Despite these protests, the Taubira Act succeeded in legalizing same-sex marriage, but there were some discriminatory provisions regarding foreign nationals. As Bruno Perreau states, "France had signed bilateral conventions with eleven countries stipulating that marriage laws in the country of origin would apply to respective foreign nationals living in France (from Morocco, Tunisia, Algeria, Bosnia-Herzegovina, Serbia, Montenegro, Kosovo, Slovenia, Poland, Laos, or Cambodia). A ministerial directive dated May 29, 2013, stated that application of the Taubira Act would confirm these conventions, thereby outlawing marriage between certain binational homosexual couples."[66] Therefore, regardless of one's French residency, you may not legally marry a person of the same sex in France, if your country of citizenship (of those listed above) has a law explicitly forbidding it.

Yet, Perreau also mentions that "LGBT movements" fought to acquire nationality for such persons to counter such discrimination. Perreau raises this point, among others, to contest Puar's argument that: "'We'—white, civilized Europeans concerned to protect homosexuals' rights—now oppose a 'them' composed of dark-skinned foreigners, immigrants from southern lands, and second-generation immigrants from certain French urban ghettos."[67] He maintains that even though "some" gays and lesbians adhere to racist and imperialist policies, this does not justify her far-reaching application of the "*portmanteau*," homonationalism.[68] I don't think Puar makes such a facile distinction, nor do I think she uniformly argues against legal protections as a recourse to justice; however, she does raise important questions regarding how narratives of "progress" tend to refer back to "pre-modern" or less progressive times. In France, such rhetoric may contrast the progressive liberal Frenchwoman with the premodern oppressed veiled[69] Muslim woman. Joan W. Scott demonstrates this interplay as she examines Marianne, the symbolic woman of the French rebellion, most famously depicted with her breasts exposed in a Delacroix painting.[70] Marianne, whose nakedness is a symbol of liberation, also appears on posters across France to remind persons that face coverings such as the niqab or the burqa are forbidden in all public spaces. For Scott, such restrictions, like the aforementioned ban of religious symbols in school, represent a failing of the French nation to consider its former colonial subjects as proper citizens. Marianne is not the only exposed woman representing French progress of some kind, for while she represents political progress in the nation, the naked statuette atop the Palace of Electricity during the 1900 Paris exposition represents technological progress and "*la promue figure de proue de la civilization*" (the promised leader of civilization).[71]

If a naked woman is symbolic of an advanced civilization, in terms of political and technological progress, how may this marginalize Muslim women who choose to veil in France, as the veil is a countersymbol to Marianne, one that represents repressed sexuality? Or, to circle back to the issue of assisted reproductive technology, how does the progress of the bioethics legislation affect Muslim women? Does extending ART to single women and lesbian couples (re)produce certain ideas about such women? The extension does not directly discriminate against Muslim women, but insofar as tenets of their religion require that sperm donation come from the husband, they are, in some way, excluded. Is it merely coincidental that an increase in access to ART correlates with an increase in European anti-immigration discourse? That is, in debating the extension, was the issue ever raised regarding who would seek access? Was it made clear that queer Muslims would be unable to seek such technology (in Puar's terms, were they deemed "improperly queer"), or were concerns of population ever broached? For example, the Hungarian government was rather explicit in its reasons for providing free IVF treatments to its citizens, noting fear of its declining birth rate in correlation with an influx in immigration. Prime Minister Viktor Orban said, "If we want Hungarian children instead of immigrants, and if the Hungarian economy can generate the necessary funding, then the only solution is to spend as much of the funds as possible on supporting families and raising children."[72] Orban is a conservative nationalist with values similar to those right and far-right French candidates whose talking points of the 2022 presidential campaign were national identity, immigration, and Islam. While it is true that right-wing conservatives tend to be more vocal in their nationalist antics, Puar points to a homonationalism that is subtler and harder to tease apart. I wonder, for example, if there is a correlation between liberals being accused of *islamo-gauchisme* and the eventual passage of the ART extension. Liberal leftists in France have been accused of *islamo-gauchisme*, because their decolonial and feminist views are said to lend support to extreme Islamic values (*islamo-gauchisme* shares certain parallels with an attack of critical race theory in the United States). What if those who initially rejected the ART extension (and not just the ultraconservatives) gave in as a way to support nationalist politics? What if the accusers of *islamo-gauchisme* supported the extension, not so much in the name of queer progress, but in the name of increasing the French birth rate contra that of immigrants? Given France's current political climate and its concerns regarding French national identity and immigration, this speculation merits discussion.

Rethinking Race and Reproductive Enframing with Heidegger

I've provided an analysis of the ways that race (and nation) is (re)produced by discourse regarding assisted reproductive technology in France. But what do we do now with this revelation? Does such an analysis offer us ways to "better wield" ART, like I previously suggested in my discussion of partial enframing?

This is tricky, because as Russell highlights, even if we consciously try to remove racial bias from scientific interventions, we cannot eliminate the "race project" from eugenics. She states,

> Proponents of contemporary eugenics argue that by ensuring that current efforts are not backed by false race science and are not conducted by racists, such efforts can reasonably be seen as free from the discredited race project of which eugenics was originally a part [. . . .] For Heidegger, the essence of technology is found in a human drive to mastery that shapes the very terms on which 'nature' is subsequently 'discovered' and investigated by science (making technology both conceptually prior and deeply linked to science).[73]

The desire to order human reproduction about in a certain way existed before the use of any particular reproductive technology. What this means is that regardless of one's intentions to remove racial bias from the use of reproductive technology, such technology is always already ideology, an ideology that necessarily orders race about in some way. If race is ideology, like technology, it cannot easily be eliminated. It is not something outside of us that can assuredly be removed. Andrew Mitchell demonstrates this point as he prefers to translate *Gestell* as positionality. According to Mitchell, enframing risks sounding like a framework or scaffolding that comes from the outside, yet there is no nature outside of *Gestell*, there is nothing extrinsic to such a technological worldview.[74] Such an acceptance of our enframed state that admits of no way out seems to be in line with my reading of Belu's notion of partial enframing. We know that in using ART, we necessarily order race about in some way, but can we order it differently? Can we queer it from the inside?

Such a manipulating of our technological "know-how" (episteme) is reminiscent of Foucault's notion of the "tactical polyvalence of discourse," the ability to reorient the meaning of discursive productions (reproductions?) as a form of resistance.[75] Heidegger, too, was aware of the disclosive power of language in his discussion of saying (*Sagen*) as showing (in terms of revealing) (*Zeigen*) and in thinking the essence (*Wesen*) of language as a revelation of the world.[76] Yet, wouldn't Heidegger critique such a "tactical" use of language and argue that such calculating further enforces our enframed state? In "The Way to Language" he asserts, "Enframing, the essence of modern technology that holds sway everywhere, ordains for itself a formalized language—that kind of informing by virtue of which man is molded and adjusted into the technical-calculative creature, a process by which step-by-step he surrenders his 'natural language.' "[77] What Heidegger means by surrendering our "natural language" is that we think language in terms of its utility, in order to exploit resources, rather than as a "saying" that is disclosive of the world. We are endowed with language to reveal what allows for being. We have already demonstrated that we cannot escape our enframed state, but do we necessarily surrender our "natural language" as revealers? What about the "saving power" in technology's essence? Surely, we must have some agency in the way that we employ discourse (thus making it tactical), for it cannot be that we are merely passive, given the interactive quality of our being-in-the-world. We should be "coresponsible" for the disclosure of something, working with it, rather than challenging it.

In reflecting on the historical truth of art, Heidegger states, "Such reflection cannot force art and its coming-to-be. But this reflective knowledge is the preliminary and therefore indispensable preparation for the becoming of art. Only such knowledge prepares its space for art, their way for the creators, their location for the preservers."[78] Thus, a reflection on the origin of art is only a preparatory stage, a necessary step in our role as preservers of history. Likewise, by reflecting on assisted reproductive technology, we use this knowledge, as preservers, to prepare a space for ART. Though, as Heidegger states, in such reflection, we should not "merely make appeal to a cultivated acquaintance with the past," as art, like language (and ART), is historically contingent and always in motion.[79] In preparing space for art/ART, we can allow other forms of (re)producing. We can use ART outside of its intended purposes, preserving through different ways of becoming, rather than cultivating an "acquaintance with the past." Though Heidegger doesn't speak about "better wielding" technology as a form of resistance, he does say that we may "prepare a free relationship to it" by questioning its essence, an essence that discloses us as revealers of being.[80]

I've questioned the essence of ART, particularly with respect to racial breeding, Heidegger's quintessential example of machinational thinking. Such thinking "prepares a free relationship to it," or as I would suggest, opens a path to resistance, a resistance to any solid grounding of reproduction. As Russell states, "once created, race can be used in ways it was not originally intended, including as a means of resistance."[81] We may not escape reproductive enframing, but how we frame it, as an epistemological problem, is subject to change.

Chapter 4

Bodyreading Grumet and Heidegger

"Setting Up" Feminist Pedagogy and "Reproducing" the Curriculum

> When we consult the etymology of the word "read," we find that "read" is lodged in the very guts of the word "ruminate," which means "to think things over." Nevertheless, the word "ruminate" is not associated with a group of animals noted for their erudition. Ruminants are cattle, also sheep (*enter Hermes*). . . . The ruminant does not give up the world in order to think about it. On the hoof it stores the world that it consumes in multiple stomachs until it has found a place of safety to bring back what has been swallowed in haste for a good chew. Actually, the ruminant's stomach has four components [. . . .] It is this fourth stomach that is called the read [*emphasis mine*].[1]
>
> —Madeleine Grumet, *Bitter Milk*

The opening quote from Grumet shares the etymology of the word *read*, the fourth stomach of the ruminant, the "one that thinks things over." Ruminants do not immediately chew what they swallow, rather they wait until they are in a place safe enough to properly digest. This chapter reads, or rather "bodyreads," Madeleine Grumet alongside Heidegger to explore how the curriculum we study is often the presence of an absence, a revealing that conceals the dialectical nature of the relationship between the domestic experience of nurturing children and the public project of educating them. In "reproducing the curriculum," passing down what we deem significant to the next generation of students, educational institutions are actively "setting up" possible worlds for its learners. Yet this "setting up" is also a "standing," one that dangerously hinges on producing classrooms akin to standing reserves that practice "banking systems of education," where knowledge is swallowed and regurgitated for the sake of an evaluation. This chapter thinks about an alternative to standing reserve classrooms, one that doesn't "repudiate the intimacy of nurture in [our] own histories and [our] work in education," one that doesn't ignore the act of reproduction in our reproduction of curriculums.[2] In bodyreading, we bring our lived generative bodies to our interpretation of texts, and we foster an empathic affective state that is concealed in traditional pedagogy.

Hermes, Messenger and Caregiver

While studying hermeneutics at university, I was taught how the etymology of the word could be traced back to Hermes, the messenger God, harbinger of the divine to "man." Hermeneutics is a study of interpretation, or more accurately, a theory that believes all truth is acquired through interpretation, through how the message is received. As Heidegger explains, "The expression "hermeneutics" derives from the Greek verb ἑρμηνεύειν. That verb is related to the noun ἑρμενεύς, which is referable to the name of the god Ἑρμενῆς by a playful thinking that is more compelling than the rigor of science. Hermes is the divine messenger. He brings the message of destiny; ἑρμηνεύειν is that exposition which brings tidings because it can listen to a message."[3] John Caputo analyzes the "two faces" of this messenger God, "Hermes the Straight Man, favoured by the mainstream, the theologians, the more tradition-bound, or Hermes the Trickster, favoured by the marginal, the outliers."[4] Any scholar familiar with hermeneutics surely knows Hermes the intermediary, whether trickster or straight. Less often taught is Hermes the god of fertility, or Hermes the fosterer and caretaker of children.[5] Where the generative nature of Hermes is referenced and linked to interpretation, reading becomes "phallic-aggressive, a cruel and violent, a destructive act," even as it appears to be a "fertilizing, a fruitful and creative one."[6] Hermeneutics is too often focused on deconstruction or *Destruktion* and not on *bodily* creation, on finitude at the expense of natality, and on "man as the shepherd of Being"[7] whose definition of care neglects the tending of his sheep.

In bodyreading Heidegger alongside Grumet, I set up a feminist pedagogy that realizes the importance of attunement in receiving the message, while also highlighting the necessity of fostering an environment conducive to such reception, an environment that doesn't ignore the act of bodily reproduction in our reproduction of curriculums. Heidegger may seem a strange candidate for advancing a feminist pedagogy built on "reproducing the curriculum," since he is notorious for his onto-somatic denial.[8] Yet his ontology of care and his later work on the body, coupled with his insights regarding the dangers of becoming part of a "standing reserve," offer important contributions to pedagogies seeking to resist "banking systems of education."[9]

Before turning to an analysis of how to resist such "banking systems," it is necessary to set the scene that allows such systems of standing reserve to emerge. I noted that hermeneutics is too focused on deconstruction and not on bodily creation. Certainly, early hermeneutics takes bodily creation and reproduction into account in classical interpretations of Christian texts, as the Virgin Mary becomes the "deliverer" of Christ and thus *secondarily* of the written word, that is, the truth. But here, bodily creation in and of itself tells us nothing of the truth. As St. Augustine, who Heidegger credits with providing "the first hermeneutics in grand style"[10] states, man was created for the contemplative life whereas woman finds her origins in corporeality and procreative purpose.[11] This association of woman with the body (reproduction) and man with the mind (production) is seen throughout the history of philosophy and is most famously exposed in Beauvoir's *The Second Sex*, where she reveals "man" as the universal standard of transcendence and woman as the other, marked by her sex and condition of immanence.[12]

We also see a gendered distinction of propagation in Plato's *Symposium*, as Diotima teaches Socrates two ways of "giving birth in beauty," reproduction of the body through a passing down of generations via childbirth and reproduction of the soul through a passing down of knowledge.[13] The latter is, of course, viewed as a higher form of love and reserved for men. The significance of Diotima's being a woman has long-perplexed scholars, but in bodyreading Grumet, in understanding how woman is viewed as mediator between the natural (mothering/reproduction) and the industrial (teaching/production), we see that Diotima can only be a woman. Woman as mediator transmits, through teaching, the law of the father. Grumet states, "[Women] were expected to be the medium through which the laws, rules, language, and order of the father, the principal, the employer were communicated to the child. Their own passivity was to provide the model of obedience for the young to emulate."[14] In making present the law of the father through the public project of educating children, woman's domestic experience of nurturing them becomes covered over. As we'll discuss in the next section, woman becomes a pedagogical tool among the standing reserve, passing down a cultural production of domination to the next generation, while being asked to forget the care that brought such generations to presence in the first place. So, too, this happens with Hermes as mediator between the mortal and divine. As students of hermeneutics, we are focused on "the message" and our attunement to receiving it, but the space in which such reception occurs, the classroom, and the *care* associated with our bodily inhabiting of it gets passed over. Here, I refer to care in both the traditional sense of nurturing and in the sense of Heidegger's ontological project (as a neutral structure from which any understanding of being emerges). Hermes the messenger god eclipses Hermes the fosterer and caretaker of children.

Why do we reiterate the story of Hermes the messenger god and repudiate the side of him that cared for and nurtured children? Of all the children Hermes fostered, perhaps Dionysus offers us the most insight regarding the importance of care in our reception of the message, particularly since a Dionysian moment can be viewed as an instant of ecstatic opening for Heidegger.

Nonnus's *Dionysiaca* states, "[Hermes] gave him [the new born babe Dionysus just delivered from Zeus' thigh] to the [Lamides] daughters of Lamos river Nymphai—the son of Zeus, the vineplanter. They received Bakkhos into their arms; and each of them dropt the milky juice of her breast without pressing into his mouth."[15] This passage recounts the rescue of Dionysus by Hermes, as he delivers him to the mountain nymphs to be nourished and protected. Zeus had turned Dionysus into a baby goat (a *ruminant* whose fourth stomach is the *read*) to protect him from the wrath of Hera. Apollonius Rhodius's *Argonautica* further highlights Hermes's delivering Dionysus to a place for sustenance, a place for milk that has not yet gone bitter: "It was Makris [daughter of Aristalos], who in Abantian Eubola, took the infant Dionysus to her bosom and moistened his parched lips with honey, when Hermes has rescued him from the flames and brought him to her."[16] The importance of Hermes's role as both messenger and caretaker is best noted in the following passage from the *Dionysiaca*: "The god [Hermes, bringing the babe Dionysos from the mad-struck Lamides] spoke to her [Ino] in friendly coaxing tones, and let pass a divine message from his prophetic throat: 'Madam, receive a new son [the baby Dionysus]; lay in your bosom the child of Semele your sister.'"[17] Here, Hermes delivers a message of care, acting as intermediary while also creating a nurturing environment in which the message can be received. I share this story of Dionysus to not only accent the dual role of Hermes but also to highlight how a celebration of Dionysus as ecstatic opening may not have been possible without such nurturance.

Mathias Warnes discusses the origin of language as the festival of poetry and the central role that Dionysus plays: "The poet-priest, as mediator between gods and men, brings gods and men together. Such a coming together of gods and men is festivity, and the center of festivity is the cult. The god of the cult of festivity is Dionysos."[18] Cult here is not supposed to indicate a herd mentality but rather a form of ritual play where such play opens space for new ways of being. While Heidegger may critique Nietzsche at times for valorizing the untamed frenzy of Dionysus over and above the Apollonian in that it further reifies a dualistic way of thinking, he sees in the Dionysian moment an opening up of possibilities. Heidegger asserts, "And yet such arousal of frenzied feeling and unchaining of 'affects' could be taken as a rescue of 'life,' especially in view of the growing impoverishment and deterioration of existence occasioned by industry, technology and finance."[19] Dionysus was first nurtured to bring about such a moment, so too was the poet-priest before initiation into language. Turning our attention to not only a reproduction of words but also a reproduction of bodies (and their "affects") and to an autonomy that is first and foremost relational also opens a path to another way of thinking.

Carrigan Wooten asserts, "Grumet argues that if curriculum is directly influenced by our relationships to our mothers and to our children in an ongoing generational conversation, then the experiences of women provide space to rupture the Father's curriculum in transformative ways."[20] The Father's curriculum is one of a standing reserve "occasioned by industry, technology and finance." But we can read differently, or rather bodyread.

Bitter Milk and Standing Reserve Classrooms

In Grumet's *Bitter Milk: Women and Teaching*, she refers to a Sri Lankan elixir, a mixture of margosa leaves and bitter milk, that is given to young women who experience "psychotic responses" as they struggle with being separated from their families. It is the same bitter milk that women apply to their nipples in order to wean their babies. Our initiation into public education is often a bitter milk, a fostering of intellectual growth, yet a repudiating of the intimacy of nurture. We are taught that we must separate ourselves from our caretakers in the pursuit of independence and favor objective knowledge over subjective experience. The "body knowledge" that we are born dependent on another and that our body actually orients our experience in the world becomes covered over for the sake of blossoming into an individual.

Grumet asserts that our neglect of the body has caused us to lose "our stomach for reading."[21] Borrowing Merleau-Ponty's notion of the "body-subject," a term for human consciousness that resists the abstraction of idealism by emphasizing the body, where it lives, and who cares for it, Grumet asks us to "bodyread." In bodyreading, we bring our experiences to language and recognize how other people influence our reading of the world. Grumet states that when we teach children how to read we fail to recognize language as something that is living; we grant authority to a text and turn children into passive learners as we request them to dutifully repeat its meaning in front of the teacher's gaze. While Grumet is concerned with elementary education, her insights can be extended to thinking about knowledge production at the university level as well.

For Grumet, mothering and teaching are intimately linked, as they are both the affairs of (largely) women. It is obvious that Grumet is talking about elementary education here as women are underrepresented at the collegial level. And yet, the role of "woman" as pedagogical tool remains the same for both. When women teach children how to read, they must initiate them into the "law of the father," as they introduce signs and symbols built on social intelligibility that cover over the "mother tongue."[22] And while university professors do not practice such elementary initiation, we often continue a tradition of similar knowledge production as we expect students to recite ideologies from the canon. Women continue to act as pedagogical tools to such a system as they pass down knowledge of largely old white men. This is not meant to entirely repudiate the knowledge of such men, for such outright dismissal would be to replace one system of domination with another. Setting up a feminist pedagogy is not just about reading different texts, but about reading the canon with one's body, to bring one's experience to the text. Grumet does not privilege the private realm over the public but rather suggests that bodyreading is a way to mediate the two. This is why Hermes is so important as both messenger and caretaker, as the word cannot be properly received without a nurturing environment.

As previously noted, Heidegger may seem an unlikely candidate for such a feminist project as he notoriously neglects the body in his work. Though in bodyreading Heidegger, I show how the canon can be read a different way, in a way that keeps language alive. I think Heidegger would be understanding of this task as he quotes Humboldt to capture the vivacity of the word: "One must not regard language as a lifeless product. It is far more like a reproducing."[23] He then goes on to suggest language as a "labor of the spirit." The choice of words here, "reproducing" and "labor" are opportune, and while neither Humboldt nor Heidegger would approach these terms in a literal sense, a project of bodyreading would ask how reflecting on the acts of bodily reproduction and labor (both bodily and affective) may transform the curriculum we teach. Heidegger says, "language is the house of being,"[24] but who takes care of the house? Maternal figures are usually responsible for setting up an abode fit for proper dwelling. Likewise, women teachers bear the burden of participating in affective labor and are attuned to care in a way that male teachers (often) are not.

Carol Hay discusses how women professors are called on to act as "mother" substitutes for their students,[25] and instructor evaluations show gender bias, as words likes *caring* are more than twice as likely to appear in student feedback of women professors, no matter the subject area.[26] Ben Schmidt, who created an interactive map to track such biases, has recently posted the following message on his site, further highlighting women's unique burden of care: "On topic reminder for everyone here that within the academy: the pandemic will hurt the careers of women with small children disproportionately."[27] Women remain the primary caretakers inside and outside of the classroom. Our current academic climate values intellectual labor (aimed at some form of utility or specialization) at the expense of affective labor, so a lot of work women do in the classroom is not regarded as actual travail. Before further discussing what setting up a feminist pedagogy that values care may look like, it is necessary to examine our current situation of standing reserve classrooms.

Paulo Freire coined the term "banking system of education" to describe classroom practices that reinforce the memorization of material rather than the genuine learning of it.[28] Like ATM machines, information is deposited (read memorized) only to be "cashed out" or withdrawn for the sake of a grade. In acting like such automatons, students may be able to recall sophisticated ideas recounted in a lecture, but mere mimesis does not involve a proper reading. Here, information is regurgitated but never properly digested. Knowledge becomes an object, placed on reserve for future utility, utility being the main goal of our technological era.

In "The Question Concerning Technology," Heidegger warns us of the dangers of technology where technology does not refer to actual apparatuses or technological devices but rather the mentality that gave birth to them. The danger of technology lies in its essence as an ideology, referred to as enframing (*Gestell*), that encounters the world as an amalgam of resources, ready to be exploited for ulterior use. The greatest danger lies in the fact that man himself, as enframed, becomes a part of this stockpile called the "standing reserve" (*Bestand*). Analyzing the way man is "challenged forth" to exploit resources as such, Heidegger states, "If man is challenged, ordered, to do this, then does not man himself belong even more originally than nature within the standing reserve? The current talk about human resources, about the supply of patients for clinic, gives evidence of this. The forester who measures the felled timber in the same woods and who to all appearances walks the forest path in the same way his grandfather did is today ordered by the industry."[29] What I find particularly telling about this passage is Heidegger's mention of a grandfather figure. On the one hand, this figure is supposed to represent a nostalgic longing for a preindustrial past, but the grandfather also conjures a generational "passing down," an ancestral "setting up." Heidegger says this man who has become a part of the standing reserve "walks the same way" his grandfather did, at least in terms of "appearances," yet this new man strides with a focus on utility, that is, cutting the trees for the purposes of industry. What sort of instruction causes the perpetuation of a mentality that "sets up" the forest as such? What sort of pedagogy views the trees (in their being) in terms of utility?

For Heidegger, each epoch is charactered by a certain understanding of being or constellation of intelligibility. Our era is governed by *Gestell*. If such intelligibility is, in part, passed down and reinforced through social conventions (*as Man*), the classroom, as a crucial space for fostering such intelligibility, is a perfect site for understanding the relation between pedagogy and ontology. As Iain Thomson states, "Heidegger defends a kind of *ontological holism*: By giving shape to our historical understanding of 'what *is*,' metaphysics determines the most basic presuppositions of what *anything* is, including 'education.' As he puts it: 'Western humanity, in all its comportment toward beings, and even toward itself, is in every respect sustained and guided by metaphysics.' "[30] Here, Thomson is interested in how Heidegger's philosophy may help us understand the current crisis of the university with its fragmentation of departments and its push toward hyperspecialization, vocationalization, and technologization, how questions of education are intricately tied to questions of being. I'm interested in the gendered aspect of such knowledge production, and how productivity eschews any understanding of reproductivity.

Grumet examines how women act as mediators between the natural and the industrial, as they must vacillate between the private realm as nurturers of children and the public realm as educators of them, where education is an initiation into the law of the father. Women read male scripts of epistemology when they teach, rather than locate their own histories and reproductions of themselves in the classroom. In doing so, they repudiate an intimacy of nurture and prepare students for inauguration into industry. Here, students become part of a standing reserve, as knowledge becomes a resource to later be exploited *for the sake of* a good grade, and the good grade is *for the sake of* a diploma, and the diploma is *for the sake of* a job; essentially, learning is only *for the sake of* being useful. Students are turned into *productive* citizens and the *reproductive* aspect of their existence is passed over. Such classroom environments teach reading as a form of mimesis. Students do not bodyread and bring their experiences to interpreting texts but rather memorize texts for future utility. Knowledge is swallowed but not digested.

Grumet notes, "The word 'institution' comes from the Latin verb, *instituere,* which means 'to set up.' The root of that verb is the same as the root of stature and state. It is *stare*, meaning 'to stand.' And it is our upright posture, argues Erwin Straus in 'The Upright Posture,' that privileges sight instead of touch, an imposture of rationality that ranks structural abstraction about textured detail as the highest achievement of human cognition."[31] Educational institutions applaud mimetic performance if those structural abstractions make it to the page for the teacher to "see." A student who engages with the text, digests it, brings it into their life to touch it in the sense of bringing it close, not at a distance, not on reserve, cannot be said to be "learning." The rationale goes that we cannot quantify or measure such engagement; learning must be objectified to be counted as learning. Institutions "stand" as standing reserves, "setting up" "banking systems"; yet, this "setting up" could be otherwise. Rather than apply the bitter milk and repudiate intimacy in the classroom, we can set up spaces for students to learn differently. In setting up a feminist pedagogy, founded on care, we open up a world for other possibilities.

Setting Up Feminist Pedagogy

Setting up a feminist pedagogy founded on authentic care entails creating a space where students are encouraged to bring their experiences to the text. Bringing our experiences to language is a working with the body, or as later Heidegger would say a "bodying forth" (*Leiben*). Such "bodying forth" is a way of "reproducing the curriculum," of understanding care as founded on an orientation of the body. To reproduce the curriculum is to both pass down the message and to nurture the one who receives it.

In reading the canon differently, in bodyreading, we keep the language of Heidegger's text alive, and we open up a space for the historical contingency of language to further reproduce. While early Heidegger may not have directly addressed the body, his later writings highlight the Husserlian distinction between *Körper* and *Leib*. While *Körper* stops at the skin, *Leib* takes into account our spatiality and ecstatic opening that allows us to encounter entities and others. *Leib* "says" something about our way of Being (where to say [*Sagen*] means to show [*Zeigen*]).[32] It is this ability to say, or rather the necessity of needing to say something, that distinguishes the human from the animal. In saying something, we bring forth that which we have gathered, and such gathering is contingent on our comportment. Heidegger expresses how this comportment is dependent on the body: "We must characterize all comportment of the human being as *being-in-the-world*, determined by the bodying forth of the body [. . . .] comportment does not simply enter an indifferent space. Rather, comportment is always already in a certain region [*Gegend*] which is open through the thing to which I am in relationship."[33] Heidegger will then go on to say that the phenomena of the body must be understood "in the context of which men are in relationship to each other."[34] Classrooms are not indifferent spaces and students orient themselves toward other students and their teacher accordingly. A classroom environment can be a nurturing one that invites engagement or a closed off one that encourages passive learners. Our being-in-the-world and the spatiality we encounter is understood by our neutral temporal structure of care, with care being a receptiveness (attunement) to an interplay of relations that designate "what is" or what has the potential to be. How entities and others appear to us depends on whether we are enacting and engaging with this neutral structure of care in a positive or negative manner. In "bodying forth," I am engaged with my environment and how it sets up my world in either a mode of concern (how I perceive/receive entities) or solicitude (how I perceive/receive others).

In chapter 1, I discussed the distinction between authentic ("leaping ahead") and inauthentic ("leaping in") modes of caring within the context of giving birth. "Leaping ahead" and "leaping in" are positive forms of solicitude in that the others with which I am engaging are not "passed by." Heidegger states,

> Being for, or against, or without one another, passing one another by, not "mattering" to one another—these are possible ways of solicitude [. . . .] With regard to its positive modes, solicitude

has two extreme possibilities. It can, as it were, take away 'care' from the Other and put itself in his position in concern: it can *leap in* for him. This kind of solicitude takes over for the Other that with which he is to concern himself [. . . .] In contrast to this, there is also the possibility of a kind of solicitude which does not so much leap in for the Other as *leap ahead* of him [*ihm vorausspringt*] in his existentiell potentiality-for-Being, not in order to take away his "care" but rather to give it back to him authentically as such for the first time.

Thus, in "leaping in," I dominate the other and propel them to act in a way most conducive to my way of "bodying forth" in the world, but in "leaping ahead," I anticipate the needs of the other while allowing them the agency to act according to their "ownmost" possibilities. While I necessarily exist alongside others in the world, I also exist as a certain "mineness," able to own my decisions in a world that solicits me according to my existential make-up and possibilities.

For example, Stephan Käufer gives an example of how our choice to become a parent affects how we navigate the world in a mode of circumspective concern: "Traffic dangers and pedestrian crosswalks, for example, are especially salient to me insofar as I exist for the sake of parenting.[(. . .] Being a parent is not a property I have. From Heidegger's existential vantage point, it is not a biological or social fact about me. Rather, being a parent is my existential make-up, constituted by deploying my parental know-how and experiencing the world as soliciting me accordingly."[35] Teachers have a certain pedagogical know-how and the way in which they navigate the classroom—ideally in an authentic mode of solicitude—determines the type of space they create. If a teacher is constantly "leaping in," students retreat into passive anonymous learners. If a teacher approaches their students by "leaping ahead," students appear to them as cases of Dasein, each with their own existential make-up to bring to the course material. A teacher who lacks this form of authentic care hears only their own voice and experiences repeated back to them. A teacher *really* cares about their students when they consider what the classroom could be in terms of its potentiality, rather than projecting their own stubborn project onto it. Our structure of care informs how things matter, and for this reason, spaces can never be indifferent. If I *see* you and *hear* you, I am enacting my care structure. Seeing and hearing are not to be taken as mere empirical senses, for I can notice your existence as an entity (or let it pass by) without weighing the different relations that allow you to exist as a certain way in my world, in the same way that saying is not just a saying but a showing (*Sagen* as *Zeigen*). What I see and hear says something (shows something) about my way of being, about how I care (positively? authentically?). Setting up a feminist pedagogy founded on this understanding of care asks teachers to reflect on the type of spatial encounters that are made possible in their classrooms. Is the classroom space a nurturing one where students can be seen and heard? Do students feel represented in discussions? As a teacher, do you listen when a student brings their experience to the text, or do you fail to hear what they say and impose your own interpretation?

Bodyreading is a form of bodying forth, as students bring what matters to them to the text. I recently stated that when a teacher cares about their students, they appear to them as "cases of Dasein." I borrow this notion "cases of Dasein" from John Haugeland as it captures the "mineness" (*Jemeinigkeit*) of existence, the existence that is "passed down to me," coupled with a certain universality of being that we all share.[36] Our being-in-the-world is determined by the comportment of our bodying forth, an orientation that must be understood in relationship to others. In seeing students as "cases of Dasein," a relationship is forged where you respect how they contribute to what allows for being, or in the words of Maria Lugones, you assume a loving perception and "world-travel," rather than force an authoritative reading of the text (an arrogant perception).

Lauren Freeman applies feminist notions of relational autonomy to reread (bodyread?) Heidegger's understanding of authentic Dasein as being-with-others. Most scholarly engagements with Heidegger's notion of authenticity rely on traditional understandings of autonomy that view the self as auto-determined and radically independent from others. Yet Freeman extracts passages from Heidegger to show that we are ontologically co-constituted by *Mitsein*: "[We are] determined by [our] dependency . . . on being already in the totality, a dependency over which Dasein itself does not have control."[37] Likewise, Anne O'Byrne examines our primordial "being-with," as she provides an analysis of being-toward-birth and imparts a historical hermeneutics of the passing down of generations. A being-toward-birth is not just a reflection of my material coming-to-be but something I take up throughout my life as I reckon with a tradition that has been bestowed on me. While the repetition of generations is a natal event in that new sociopolitical events are born and new forms of existing in time emerge, such repetition is intimately linked to our bodies, making this "biological" act an ontological one. O'Byrne asserts, "Bodies can no longer be ignored because our generative—creative and procreative—capacities must now be given their due."[38] In bodyreading, in "reproducing the curriculum," our procreative capacities are given their due, as we return to an initial natal event of which we all have body knowledge. In bodyreading, we find anew our stomach for reading.

Part II
Heidegger's Grounding of Sex/Gender and the Politics of Birth

Chapter 5

A Feminist Reading of the *Black Notebooks*

The Eternal Feminine, Peasant Women, and "Being a People"

We are again approaching the truth . . . paths which kept mother's blood, and that of her ancestors, circulating and pulsing.

—Martin Heidegger

Mother—my untainted memory of this pious woman—without bitterness, and in a surmising prescience, she countenanced the itinerary of a son who had *apparently* turned away from God.

—Martin Heidegger

It's no surprise that I turned my mother into an idea. Transference of an emotional *affect* into a conceptual one helps the thinker distance themselves from the origin of pain that brought them to ruminate the subject in the first place. (I could say something about pain here, but pain is not logical the way a cloud is not logical the way a war is not logical the way a motherless child is not.)

—Kimberly Grey

In his *Black Notebooks*, Heidegger critiques scientific explanations of biological racism, largely influenced by Darwin, that politicize the superiority of the German people. This is not to say that the Germans (as "a people"), according to Heidegger, are not superior; rather, their supremacy rests on something other than genetic lineage and blood ties. It is founded on a historically privileged attunement to being (beyng).[1] I examine how sex/gender facticity comes into play within such attunement. That is, in the rare instances that Heidegger references "woman" or the "feminine" in the *Black Notebooks*, how does she figure within his larger ontological project of understanding beyng? I then demonstrate that despite attempts to critique the "self-conscious thought of race,"[2] Heidegger reifies the ontological significance of race via a "blood and soil" ideology symbolized in the peasant woman. Next, I tease apart what it means to be "a people" as "one generation" in Heidegger's reading of Trakl's poetic work. Here, Heidegger's open-ended question, "Problem: what is woman?," raised in his 1923 *Ontology—The Hermeneutics of Facticity* (GA 63), resurfaces as he tries to destroy a sexual duality founded on Judeo-Christian origin stories of the flesh in favor of a "gentle twofoldedness," a struggle that bears parallels with the German's struggle over their essence in the *Black Notebooks*. Throughout this chapter, I demonstrate how Heidegger manipulates tropes of the feminine through his discussion of the eternal feminine, mother, peasant woman, and sister to advance a politico-poetic project of Nazi politics.

The Historicity of Beyng and the Eternal Feminine

In *Ponderings V* (GA 94), Heidegger asserts, "One must of course not fall into the basic illusion—that everyone's easily possible insight into the biological condition for breeding of a 'people' could touch what is essential—whereas the predominance of this naturally crude and common biological way of thinking precisely suppresses meditation on the basic conditions of being a people."[3] The biological condition of breeding cannot account for what is essential about "a people." This claim is reminiscent of Heidegger's assertion in *The Metaphysical Foundations of Logic* (GA 26) that the "species-being of sexually differentiated bodily creatures" cannot account for the primordial being of Dasein.[4] Heidegger dismisses "survival of the fittest" claims based on blood or genetics, indicating that belief in such facile biologism erases meditative thinking. Meditation is "the leap ahead into the truth of beyng."[5] And while Heidegger rejects "the fittest" founded on relations of blood ties, he supports a notion of supremacy based on those who are capable of taking such a leap toward truth, through an *attunement* to beyng. He states, "*Only a few, only mastery, only what has already long since grown up, only what possesses the basic attunement and has style* can lead here and can introduce an actual rebellion that does not end in slogans and abusive language."[6] Heidegger is referring to the slogans and abusive language of the Nazi Party, but what he seems to find unsettling here is not so much the discriminatory nature of this party but its unfounded *inclusivity*. Heidegger not only believes in the superiority of "*a few*," he also disparages democratic mediocrity and the leveling off of ranks for the sake of "community." National Socialism, and its scientific supporters, declassify the privileged attunement of certain Germans by speaking of "people" in terms of biology. An intriguing aspect of this thought is that Heidegger will compare such erasure of ranks (for the sake of uniform mediocrity) to Nietzsche's concept of the eternal feminine.

Heidegger raises the notion of the "eternal feminine" in a vehement critique of Alfred Baeumler. Baeumler was a philosopher, pedagogue, and author of *Male Confederation and Science* (*Männerbund und Wissenschaft*). In this text, he cites the "political soldier" as the "ideal student" and calls for "men's schools" and the exclusion of the "feminine-democratic." He used Nietzsche's philosophy of "heroic realism"[7] to justify National Socialism (founded on racial superiority and heredity) and to train men to become proper (read manly) soldiers. Heidegger asserts,

> *Male confederation and science*—a quite cleverly fabricated fig leaf, but one which, despite everything, does not altogether cover the nakedness: male confederation! That signifies a complete lack of manliness of spirit; it is the flocking together and promotion of those who otherwise would fall too short [. . .] in order then to degrade "with power" all distinctions of rank down to a comfortable mediocrity. Then why are there strata! The "eternal feminine" in this male confederation! Just like the metropolitanism in the petty bourgeois "blood and soil."[8]

Heidegger is using Nietzsche against Baeumler in two important ways. First, while Baeumler uses Nietzsche's philosophy of the heroic masculine Overman to support the ideology of the Third Reich, in that science (via eugenics) can prove or propagate "Overman" qualities of the German people, such use betrays Nietzsche's philosophy as the coupling of "male confederation and science" works to disregard any "manliness of spirit," a manliness that is necessary to become the Overman.[9] The nude virile male was a popular symbol of German superiority, yet such "manliness of spirit" is covered with a fig leaf that is "science" (eugenics). Science as fig leaf shamefully reveals (by concealing[10]) the general mediocrity of the German people by telling racial lies of superiority. Heidegger is critiquing Baeumler for making biological claims regarding the universal privileging of Germans. That is, a German man does not automatically become an Overman, simply by virtue of his blood. Such universality leads to a "comfortable mediocrity" as all persons are placed on the same level, that is, the shared blood of the Germans makes them a superior "people." Yet, as Heidegger asks, if all Germans are the same, why are there strata?

Second, such leveling off draws similar parallels to Nietzsche's discussion of the "eternal feminine" and the ranking of women. Heidegger seems to imply that the equalizing of German people, asking that they all be treated in similar regard, is just as ridiculous as the demand for women to be treated like men, for they lose their "rank" in demanding equal rights. Nietzsche states, "The more womanly a woman is, the more she fights tooth and nail against rights in general: the natural order of things, the eternal war between the sexes, assigns to her by far the foremost rank."[11] Clarifying Nietzsche's viewpoint, Fredrick Appel asserts, "Although the feminist woman remains convinced that she is working for the true interests of the female sex, she in fact ensures a contrary result [. . .] [feminist] women actually abandon their great natural advantages in exchange for the opportunity to compete with men in a man's game, thereby 'lowering the general rank of woman.'"[12] Just as a woman loses her "rank" in attempting to be equal, the Germans lose the few who are actually of a higher rank in demanding universal superiority.

I see Heidegger engaging with two aspects of the "eternal feminine." First, there is no "eternal feminine," no essence of what it means to be a woman outside of an historical discourse. Second, such discourse regarding the "eternal feminine" equates "woman" with "breeder."

If, for Nietzsche, women are of a higher rank, it is due to the power conferred her by male discourse by first dubbing her inferior and then subsequently endowing her with a mysterious quality and seductiveness. Sarah Kofman states,

> It is the "becoming-Woman" of woman that made life on earth interesting: if "God" created woman, Nietzsche says elsewhere, it was to rescue man from boredom. But God has been dead for a long while: the myth of the "creation" of Eve signifies that it is men themselves (and the women who are in league with their interests) who, at a given moment when it was entirely in their interest, created woman as the "weaker sex" or Eternal feminine, transforming her into an interesting enigma.[13]

Here, there is an emphasis on "becoming woman," the "how" and not the "what," a distinction that we have previously shown to be of paramount importance for Heidegger.[14] There is no uniformly superior "male confederation" that can be explained by science any more than there is an unchanging "eternal feminine." Both are opportunistic creations. There is no eternal essence of what makes one a woman, but neither is there an eternal essence of what makes one "a people." There is no unchanging "what is," but rather a questioning of how "what is" became grounded as such. Nevertheless, the Germans find themselves in a privileged position as "a people." How can this be?

Heidegger begins *Ponderings VII* (GA 95) with the following insight: "*The essence of the Germans:* That they may be chained to the *struggle* over their essence, for only inasmuch as they take up this struggle are they the people they alone can be. Suitable for this struggle is only that which, with unwavering confidence in its essential pride, is able to suffer the highest question—worthiness of what is most question-*worthy* (beyng)."[15] The Germans must "struggle" to reach their full potential by opening themselves to the question of *beyng*. However, as Heidegger will continue to discuss, such a receptiveness to what he calls historical "thrusts of beyng," are often concealed by "culture, as an organization of lived experience."[16] Heidegger seems to imply that, for Baeumler, the Germans passively accept their superiority as a given, based on blood, when the owning of such superiority consists of a struggle, one that must not "parry" these "thrusts of being."[17] Heidegger's comment, "The eternal feminine in this confederation!" is thus a grave insult to Baeumler's "men's school," as he accuses Baeumler's students of being that which they are trained to reject—passive women. Fascist ideologies of that time glorified men as active warriors in opposition to passive women, as evidenced in Marinetti's manifesto: "We want to glorify war—the only cure for the world—militarism, patriotism, the destructive gesture of the anarchists, the beautiful ideas which kill, and contempt for woman."[18]

The "eternal feminine," or an unchanging ideal of passivity, should not exist in the male confederation; rather, such men, according to Heidegger, should actively engage with "thrusts of beyng." Yet, what are these seemingly violent thrusts of beyng? In *Introduction to Metaphysics*, Gregory Fried and Richard Polt have found a similar violent portrayal of beyng, as the aforementioned "few" are "literally violated" or "raped" by beyng. Heidegger asserts, "Not-Being-here is the ultimate victory over Being. Dasein is the constant urgency of defeat and of the renewed resurgence of the act of violence against Being, in such a way that the almighty sway of Being violates Dasein (in the literal sense), makes Da-sein into the site of its appearing, envelopes and pervades Dasein in its sway, and thereby holds it within Being."[19] As Fried and Polt mention in a footnote, "*ver-gewaltigt: vergewaltigen* (root *Gewalt*, violence) means to violate, and specifically to rape." This seems to insinuate that the "few" who are able to take the "leap toward beyng," through a basic attunement, must allow themselves to be rendered passive, to be violated by beyng. This act of violation, where an unfolding of ontological difference occurs (Dasein is held "within Being"), is also an unfolding of sexual difference. Fried suggests that " 'Thrust,' in addition to its sexual connotation, is applied to the attack of the sword; one speaks of sword thrusts. The Latin root of 'vagina' means a sheath for a dagger or a scabbard for a sword."[20] On the one hand, these "thrusts of beyng" are metaphorical, representing a certain spiritual attunement necessary for "being a people." On the other hand, literal sexual procreation (thrusts) is needed to sustain such people. Heidegger may not have advocated for eugenics, but in his analysis of Trakl, which I will examine in the next section, his discussion of a "twofoldness" founded on sexual difference, a twofoldness that is required for "one generation," points to a pronatalist discourse.

Whereas culture is organized and calculated in the form of "cultural politics, cultural concern, Christian cultural assimilation," thrusts of beyng are "incalculable."[21] We can say that *the few* who are able to open themselves up to the incalculable, a form of meditative thinking rather than machinational thinking (*Machenschaft*), are superior in their attunement to beyng, for they are able to overcome the "struggle over their essence." These *few Germans* sound a lot like Hegel's world historical figures that are appropriated by the cunning of reason throughout different stages in history,[22] but Heidegger contends that the incalculable is not grasped via reason, as it is not synonymous to that which is irrational. He asserts, "*The incalculable*: if this were only the irrational, then rationalism could ultimately triumph over it. But the *in*calculable is that which first provides an abode for calculation and its limits—and opens itself only to those who no longer 'reckon' with the incalculable but instead undergo its thrust as an appropriation into beyng—and who are prepared for thrusts."[23] The incalculable is invited through a meditative thinking that views "nature" as "self-emergent."[24] That is, nature is not "challenged forth" and exploited as a resource for the sake of utility.

As referenced in chapter 3, Heidegger posits racial breeding as the quintessential example of machinational thinking. Once again playing with the language of "nakedness," presumably to critique the male confederation of such thought, Heidegger quotes Nietzsche's *Will to Power* to make his own point: "A period in which the old masquerade and the moral adornment of the affects provoke aversion: *naked nature*; in which the *power quantities* are simply conceded as *decisive* (as *determinative of rank*) (. . .) (*Will to Power*, no. 1024), 'Nature' has now been taken up into 'breeding'; i.e., the forces of nature are consciously *stored*."[25] The male confederation, symbolically represented as a (virile) nude male, has determined rank (German superiority) based on blood ties that can be controlled through techniques of breeding. Such techniques disrupt "naturally evolving races" by manipulating race as a "self-conscious thought";[26] that is, through racial breeding, race is no longer something that historically occurs in nature but is manipulated to evolve (or not) through machinational thinking. The concept of race, as something that can be bred, thus becomes ontologically significant.

This is where a second reading of Heidegger's mention of the eternal feminine comes into play. Whereas Nietzsche talks of "becoming woman," in a way that, at times, lauds her versatility, he praises her role (and trope of the eternal feminine) as breeder, as mother. Nietzsche is resentful of women who do not bear offspring, disparaging the "emancipated ones who lack the wherewithal to have children."[27] Thus, when Heidegger interjects, "The 'eternal feminine' in this male confederation!" is he also denigrating rhetoric that equates and manipulates "woman" as "mother/breeder"? How Heidegger understands "woman" or manipulates tropes of the feminine in the *Black Notebooks* is important, as these personal journals point to an anti-Semitism that can no longer be chalked up to either a political naivete or a political motivation to save his university career. One of the overall projects of this book is to demonstrate how totalized definitions of "woman" lead to harmful exclusionary politics. In the case of Heidegger, how did he manipulate understandings of "woman" to this end?

The Blood and Soil of Peasant Women

On the one hand, Heidegger is quite clear that breeding techniques cannot reproduce a superior "people." As previously noted, such supremacy cannot be calculated via machinational thinking but through meditative thinking. His privileging of *a few* Germans is thus not founded on biology but on a sort of intellectual or spiritual attunement to beyng. After remarking, "The 'eternal feminine' in this male confederation!" he follows up with, "Just like the metropolitanism in the petty bourgeois 'blood and soil.' " "Blood and soil" (*Blut und Boden*) was a popular slogan used by National Socialists to highlight the blood of the Germans (as a nation) and to call for a return to the "soil" of preindustrial peasant life. For example, Clifford Lovin states, "That industrial capitalism with its attendant evil of urbanism was responsible for the deterioration of the German nation and that only a return to the soil could halt the decline were commonplaces. Popular German novelists such as Berthold Auerbach and Conrad Ferdinand Meyer idealized the peasant as the true representatives of the German race."[28] Thus, "blood and soil" ideologies romanticize farm life and peasant living, and yet Heidegger accuses the speakers of such slogans of "metropolitanism." It appears that Heidegger is not critiquing "blood and soil" ideologies in and of themselves but is rather accusing Nazi propaganda of not returning to the soil far enough, of being urban despite claims to be otherwise.[29] Nationalist chants of "blood and soil" that seek to unify and equalize the Germans based on an idea of (biological rather than historical) race actually make the Germans lose their essence as Germans (as a people) in the same way that Nietzsche's discussion of the eternal feminine suggests that women lose what is "feminine" about them when they demand equality. Thus, Heidegger's remark on the eternal feminine is about essences. On the one hand, there is no eternal essence in an absolute sense. On the other hand, the Germans are in a unique historical situation whereby they can appropriate their essence by not "parrying thrusts of beyng," by being attuned to beyng. Such attunement is tied to notions of the eternal feminine and blood and soil, but they have been misappropriated.

As Heidegger elucidates in *Ponderings II* (GA 94), *woman* as mother (a trope of the eternal feminine) is key to the truth (revealed as an attunement that dwells on native soil).

> We are again approaching the truth and its essentiality—we are becoming mindful of everything the truth requires to take it up and to take a stand within it—to become ones who are indigenous, who stand on native soil [. . .] that is what often vibrates in me through body and disposition—as if I went over the fields guiding a plow [. . .] paths which kept mother's blood, and that of her ancestors, circulating and pulsing.[30]

Thus, a key to discerning the truth, to understanding beyng, relies on an embeddedness to native soil, soil that is intricately tied to the blood of the mother. This is not the only instance in the *Black Notebooks*, where "woman" is referenced in connection to the soil and a romanticized peasant life. The rural woman appears in *Ponderings III* (GA 94), as Heidegger reproaches students with their pretentious socialism, "meanwhile the fields and the harvest go to the devil—or a few women work themselves to death."[31] Here, a communitarian philosophy of (an urban intellectual) "socialism" is denigrated, while rural life is valorized. What is particularly communicated here is the sacrificial role of the hardworking woman. The trope of the "sacrificial mother" who laboriously toils in fields is also dominant in "The Origin of the Work of Art" (OWA), as the truth of the artwork is revealed by examining a painting of shoes, shoes that Heidegger imagines belong to a peasant woman. The truth of these peasant shoes is made manifest through a setting up of the woman's world in relation to the equipmental being of the shoes: "This equipment belongs to the *earth*, and it is protected in the *world* of the peasant woman."[32] The shoes "set up" as an artwork reveal a certain historical truth about the life of the peasant woman and the hard, yet revered, conditions of agricultural life. Heidegger asserts,

> On the leather lie the dampness and richness of the soil. Under the sole stretches the loneliness of the field-path as evening falls. In the shoes vibrates the silent call of the earth [. . . .] This equipment is pervaded by uncomplaining worry as to the certainty of bread, the wordless joy of having once more withstood want, the trembling before the impending *childbed* and shivering at the surrendering menace of death [*emphasis mine*].[33]

The peasant woman is not only a hard worker but a "sacrificial mother," as evidenced by her reason for working—to stave off the death of her child. The world of the peasant woman (and her inferred children) is protected by the care the peasant woman takes in toiling the field, in her relation to the equipment. As previously stated, "This equipment belongs to the *earth*, and it is protected in the *world* of the peasant woman." Why does a woman, and more importantly, a peasant woman, secure a privileged position in Heidegger's discussion of the artwork? Again, these questions are important for analyzing how Heidegger understands "woman" in constructing what turns out to be a Nazi politics. How can a thinker who celebrates the diversity of *becoming* fall prey to an identity politics that universalizes the truth of being in a way that only a few superior Germans can ascertain it? How can one of the most important philosophers of the twentieth century, at one time, claim the sex/gender neutrality of Dasein, and at other times, wield sex/gender in such a way as to support pronatalist and national discourse? These questions are important for feminists who seek to understand Heidegger's disastrous politics.

After Heidegger's remarks regarding "mother's blood" that keeps the "paths" of "native soil" circulating (that invoke a *Blut und Boden* ideology), should we follow thinkers such as Philippe Lacoue-Labarthe, Victor Farías, Theodor Adorno, Peter Trawny, Richard Wolin, Adam Knowles, and Emmanuel Faye, and declare the corpus of his work tainted by National Socialism?

Lacoue-Labarthe views Heidegger's philosophy of art as an extension of the "aestheticization of politics" in line with Goebbels's assertion that "Politics is the plastic art of the state."[34] Goebbels emphasizes,

> Politics, too, is perhaps an art, if not the highest and most all-embracing there is (. . . .) As a German politician I therefore cannot recognize the dividing line you hold to be the only one, namely that between good and bad art. Art must not only be good, it must also be conditioned by the exigencies of the people or, rather, only an art that draws on the *Volkstum* as a whole may ultimately be regarded as good and mean something for the people to whom it is directed.[35]

Thus, only "good art" is constitutive of a historic people. This dividing line between "good" and "bad" art is referenced in Heidegger's OWA, as he highlights, "It is precisely in *great* art—and only such art is under consideration here—that the artist remains inconsequential as compared with the work, almost like a passageway that destroys itself in the creative process for the work to emerge [*emphasis mine*]."[36] The emergence, or the revelation of the artwork, defined as an historical truth, is only made manifest in *great* art. Such art is in contrast to "bad" art or the "art business." Heidegger states, "As soon as the thrust into the awesome is parried and captured by the sphere of familiarity and connoisseurship, the art business has begun."[37] This mention of "thrusts" being "parried" is similar to his remarks in the *Black Notebooks*, as he discusses the "parrying of thrusts of being," an evading of the rare instances in history when an appropriation of beyng is possible.[38] That is, bad art parries such thrusts, whereas good art embraces them. Similarly, Heidegger's assertion that great art emerges in the struggle between earth and world sounds like his remarks in the *Black Notebooks* that the question of beyng is a question of the German's struggle over their essence (as a people). Farías would agree with this reading of Heidegger, as for him, the origin of the artwork is really a question about the origin of the state and the constitution of a German people. That is, his discussion of good artwork is intimately tied to his discussion of a good historic people. Farías asserts, "The subject in which the truth appears, truth embodied in the work, is the people. The categories of earth, of world, and those things that flow from them are grounded in the act by which a 'historic people' constitutes itself, makes truth concrete, makes it an artwork. Thus, Heidegger interprets his own work as a moment in the struggle of the German people for its own identity."[39] Here, Heidegger's work as a philosopher is made comparable to that of the peasants, as both works reveal something essential about the constitution of an "historic people." Farías quotes Heidegger stating, "Philosophical work does not develop over time without revealing a pattern. It has its place right alongside the work of peasants."[40] The truth of such work is made manifest in Heidegger's discourse, cited by Farías:

> Peasant remembrance, on the contrary, gives witness to simple fidelity, proven and unflinching. Lately an old peasant woman up there reached the time of her death (. . . .) She kept in her powerful and vivid language many old words and proverbs that had dropped from the living language and that the youth of the village could no longer understand (. . . .) She spent the night of her death talking with family members. Then again, about a half-hour before her death, she told them to greet "The Professor." Such a remembrance is incomparably more valuable than the most able reporting in a world-famous journal on my supposed philosophy.[41]

Heidegger's "remembrance" of the peasant woman equates her with the language of truth. Her "powerful" and "vivid" language has been passed down to "The Professor"—that is, Heidegger himself—whom she called on her family members to "greet," upon her death. Just as Nietzsche says to the old woman, "Give me your little truth, woman,"[42] Heidegger views the old peasant woman as the harbinger of such veracity.[43] Prior to her death, Heidegger says, this "*eighty-three*-year-old peasant woman several times climbed the rather steep slope to come see me [*Heidegger's emphasis*]."[44] The emphasis on her age highlights a certain wisdom and proximity to death, and the "rather steep slope" can be read as a "going down," one that is necessary for the "new beginning" that Heidegger references in both the *Black Notebooks* and "Language in the Poem: A Discussion on Georg Trakl's Poetic Work."

Sexual Tension in Trakl's Poetic Work: (Pro)Creating a People

Could the climb of the steep slope and the death of the woman echo the death as a "going down" in Heidegger's interpretation of Trakl's "Seven-Song of Death"? While Heidegger is the mouthpiece of this "new beginning," the source or site of the truth stems from the feminine, depicted as a peasant woman, mother, or sister, feminine tropes that (pro)create "a people."

Heidegger dissects Trakl's poetry without providing any of the poems in their entirety; rather, he chooses certain sections and provides his own hermeneutic reading. At times, I will counter his interpretation, like when I bring Irigaray into the conversation to highlight the ambiguity of language. Many scholars read Heidegger's work on poetry as a meditative thinking on the truth. Poetry, in its use of ambiguous terms, resists a metaphysics of presence by not directly representing (through signs) what it purports to speak (that is, a poem may talk about a plum but not be about a literal plum at all). Poetry is the revealing/concealing that is *alētheia* in that language has the ability to say something ontologically disclosive about our world. Though poetry certainly has its merits, there is a danger that the ambiguity of such words may lend itself to fascist rhetoric (poetry turned propaganda). I will say more about this, but I want to highlight why I will spend time looking at the individual words that Heidegger clings to and chooses to interpret. Words are never only words, but worlds. Heidegger's interpretation of these words tells us the kind of world he wants to build.

Of Trakl's "Seven-Song of Death," Heidegger says, "Death is not understood here vaguely, broadly, as the conclusion of earthly life. 'Death' here means poetically the 'going down' to which 'something strange' is being called."[45] This "going down" that Heidegger reads into several of Trakl's poems could be a reference to Nietzsche's Zarathustra, who must destroy the old in exchange for the new (by going down to the earth), or it could refer to Heidegger's looking south to the countryside as the spiritual and political impetus of Germany.[46] Heidegger sees a new beginning in this "something strange" that he illustrates is not a strangeness of unease but of the Old High German *fram*, which means: "forward to somewhere else, underway toward . . . onward to the encounter with what is kept in store for it. The strange goes forth ahead. But it does not roam aimlessly, without any kind of determination [. . .] the strange is already following the call that calls it on the way into its own."[47] This sense of strangeness is passed down to a "friend" who follows the stranger, upon his death. Heidegger asserts, "When mortals follow after the 'something strange,' that is to say after the stranger who is called to go under, they themselves enter strangeness, they themselves become strangers and solitary."[48] He further notes, "A friend listens after the stranger. In listening, he follows the departed and thus becomes himself a wanderer, a stranger. The friend's soul listens after the dead."[49] This sense of being "solitary" will be characterized as an "apartness," a sort of wandering into one's own, yet such meanderings will lead to a "homecoming" or a final location.[50] This "strangeness" is "of the spirit," but not in any Platonic sense, as a language of metaphysics.[51] Heidegger links the spiritual to the "ghostly," as an experience of being terrified to the point of an *ek-stasis*, a spirit or ghost that is both gentle and destructive.[52] This *ek-stasis*, this standing outside of oneself, is governed by an "apartness" that must destroy in order to usher in a "new beginning," founded on a "gentle twofold." This new beginning requires that this wanderer be parted from "others" who are molded in the cast of the "decomposed man," for they have been removed from their kind of "essential being."[53] Of this cast, Heidegger says, "A human cast, cast in one mold and cast away into this cast, is called a kin, of a kind, a generation [*Geschlecht*]. The word refers to mankind as a whole as well as to kinship in the sense of race, tribe family—all of these in turn cast in the duality of the sexes."[54] Thus, the wanderer must separate himself from this "decomposed man" and find his "proper cast." Heidegger states, "Its proper cast is only with that kind whose duality leaves discord behind and leads the way, as 'something strange,' into the gentleness of simple twofoldness following in the stranger's footsteps."[55] That is, in Heidegger's reading of Trakl's work, in death (of the stranger), the friend becomes a wanderer toward that "something strange," into his "own," into his "proper cast" of a "twofoldness." The wanderer leaves a former generation and follows the stranger's footsteps home to "one generation," founded on such duality. This friend, this wanderer, is referred to as "he," who I take to be Heidegger as the mouthpiece of the old peasant woman (I will return to a discussion of this).

There is a lot to unpack here in terms of what Heidegger means by "generation" (*Geschlecht*) and how this involves a duality. In chapter 2, I discussed Heidegger's reference to *Geschlecht* in GA 26, and whether this term could be translated to indicate a sex or gender neutrality. Here, in Heidegger's interpretation of Trakl, he states that "The word refers to mankind as a whole as well as to kinship in the sense of race, tribe, family—all of these in turn cast in the duality of the sexes."[56] Later on in the text, Heidegger reiterates the multifariousness of this term while highlighting that

"At the same time, the word [*Geschlecht*] always refers to the twofoldness of the sexes."[57] As noted in chapter 2, Heidegger privileges the predicates of sex/gender difference in his assertion of Dasein's neutrality in GA 26, and continues to emphasize sexual difference in "On the Essence of Ground" as he stipulates the neutrality of selfhood "above all with respect to such things as sexuality."[58] Are we once again led to think, as Derrida does, sexual difference as ontological difference? What does sexual difference have to do with Heidegger's remark that the generation of the "decomposed man" has "been removed from its kind of essential being?" How does sex/gender facticity figure into a question of being/beyng in Heidegger's reading of Trakl?

As Rodrigo Therezo highlights, Derrida's reading of Heidegger in *Geschlecht III* is primarily concerned with the "curse" or "discord" that is purported to strike (*Schlag*) or disrupt the "gentle twofold" of the sexes into competing forces of good and evil, portrayed in a struggle between an old decaying Geschlecht and "the beauty of a homecoming Geschlecht."[59] Therezo asserts, "As Derrida remarks, Geschlecht is struck a first time by a generic blow that *specifies* it into a species or type, and then secondly by a blow held responsible for the sexual differentiation occurring within each species, a differentiation that will *itself* allow for two kinds of sexual difference, a 'good' and a 'bad' one [Derrida's emphasis]."[60] Given Derrida's resistance to phallogocentrism, a term he coins to signify the privileging of the masculine in constructions of meaning, Derrida would have liked for such a "*Schlag*" to upset a binary sexual logic or to upset a system that erases difference for the purpose of masculine self-sameness. Yet Heidegger's understanding of such rupture that purports a distinction between a "good" and "bad" sexual difference is, according to Derrida, "Platonic and Christian," despite Heidegger's protests otherwise.[61] By speaking of a "good" and "bad" sexual difference, does Heidegger reify platonic dualisms? Does he embrace a system of Christian dialectics?

On the one hand, as demonstrated in chapter 2, Heidegger criticizes Judeo-Christian origin stories of the flesh founded on an unequal sexual difference. In GA 63, he purposefully highlights the gendered masculine language of Genesis (that is, son, brethren, man) to raise the question, "Problem: what is woman?" He illustrates that Dasein and not "man" will be used in his existential analytic, since "man" supposes predetermined predicates (founded on sexual inequality) prior to an investigation of facticity. Highlighting the privileged position of "man" in this dialectic of sexual inequality, Rosemary Radford Ruether states, "The nineteenth-century concept of 'progress' materialized the Judeo-Christian God concept. Males, identifying their egos with transcendent 'spirit,' made technology the progressive incarnation of transcendent 'spirit' into 'nature.' "[62] While males are associated with the "spirit" and a progressive infinite expansion, women are associated with the "flesh," and subsequently, death. Heidegger rejects such dialectical constructions of "flesh/spirit," "death/life," "sin/righteousness," and "slavery/sonship,"[63] as he highlights: "[Dialectic] steps into an already constructed context, though there really is no context here [. . . .] Every category is an existential and *is* this as such, not merely in relation to other categories and on the basis of this relation."[64] Heidegger thus rebuffs the existence of something founded merely in relation to something else (that is, the existence of man cannot be determined as "not woman," righteousness cannot be determined as "not sin"). Yet how are we to read GA 63 alongside his reading of Trakl?

As I state in the Introduction, Heidegger has two distinct ways of treating "the woman question." In GA 63, he suspends "the woman question" and refuses to define her in relation to man, offering resources for thinking the historical contingency and fluidity of sex and gender. However, in other works, such as the *Black Noteblacks*, "Language in the Poem: A Discussion on Georg Trakl's Poetic Work," and "Building Dwelling Thinking," there is a certain grounding of meaning as he manipulates feminine tropes to speak of "one dwelling space" or "one generation." Moving between these conflicting perspectives offers us insight into how Heidegger's thought can and does lead to Nazi politics. As we've seen throughout history, and in our politics today, "the woman question" accompanies attempts to define "what is." That is, there is a relation between being and woman, as we believe we can't understand the former without defining the latter. Fried has said that what is at stake in understanding Heidegger is the "very being of our politics," because of the questions of identity and difference that emerge in his work. I would add that what is at stake in understanding Heidegger's position of "the woman question" is our "very understanding of being."

Heidegger critiques Christian dialectics in both GA 63 and in his reading of Trakl; however, in the latter, he upholds a certain understanding of sexual difference founded on the flesh, even though such dialectic is masked as a "gentle twofoldness." That is, in his reading of Trakl, he seems to glorify an aspect of the feminine (and her sexual difference), in that she is necessary to propagate the "one generation" of the German people. While Ian Alexander Moore recognizes the polyvalence of the term *Geschlecht*, he chooses to render the term as "lineage" in interpreting Heidegger's reading of Trakl, and he further points to its emphasis on generation by highlighting a remark that Heidegger leaves atop the poem "Into an Old Family Album": "The *book of the Geschlecht* and its essence!"[65] How can the essence of *Geschlecht*, a term that always refers to the twofoldness of the sexes, be found within such a poem, a poem initially titled "To Melancholy?" This poem harbors a sadness due to the recurrence of time that is not, as Moore notes the sameness of Nietzsche's eternal return, but an ever-increasing decline. We can surmise that such decline, interpreted by Heidegger, is the Western decline into nihilism from which only a "few" Germans can save us. While only a few may be properly attuned to beyng, Heidegger recognizes the role of the feminine and procreation in ushering in this new "one generation." The association between melancholy and an *old* family album is also intriguing, given a political discourse of that time that lamented the declining birth rate. As Charu Gupta notes, the National Socialist Party believed that the women's movement, which encouraged voting and birth control, was part of an international Jewish conspiracy to destroy the German family and German race.[66]

In Heidegger's reading of Trakl's poetry, there is a decaying or old *Geschlecht* versus a new homecoming *Geschlecht*, the latter being the "proper cast," or good one. The decaying *Geschlecht* is the former Christian "mold" of sexual difference.[67] However, the "proper cast" of *Geschlecht*, the gentle twofoldness, is not (or, so it appears) a dialectical relation in that man is not defined in relation to woman, it is not a question of "is" versus "is not"; rather both must be negated so that a new twofold can emerge that allows each "fold" to exist as they are, on their own. This double negation, or complete destruction, ushers in a new beginning founded on a twofoldness that is described in a brother/sister relation.

In his reading of Trakl, Heidegger appears to say that the discord that disrupts the sexes is particularly strong when it invades the realm of brother and sister. In once again referencing the "apartness" that is necessary for the new beginning, he describes it as a "gathering power" that "carries mortal nature back to its stiller childhood" from where future generations can be born for the "rebirth" of mankind.[68] This gathering power is described as a spirit of gentleness that stills the spirit of evil. Heidegger elucidates, "That [evil] spirit's revolt rises to its utmost when it breaks out even from the discord of the sexes, and invades the realm of brother and sister."[69] While Heidegger does not say he interprets the brother and sister as Antigone and Polyneices, the tension between siblings that occurs on the "night's starry pond—which is the sky above earth" (earth, sky, divine, mortals) sounds like an earth/world strife similar to that of the human law (earth/mortals) versus divine law (sky/divine) in Sophocles *Antigone*.

As Michael Zimmerman states, Antigone played a central role in "Heidegger's changing vision of Germany's Tragic destiny."

> Like Hegel, [Heidegger] regarded Sophocles' *Antigone* as the "foundation of the whole Greek Dasein." [GA, 39: 216] Antigone resisted the command of her uncle, who—representing civil authority—refused permission for her to bury her brother, who had been killed in civil war against him. Torn between her loyalty to the state and her obligation to the law of the gods and family, Antigone—in courageous struggle with her destiny—illuminated and held open the enduring rift between what Heidegger was to call "world" (the open historical-political realm) and "earth" (the self-concealing dimension of "nature"). Antigone's death was the unavoidable accompaniment of a greatness that involved distinguishing world and earth in such a way that each could be itself. Only has thus set apart could world and earth enter into a dynamic relationship, a mysterious and hidden unity.[70]

Antigone is thus responsible for the unification of the earth/world struggle, but such wholeness is not founded on sameness, as her death precipitated a "greatness" that allowed earth and world to exist "in such a way that each could be itself." The earth, "the self-concealing dimension of nature" can be read as human law, as earth is often associated with a material grounding, with such grounding of "what is" being established by mortals. The world, as "the open historical-political realm," can be interpreted as the divine realm, that toward which humans transcend. As I demonstrated in chapter 1, transcendence is a necessary condition of any sense of world-forming. In order to overcome a metaphysics of presence that purports to know "what is" through *logos*, earth and world must be able to exist "in such a way that each could be itself." That is, language as a set of universal signifiers cannot simply speak the truth of something that is present by virtue of its symbolic communication. Language, as a present form of symbols, may communicate an absence, but it cannot be said to represent the truth of that absence. For example, insofar as men have historically created meaning within the world, language represents a masculine point of view. This is what Derrida calls phallogocentrism, and something he accuses Heidegger of doing in his discussion of the brother/sister relation.

Derrida makes reference to Hegel's Antigone in his reading of the brother and sister, as he describes their relation as one of "a double homosexuality, a reflection without appropriation of the desire of the other."[71]

Here, the brother becomes the sister and the sister becomes the brother in an effacement of sexual difference, though such erasure seems to privilege the brother via a Christian phallogocentrism. Likewise, Irigaray in commenting on how it is the death of a *boy* that is the source of a new possible future inquires, "*Encore de l'homme*?" (Man, again?)[72] Patricia Huntington also accuses Heidegger of espousing a "masculinist ethos" and follows Irigaray in her critique of the "masculine imaginary," fantasies that "center around the drive for unity, noncontradiction, and fullness of presence at the expense of the inassimilable particularities of things."[73] Furthermore, Jennifer Anna Gosetti demonstrates how the "feminine" is "explicitly rejected and implicitly opposed to destinal-historical founding" in Heidegger's reading of "Germanien," because he accuses Hölderlin's projected image of Germania as being "too feminine," offering a more "masculine" substitute.[74] And yet, Gosetti suggests that Heidegger "symbolizes the ontological disclosure of language in terms of femininity"[75] That is, the between or rift, that language opens, the struggle between the presence of symbols and the truth of an absence that they represent, is expressed in feminine terms. How is this rift captured in the figure of the sister or Antigone?

If we liken the sister in Trakl's poem to Antigone, is she not privileged as the one responsible for opening the "enduring rift" that is necessary for the "mysterious and hidden unity" of the "one generation" of the "twofold"? In Trakl's poem "Ghostly Twilight," the sister's lunar voice overtakes the sun and is responsible for the ek-static (ghostly) state of the brother. There is a certain overarching gathering of the "Dame Moon;" as Heidegger put it, "All around her radiance, as the ancient Greek verses tell us, the stars turn pale and even cool. All things become 'lunar.' The stranger going through the night is called 'the lunar one.'"[76] This privileging of the moon could be read as a counter to Plato's metaphor of the sun in his "Allegory of the Cave," as the sun represents an enlightenment founded on a dualistic way of thinking, a thinking that Irigaray demonstrates as leading the way to phallogocentrism. Irigaray states, "The Copernican revolution has yet to have its final effects in the male imaginary. And by centering man outside himself, it has occasioned above all man's ex-stasis within the transcendental (subject) [. . . .] Exiling himself ever further (toward) where the greatest power lies, he thus becomes the 'sun' if it is around him that things turn, a pole of attraction stronger than the 'earth.'"[77] Irigaray likens man to the sun in that all revolves around him, all images are created in his likeness, and "woman" disappears in his self-sameness. Everywhere man looks, "he runs into the walls of his palace of mirrors."[78] Nevertheless, Irigaray offers a way of looking at "woman" beyond the male gaze, of seeing beyond the fire "lit by the hand of man in the image of the sun."[79] Irigaray offers the image of a speculum that symbolizes a curved mirror, in contrast to the flat mirror that represents a self-same reflexivity. The speculum distorts any parallel reality and offers the "woman" a means to examine herself beyond the male gaze. She asserts, "A living mirror, thus, am I (to) your resemblance as you are mine. We are both singular and plural, one and ones, provided that nothing tarnishes the mirrors that fuse in the purity of their ex change. Provided that one, furthermore, does not exceed the other in size and quality. For then the other would be absorbed in the One (as) to infinity."[80] Such a mirror offers subjects the possibility of being "singular" and "plural," joined in their difference.

In Heidegger's reading of Trakl, he appears to want to break with such logic of self-sameness, as he references a moment when the brother sees himself in the pond but is taken aback by the light from the moon. He states, "The waters which are sometimes black and sometimes blue, show to man his own countenance, his countering glance. But in the nighting pond of the starry sky there appears the twilight blue of the ghostly night."[81] Under the twilight of the moon, man does not just see himself but is called by "the lunar one." Could Heidegger's reading of the moon challenge not only Plato's dualistic way of thinking but also a patriarchal Christian logic that privileges the masculine spirit (sun) over the feminine flesh (moon). Heidegger defends Trakl against an alleged Christianity, thus presumably wanting to separate himself from such a religious doctrine, as he conjectures, "If indeed this poet is so resolute a Christian, why does he not here in the extreme agony of his last saying, call out to God and Christ? Why does he instead name the 'sister's swaying shadow' and call her 'the greeting one'? Why does the song end with 'unborn grandsons' and not with the confident hope of Christian redemption? Why does the sister appear also in the other late poem, 'Lament.' "[82] Heidegger appears to be saying that if Trakl were such a Christian, he wouldn't have privileged the feminine side of the dialectic. He wouldn't have given the sister the power of being "the greeting one." The sister as the "greeting one" is intriguing as we return to the old peasant woman who upon her death told her family to go "greet the Professor" (Heidegger). In such greeting, does Heidegger become the mouthpiece for the old peasant woman who is thus privileged in her relation to the truth? Or is the feminine at least associated with a different kind of truth than the logic of the self-same?

While the stranger is a "brother" (masculine), he wanders toward the "something strange" that is the "soul on the earth," a strangeness that is feminine. Heidegger states, "The soul only *seeks* the earth; it does not flee from it. This fulfills the soul's being: in her wandering to seek the earth so that she may poetically build and dwell upon it, and thus may be able to save the earth as earth."[83] *She* may poetically dwell in *her* wandering, a wandering that leads to the earth in contrast to Plato's ethereal realm of forms illuminated by the sun. Furthermore, even though the stranger is masculine (being a brother), the friend becomes the "brother of the stranger's sister whose 'lunar voice rings through the ghostly night.' "[84] It is only after becoming the brother of the stranger's sister that "soul then is purely a blue moment."[85] It is in that moment that a "stiller childhood" is met from which can rise a new generation, "one generation," a new beginning, a homecoming.

I read Heidegger as being that friend that follows Antigone and the peasant woman after their deaths. He becomes a mediator in the same way that Socrates speaks through Diotima in *The Symposium*. Yet while Socrates privileges a "giving birth in beauty" via intellectual creation, while devaluing bodily procreation,[86] Heidegger plays with the language of procreation in a way that reverses the supremacy of the former. Antigone's tale of brother and sister demonstrates that the realm of the family is where the tension between human and divine laws meet, because of its connections with sexuality, birth, and death. In the tale of Antigone, both brother and sister must die to give birth to a new order. Their deaths lead to a fertility of sorts, though it is not a fecundity founded on the difference of sexual desire (even though Trakl's relationship with his sister is said to be an incestuous one). Rather, the brother/sister relation is, according to Hegel's reading of Antigone, the only relation that assures mutual recognition, free from desire.[87] The birth stemming from their relation is thus not founded on biological reproduction.

The kinship of brother and sister (incest taboo) appears to foreclose a Judeo-Christian beginning founded on a sexual difference of bodily generation. Heidegger emphasizes, " '*One generation*' here does not refer to a biological fact at all, to a 'single' or 'identical' gender." He thus appears to reject breeding of the self-same (Aryan eugenics and racial breeding). And yet, birthing metaphors that would hint to bodily procreation are there as "pain feeds the hot flame of the spirit, The grandsons yet unborn."[88] Heidegger accentuates that the "unborn" must be "grandsons" and not "sons," because "they cannot be the immediate descendants of the generation that has gone to ruin."[89] The descendants' lack of generative power is described as "a blue flower" that withered to "stone." This decaying generation, founded on a metaphysics of presence (Platonic and Christian) is elsewhere described as "miscarrying." As Shane Ewegen notes, Heidegger, in his Heraclitus lectures, describes logic (binary logic as a dualistic way of thinking) as "a miscarriage of a miscarriage," or the *misbirth* of metaphysics.[90] In OWA, when earth is effaced, as when a sculptor "uses up" the material, the work of art is said to "miscarry."[91]

In "Gestures of the Feminine in Heidegger's 'Die Sprache,'" Ewegen gives a reading of "Die Sprache" that demonstrates how language speaks in a feminine form. Ewegen conjectures that to read this text as an expression of Heidegger's "interior thoughts" would be "a monumental failure and would merely serve as yet another addition to the already long list of metaphysical analyses of language."[92] Turning to the words themselves, he shows how the ontological difference is understood as a carrying to term or as a giving birth of the world, a world that emerges through the intercourse of human beings and things.

Likewise, Jean Graybeal examines "the feminine" in Heidegger's language by searching for passages of what Julia Kristeva refers to as *jouissance*, ecstatic moments where signification is suspended and an interrogation into the unnamable is possible. For Graybeal, Heidegger turns to the realm of the semiotic, associated with the maternal and the erotic as he searches for an escape from metaphysical thinking. In its search for a unification of meaning, metaphysical thinking belongs to the realm of the symbolic, a realm associated with the paternal and the rational. According to Graybeal, moments of *jouissance* teeter between the semiotic and the symbolic. Graybeal particularly pays attention to the figure of *la mère qui jouit*, the mother who is both maternal and erotic, the woman caught between the dualisms prescribed by metaphysics. "Feminine" language is a rift where meaning is not yet grounded.[93]

For Ewegen, the difference, or rift, that pain holds apart is vaginal. Playing with the close association of the words division (*Schied*) and vagina (*Scheide*), he writes, "Pain is the tearing of the difference that holds together by pulling apart. One notes, here, the visibly and audibly significant language used: Pain separates (*scheidet*); it is the separating (*das Scheiden*). These terms carry within themselves, both literally and figuratively, the vagina: they announce *die Scheide*."[94] That is, the pain that Heidegger describes as being essential to being is likened to the pain of childbirth. Literally, the vagina births a child, but what of this metaphorical rift that brings forth the homecoming of a new generation? What exactly is birthed in this "one generation"?

Analyzing another of Trakl's poems, Heidegger associates the pain of this new birth with "blueness," interpreting blue itself as "the holy," a holiness that he describes in OWA as opening a clearing where that which was invisible comes to light. What becomes clear in the blueness that Heidegger at other times associates with the lunar one or sister is a "mirror of truth" (speculum?). In this truth, Heidegger says, the "wild game's face retracts into gentleness [. . . .] The animality of the animal here intended thus vacillates in the indefinite. It has not yet been gathered up into its essential being. This animal—the thinking animal, *animal rationale*, man—is, as Nietzsche said, not yet determined."[95] Here, the decaying generation, the *animal rationale*, founded on a metaphysics of presence dies and becomes "not yet determined," recalling Heidegger's earlier work in GA 63, where he tries to understand Dasein prior to predetermined predicates. We thus circle back to his question, "Problem: what is woman?" What is woman, sister, the blue that opens the holy? Who is *she* that ushers in a new beginning?

While Heidegger explicitly rejects racial breeding, forced breeding (discord) through machinational thinking, does he reject a carnal breeding (gentle) through meditative thinking? In rebuffing artificial reproduction incited by the "self-conscious thought of race," does that mean that he likewise renounces a *phusical* way of birthing, a breeding that lets things come forth without challenging (as Heidegger formerly stated, a letting be of the "naturally evolving races")?[96] I pose these questions because in reading these texts alongside the *Black Notebooks*, it's hard not to conjecture that the "one generation" the feminine figure is supposed to bring forth is the German people. That is, even though Heidegger rejects German supremacy based on biological blood ties, women are still necessary for bringing forth future generations of the motherland, through a literal and metaphorical birth. If we think about the "enduring *rift*" that is necessary for a "new beginning," a new beginning that doesn't "parry *thrusts* of being," it is hard to ignore the violent gendered aspects of this ontological/sexual difference. In the *Introduction to Metaphysics*, beyng violates Dasein, and here, a masculine Dasein violates a feminine Dasein.

Therezo highlights Derrida's argument that despite Heidegger's outright renunciation of biological racism, his ambiguity of speech with respect to *Geschlecht* is comparable to Fichte who uses an equivocality of language as a means of espousing nationalism.[97] Derrida's reading of Heidegger's Trakl points to a nationalist reading of "returning home," as a "nostalgic withdrawal towards the originary habitat, the colonial expansion, the future as an adventure of culture or of colonization, of the cultivated and colonized habitat on the basis of new routes."[98] That is, even though Heidegger rejects National Socialism (he *says* these words), the ambiguity of his language strategically lends itself to fascist interpretations (did he really *mean* to intend *x* with such words?). There is thus a potential danger in Heidegger's poetic way of thinking as it risks eschewing accountability. I'll return to the danger of this ambiguity in the next chapter, but for now, I want to focus on the importance of the feminine in his ambiguous reading of "homecoming."

The feminine is that "something strange," or "the pole" that leads the wanderer home to this dwelling place. Heidegger's focus on "the pole" that leads to a "dwelling place" is hard to consider outside of fascist rhetoric, as "Alfred Rosenberg, the self-proclaimed Nazi philosopher, represented the female sex as the 'lyrical' pole, the male as the 'architectural.' "[99] This "pole" and the importance that Heidegger gives language in uncovering the "dwelling place," is not without its bodily elements. As Gosetti highlights, "What the classical theory of expression neglects, according to Heidegger, is that the sensuality of language is our connection to the earth, which Heidegger links, particularly in the interpretations of Johann Peter Hebel, to the 'mother tongue,' that is, to dialect and the speaking that occurs in a region or landscape."[100] We see this "mother tongue" as Heidegger meticulously breaks words down into the Old High German, the earliest *origin* of the German language, but we also see the "mother tongue" in the *Black Notebooks*, as the "native soil" to which Germans must return are "paths which kept mother's blood, and that of her ancestors, circulating and pulsing." Heidegger's poetic readings view the feminine as a beacon of the homecoming, symbolic of blood and soil. Just as the wanderer of Trakl returns home after an "apartness," a strangeness that is characterized as feminine, Antigone guides the path from "unhomeliness" to the "homely." As Gosetti remarks, in *Hölderlin's Hymn "The Ister,"* "Antigone's polis is the 'pole' to which the human being turns in becoming homely through unhomeliness."[101] The old peasant woman of Heidegger's remembrance is also a "pole" to which Heidegger must turn in his "greeting" to go home. This relation between "remembrance" and "greeting" is explored by William McNeill in his reading of Hölderlin's Hymn "Andenken." McNeill states,

> Remembrance is poetized as a greeting. As a greeting, it is a thoughtful turning toward that which is greeted. Yet this thinking in the direction of what is greeted does not lose itself in something that is past [. . . .] Something more than a personal "experience" (Erlebnis) is at stake, Heidegger insists, something that demands of us an "other thinking" (50); and the mystery of this "other thinking," as remembrance, is perhaps that of thinking itself, the very essence of thinking, which is something entirely other than what Western philosophy conceives as logic (55).[102]

Here, remembrance and greeting must turn to the past but not in a way that takes up a repetition of the same. This greeting is an invitation to a new way of thinking that parts with "logic," a logic previously defined as the "misbirth of metaphysics." This is very much in line with Heidegger's reading of Trakl, as brother and sister must die after greeting the friend; only with their deaths can the friend turn wanderer and go home. The wanderer must abandon the old decaying generation (binary logic) and turn toward "his proper cast." Likewise, the old peasant woman had to die in order for the professor to be greeted; she had to "go down." We previously mentioned that this "going down" could be a reference to Nietzsche, or it could be a reference to Heidegger's argument that the spiritual and political impetus of Germany should be located south in the countryside and not in the metropole of the northeast. Such geography is hard to ignore as the "going down" of the wind expressed in *Andenken* is a "northeasterly wind" that travels south to La Garonne.

> The Northeasterly blows,
> Most beloved of the winds to me
> For it promises fiery spirit
> And good voyage to those at sea.
> But go now, and greet
> The beautiful Garonne,
> And the gardens of Bordeaux[103]

Whether or not Heidegger intended to poetize politics in highlighting such geography is speculation, yet there is enough evidence from aforementioned scholars such as Lacoue-Labarthe, Farías, Adorno, Trawny, Wolin, Knowles, and Faye to demonstrate a collapsing of his politics and his project of overcoming metaphysics. What interests me as a feminist scholar is how "woman" or the "feminine" may be manipulated toward this end and how such handling participates in harmful exclusionary politics. If Heidegger's discussion of "great art" promotes an aestheticization of politics that creates an historical "people," what kind of "people" are excluded? Is Heidegger's characterization of an "old decaying Geschlecht" versus a "new homecoming Geschlecht" another formulation along the lines of "good" versus "bad" art, a "people" construed in terms of "us" versus "them"? Who is the "decaying generation" that must die in Trakl to give birth to a new unity, a unity that is unmistakably German in the *Black Notebooks*?[104] After the *Black Notebooks*, how do we think constructively with Heidegger? In the next chapter,

"Bridging Heidegger after the *Black Notebooks*: Of Worlds, Not Words," I attempt to read Heidegger against himself by examining his philosophy alongside Latina feminist thinkers (Lugones, Anzaldúa, Ortega) and Perry Zurn's trans poetics of dust.

Chapter 6

Bridging Heidegger after the *Black Notebooks*

Of Worlds, Not Words

Heidegger uses tropes of the feminine to advance a politico-poetic project that privileges the German people. While there is power in poetry to disclose certain truths, the ambiguous character of its language, may lend itself to malicious ends. Heidegger's interpretation of Trakl's poetry does just that. Nevertheless, Heidegger's poetic thinking offers important insights insofar as he emphasizes the ability of poetry to *say* the truth, where to say is to reveal (*Sagen* as *Zeigen*). *Words* can reveal many *worlds*, and yet, Heidegger speaks of *one* historical destiny and *one* dwelling space, foreclosing the very possibilities his philosophy has often lauded. In this chapter, I suggest that Heidegger's thinking goes astray because of his inability to think *words as worlds*. By drawing from Latina feminist scholars such as Mariana Ortega, Gloria Anzaldúa, and Maria Lugones, I read Heidegger against himself to focus on the in-betweenness of worlds, that space of possibility prior to dwelling. Then, I turn to Perry's Zurn's trans poetics to explore the in-betweenness or border-consciousness of sex/gender facticity. Poetically relating trans experience to dust, Zurn allows us to think the bridge (symbolic of an in-between), or *apeiron*, of sexed/gendered existence. By emphasizing the "bridge" rather than the "dwelling," Ortega, Anzaldúa, Lugones, and Zurn are also able to speak of collective identities (that is, Latina, trans) and rootedness without following Heidegger's path toward privileging any one people.

Worldless Jews, Genos, and Polemos

One of the most outrageous statements from the *Black Notebooks* is Heidegger's assertion that Jews are without world. He asserts, "One of the most secret forms of the *gigantic*, and perhaps the oldest, is the tenacious skillfulness in calculating, hustling, and intermingling through which the worldlessness of Jewry is grounded."[1] To be without world is worse than the existence of animals, as Heidegger had previously suggested that stones are "worldless" and animals are "poor in world."[2] Jews are thus not "cases of Dasein"[3] that participate in world-forming. They are hence incapable of any attunement to being/beyng. For Heidegger, to be worldless is to be incapable of dwelling, that state of preservation that is essential for mortals.

In "Building Dwelling Thinking" (BDT), Heidegger states, "The way in which you are and I am, the manner in which we humans *are* on the earth, is *buan*, dwelling. To be a human being means to be on the earth as a mortal. It means to dwell."[4] *Dwelling* is essential to the *being* of humans. If dwelling as mortals is a requisite for being human, then Heidegger's statement necessarily deprives Jews of humanity. To dwell is "to preserve and care for, specifically to till the soil."[5] It is hard to once again dismiss the undertones of a blood and soil ideology (*Blut und Boden*) that we previously analyzed in the trope of the peasant woman and in Heidegger's remark on dwelling on native soil that preserved "paths which kept mother's blood, and that of her ancestors, circulating and pulsing."[6] Despite Heidegger's rejection of eugenics and his critique of German superiority founded on biological racism, mother's blood drives the historical becoming of the Germans as the "homecoming" of "one generation." To think that a new beginning could arise in "one generation," determined by a singular worldview of dwelling, grounds a presence of meaning that Heidegger had previously sought to overcome. In this section, I show that Heidegger's speaking of *genos*, rather than *genera*, leads to fascist thinking capable of genocide.

In *The Genocide Paradox*, Anne O'Byrne states, "Yet, there is never a *genos*, only genera. We may belong to several of them—why not?—and what we experience or long to experience as belonging to a single, self-evident, self-generating group requires the generation and policing of boundaries: this and not that, this because not that, us because not them."[7] Speaking of a single *genos* necessarily creates delimitations and participates in an exclusionary politics that creates an "us against them" mentality, or an "old decaying generation" versus a new "one generation." Even though the "old decaying generation" is supposed to represent the binary logic of metaphysics and Christian dialectics that must be destroyed, the new "one generation," founded on a "gentle twofoldness" participates in a form of boundary policing, as this "one generation" is the only acceptable destiny of the German people. For Heidegger, the Germans are in a privileged historical position as they are capable of a certain attunement to being/beyng of which worldless entities (Jews) are not. Bridging the connection between the acceptance of one *genos* and genocide, O'Byrne suggests, "Genera are necessarily plural, and the distinctive worlds we live in abut and intersect. The world consists of many worlds. So long as we think of genera as fixed and worlds as closed, we have no language for what happens when apparently sharp boundaries run right through us. Overlaps and intersections become occasions for fear and, in the absence of a worldly (political) space where contestation happens without guns, they become the place of genocidal violence."[8] Genocide is possible because of our desire to know ourselves and our world as a totality, a totality that is closed off from other worlds. Believing that our very being is defined by an origin of blood or geography may give one a sense of belonging and purpose, but it may also create an isolated sense of self that rejects otherness. I am not trying to downplay the significance of cultural identity or the importance of tracing one's roots, rather I am cautioning against the *privileging* of any singular identity that occurs "in the absence of a worldly (political) space where contestation happens without guns," where genocide becomes possible. It is not the owning of an identity that is problematic but a *privileging* of such an identity, particularly at the expense of others. In determining (privileged) boundaries of Dasein, Heidegger erodes potentially useful resources in his poetic thinking.

Whereas texts such as *Being and Time* (GA 2) and *The Metaphysical Foundations of Logic* (GA 26) characterize Dasein in terms of its possibilities, in works such as his *Black Notebooks* and "Language in the Poem: A Discussion on Georg Trakl's Poetic Work," possibilities become foreclosed as there is only *one* historical destiny of the Germany people. I am not suggesting that we remain in a world of pure potential forever, as if we could. As discussed in the introduction, we eventually have to provide a resolution to the conflict of meaning, or *polemos*, that characterizes all sense-making. We want to acknowledge possibility and potentiality that is inherent in beings, though we must, to some extent, place such potential in stasis in order to speak of any particular being in concrete terms (that is, we must be able to say *x is*). However, it is important to understand that prior to any grounding of meaning, it could have been otherwise. How does meaning take shape? How does a thing become what it is?

In his essay "The Thing," Heidegger says a thing comes to presence through the "gathering in" of the fourfold of earth, sky, divinities, and mortals.[9] What comes forth through this gathering cannot be understood in terms of a strict subject/object distinction but is a gathering of phenomenological perception and environment. Here, the fourfold sounds like a riff on Aristotle's four causes, three of which, have long been forgotten in favor of the efficient cause—man, as master and creator. In BDT, the gathering of the fourfold is what necessitates preservation through dwelling. Thus, mortals as dwellers gather the fourfold in order *to be*. Dwelling is "*the basic character* of being."[10] In GA 2, the being of Dasein was defined as care, insofar as our existential make-up consists of this neutral temporal structure that makes sense of how we navigate our environment and constitute our world; our structure of care may be negatively or positively enacted, thus informing whether we engage with entities in an authentic or inauthentic manner. The entities and others that show up in my environment and that constitute my world are navigated in modes of concern (things) or solicitude (others). Yet, what shows up and seems to appear as a closed-off entity, in its presence before us, is always riddled with strife. There is potential for a thing/other to have been otherwise.

In "The Origin of the Work of Art" (OWA), the strife between earth and world is responsible for the coming-to-be of the artwork. In BDT and "The Thing," it is the gathering of the fourfold, a tension that works in similar ways as the struggle between earth and world, in that separate poles unite to form an intelligible, seemingly singular site of meaning. Gregory Fried centers in on this notion of struggle, of *polemos*, as being essential to the characterization of Dasein. It is this confrontation at the heart of Dasein's being that allows something like exclusionary politics to take place. Fried asserts,

> *Polemos*, or *Auseinandersetzung*, is an *ontological* concept for Heidegger. It describes the way in which Being happens and how it concerns us, and it also describes our relation to Being as what Heidegger calls Dasein, the site, the There, in which Being manifests itself. Our Being is polemical [. . . .] *Polemos* belongs neither exclusively to Being nor exclusively to Dasein; it is neither objective nor subjective. Heidegger frequently speaks of Being's *needing* us for its happening, even as it destroys us. Being and Dasein belong together in *polemos*. *Polemos* takes place *between* ourselves (Da-sein) and Being (*Sein*). *Polemos* is Da-Sein.[11]

Even though Dasein is always understood from a certain historical period and thus always in flux (without ground), we must necessarily ground the ground in order to make sense of "what is" here at this particular time. *Polemos* is Da-sein in that there is necessarily a struggle of meaning in terms of making sense of what matters to us and in understanding the "what" and "how" of our world-forming. Furthermore, this world-forming is always intersubjective and so our encounter with others is also one of *polemos*. Fried states, "Heidegger understands the proper relation of peoples to be one of *polemos*. Just as individual Dasein, confronting its world or another thinker, must take seriously the possibilities offered by the Other in a respectfully agonal encounter, so, too, must entire peoples set other peoples within discernible boundaries, both physical and philosophical, in order to be able to take this Other seriously *as* an Other in conversation."[12] This is a generous understanding of polemos, as the tension between two peoples need not end in war but may lead to a respectful conversation in which people can exist on their own and with their own understanding of history. And yet, as we've seen in Heidegger's reading of Trakl, *polemos* can lead to destruction and war, as an old generation must die to make way for a new beginning. The problem with *polemos*, whether this is a tension within ourselves or with other people, is that it inevitably sets limits on a particular site or locale of meaning. As previously noted, we must, in some way "ground the ground," as we cannot remain in an ontological struggle over meaning forever. Our worlds would never make sense. However, we must remain cognizant of the ambiguity of such grounding; we must, in Heidegger's own terms, recognize the simultaneous revealing/concealing (*alētheia*) that is truth. And yet, Heidegger betrays his own words by concealing the possibilities of other worlds in his revelation of one dwelling space and one historical destiny.

We can own identities and belong to "a people" without following Heidegger's path toward Nazi politics. Understanding Gloria Anzaldúa's theory of borderlands, Mariana Ortega's multiplicitous self, and Maria Lugones's playful world-traveling helps us think a hybridity of meaning that Heidegger forecloses despite his initial efforts to contest grounding.

Borderlands, Multiplicitous Selves, and Playful World-Traveling

> I am multiplicitous. Multiple and one [. . . .] Latina, de las otras, daughter, sister, lover, student, teacher, philosopher. English. Spanish. Other languages, but not of words. Of worlds, many of them.
>
> —Mariana Ortega

This focus on *worlds*, rather than *words* offers important insights for readers of Heidegger. Whereas Heidegger's Dasein exists in a world that is historically contingent and thus in flux, the "there" (*Da*) of Dasein, the site by which Da-Sein understands its relation to being/beyng, is reduced to a single origin or dwelling. Heidegger's poetic thinking focuses on many words, but a singular world. Heidegger is meticulous in his translations and takes great care in choosing the roots of Greek and Old High German words, but a plurality of worlds becomes unthinkable. Ortega invites us to think in-*between* worlds rather than *in* worlds, as the former expresses a possibility, if not necessity, to think across boundaries, and to create new meaning in the margins of seemingly closed-off worlds.

Ortega draws from Gloria Anzaldúa's notion of *mestizaje*, Lugones's account of world-traveling, and Heidegger's understanding of Dasein as being-in-the-world to provide an account of multiplicitous selfhood as being-between-worlds and being-in-worlds. While there are similarities between Heidegger and Latina feminist phenomenologists in that they both highlight how the self is not purely substantial but rather always "in the making," the latter focus more on the material conditions of human beings and the power relations that inform the "there" of Dasein. For example, Anzaldúa's mestiza is "thrown into the US-Mexico borderlands and has to negotiate her various social identities in this complex in-between territory."[13] It is this in-between character of the mestiza that causes a form of anxiety (*Coatlicue*) whereby the self is forced to make choices in light of her multiple social positionalities.[14]

For Heidegger, anxiety is a similar disclosive state in that this mood forces one to own one's possibilities of existence, or to make an authentic choice. Such an affective state is individualized in that the self is laid bare apart from the chatter of the *they*, typically understood as an amalgam of social and cultural conventions. Such instances of anxiety are rare, and they ultimately end with a moment of resoluteness whereby Dasein can make owned choices and absorb themselves back into the *they* (*Das Man*). That is, Dasein can never fully exist as an individual separate from a shared community of understanding. Dasein is being-with-others (*Mitsein*), and thus any decision Dasein makes will have to make sense within the shared social conventions of the *they*. Yet, for Anzaldúa, anxiety is a result of being between several *theys*. There is not a singular public from which she must become individualized. As Ortega states, "Considering the fact that the multiplicitous self occupies various social locations and is immersed in various cultures, she might hold contradictory norms."[15] Living in-between such contradictory norms amounts to a continuous feeling of not-being-at-ease and of thus not being fully able to return to a singular *they*. The mestiza's experience is not one of average everydayness where practical involvements with the world distract from authentic moments of existence. The multiplicitous self doesn't always return to the same historical world of possibilities set forth by the *they* but rather creates new possibilities and histories. Jennifer Gammage asks whether this self that creates multiple and conflicting histories can be explained through an expansion of Heidegger's "unified temporal horizon of Dasein," stating, "I struggle to find this in Heidegger's work in *Being and Time*, wherein the creative aspect of the *Augenblick*, or moment of decision, is only ever a modification of our historical existence in which we are given the chance to become responsible for which possibilities we carry forward, but never to create a radically new world or history that drastically breaks with extant norms."[16] That is, Dasein, after a moment of decision, is able to absorb itself back into the established norms of the they. Such absorption may be characterized as authentic in that this decision is now owned rather than taken up without reflection, but what is owned seems to be an already established possibility within a singular world. Gammage thus wonders whether Ortega's multiciplicitous self, whose capacity for historical transformation is made salient via Anzaldúa's *Coatlicue* state, can be reconciled with Heidegger's notion of Dasein.

I find what Gammage is looking for can be found in Heidegger's notion of transcendence as "world-forming," where such formation depends on our neutral temporal affective structure of care. While we necessarily understand what allows for being according to a certain historical awareness, there must be an ecstatic opening where we are diversely attuned to how "temporality temporalizes." If our understanding relies on a certain historical contingency, and if we do not exist outside of history, there must be something about our structure of care that allows us to interact differently with the phenomenological relations that gather an understanding of being. As transcending, as being in the process of world-forming, there is a momentary suspension of meaning as I am no longer able to navigate my world in a mode of average everydayness. Here, I am not at ease with my environment as it is placed under theoretical examination. It is during this moment of vision that I am able to reassess the nexus of relations that give my world meaning. My ability to be factically dispersed, into one world among others, depends on this state of transcendence where things in the world do not yet show up as intelligible, do not yet *really* matter, where they are in the process of being formed.

To relate this back to Ortega and Anzaldúa, in such *Coatlicue* states, the multiplicitous self experiences an *Augenblick*, that moment of vision that allows for a bracketing of meaning where she is in the process of world-forming. Even though Heidegger speaks of a singular site of dwelling and a seemingly unified world, his discussion of transcendence allows us to read him otherwise. Given my neutral temporal structure of care that allows for transcendence, a transcendence that Heidegger qualifies as a "freedom for ground,"[17] why must I assume that the formation of my world, the world toward which I transcend, will "ground the ground" in the same manner prior to an *Augenblick*? There have to be additional possibilities of which I was heretofore unaware. If this were not the case, how could historically contingent notions of being emerge?

While this place of in-betweenness, prior to a moment of decision, is described by Anzaldúa as the *herida abierta*, the open wound, there is also space for "strategies of resistance that allow her to reinterpret herself and her cultures."[18] In Heideggerian terms, in a moment of vision (*Augenblick*), I am able to choose among different possibilities of existence and not just follow the public conventions of the *they*. By traveling in-between many worlds (and many *theys*), a multiplicitous self is able to decipher even more potentialities of existence. Such potential resists dichotomous thinking and dualisms, binaries that Heidegger has likewise rejected throughout the corpus of his work. It is not just self against world, but many *worlds*.

I began this book with Heidegger's problem, "what is woman?" and demonstrated his critique of Judeo-Christian dialectics of the flesh where human beings are reduced to substances of sexual difference. In his reading of Trakl, he once again critiques a metaphysical tradition founded on such dichotomous thinking, and yet, when all is said and done, we are left with "one generation" (*Geschlecht*) where no matter the complexity of the term, it "always refers to the twofoldness of the sexes."[19] According to Heidegger, this twofoldness culminates in the "one generation" of the German people, the only people capable of proper dwelling in their attunement to being. Heidegger's thinking goes astray because of his inability to imagine an in-betweenness of worlds. His language lends itself to fascist thinking and ends up privileging a single German world and its relation to being. And yet, right here, we also find strategies of resistance to just this thinking.

In chapter 1, I discussed Heidegger's notion of neutral Dasein and his assertion that "Dasein harbors the intrinsic possibility for being factically dispersed into bodiliness and thus into sexuality."[20] Essential to such facticity is Heidegger's insistence that dispersion is an affair of "multiplication (not 'multiplicity') which is present in every factically individuated Dasein as such."[21] I previously highlighted how the distinction between multiplication and multiplicity is key here, for multiplicity implies that a plethora of attributes is already found in Dasein that then becomes factically dispersed, whereas multiplication signifies the *process* of such dispersed multiplicity (the how and not the what). Implicit in this distinction is that neutral Dasein is not closed-off or predetermined; we do not exist as possibilities of existence prior to our interaction with our environment and others. We, as "cases of Dasein," are always in the process of world-forming, so it seems very contrary to Heidegger's thought to suppose that Dasein's world is formed at a single site of dwelling. Dasein must always speak from the position of an "I" that is in some sense unified, but this "I" is never static. Heidegger states, "Because Dasein has *in each case mineness (Jemeinigkeit)*, one must always use a *personal* pronoun when one addresses it: 'I am,' 'you are.' Furthermore, in each case Dasein is mine to be in one way or another. Dasein has always made some sort of decision as to the way in which it is in each case [je meines]."[22] While such "mineness" implies an individualized or unified self, Heidegger also emphasizes the shared community or being-with (*Mitsein*) of Dasein. Furthermore, Dasein's moods constantly disrupt the world-forming of this seemingly unified self, so Dasein's decision regarding the way it takes up its mineness may change according to its affective state. It is this fluidity of selfhood that bridges Heidegger's thinking with Latina feminist phenomenology.

However, whereas Heidegger undergirds "multiplication" rather than "multiplicity" in describing the how of Dasein's world-forming, Ortega highlights how she prefers the term *multiplicity* to *plurality*; She asserts, "In my view, the term 'plurality' suggests multiple selves, while the term 'multiplicity' suggests a complexity associated with one self [. . . .] I appeal to a multiplicitous self as being-in-worlds and being-between-worlds, a singular self occupying multiple social locations and a condition of in-betweenness."[23] While Heidegger and Ortega disagree on whether the term "multiplication" or "multiplicity" best captures the way in which Dasein comes to form a world and take up a position of mineness, there are important parallels, as both are interested in how the self is always in the process of being made. Furthermore, both are concerned with how phenomenological perception (that is, moods) and one's environment influence the type of self one is able to become. However, while Heidegger acknowledges the possibility of forming many different worlds, his later thinking on poetic dwelling privileges a singular site of world-forming, as there is only one correct historical attunement to beyng. There is only one world in which Germans *should* dwell; only one struggle to realize their essential relation to beyng.[24] I emphasize *should* to highlight the moral implications of this assertion. While Heidegger has always touted ontology as first philosophy, in that he is first and foremost concerned with the question of being, he nonetheless prescribes conditions under which such an attunement to being/beyng becomes possible. Meditative thinking becomes the means through which Germans are able to grasp their essential (and singular) relation to being. It is this lack of meditative thinking, in favor of a supposedly calculative thinking, coupled with an inability to dwell at a single site of origin that leads Heidegger to assert that Jews are worldless.

In part, Heidegger is able to make such a deplorable statement because of a political motivation to conflate a *geographical world* with a *phenomenological world*. As argued in chapter 5, Heidegger references the necessity to center the political impetus of Germany in the South, in the countryside. He speaks of a rootedness to a particular German soil. Heidegger uses an ontic anti-Semitic myth of the "wandering Jew" to make a seemingly ontological statement about the Jewish community, which he implicitly understands as monolithic. It is important to highlight this ontic/ontological entanglement and to once again use Heidegger as a cautionary tale to demonstrate how philosophy is led astray in trying to neatly delineate the ontic concerns of lived experiences from ontological issues. As I've demonstrated throughout this book, narratives that define "what is" are necessarily involved in ethical assertions, because what we take "to be" depends on how things show up and matter to us. And yet, feminist philosophy that focuses on situated knowledges and lived narratives is often questioned for not being philosophical enough.

Jessica Elkayam highlights this concern in reference to Ortega's work: "If we say that Heidegger lacks the ontic dimension of the lived experiences of the marginalized developed by Latina feminist phenomenologists because he too heavily favors the ontological, does this position classical theorists to dismiss Latina feminist phenomenology on the grounds that it is not 'proper philosophy'? Ortega is not unaware of this tendency to dismiss Latina feminist phenomenology as 'improper philosophy' precisely because it grounds an ethics in the testimonials of lived experience rather than in theory."[25] Contrary to not being "proper philosophy," Latina feminist phenomenology may be closer to seeking wisdom (that is, philosophy) in that it attends to Harding's rules of "strong objectivity." That is, by emphasizing *situated knowledges* and the way that our social location and history inform our ways of knowing, we are able to arrive at closer approximations of the truth.[26] Especially from a Heideggerian viewpoint, if Dasein is that being for whom being is an issue, we must start with the ontic concerns of the self that has any conception of being at all. By focusing on the experiences of marginalized selves, those beings that escape determinate meaning, or those bodies that evade normative institutions by teetering between *theys*, Latina feminist phenomenologists, offer us insights into better understanding "what is" outside of a totalized presence of meaning. Such phenomenology understands being as *physis* as a coming-to-be of world-forming, not as *ousia*, in the sense of a substantial self who is always already present in its "there." Lugones captures this ability to be "there" in different worlds, this capacity for world-forming, in her notion of playful world-traveling.

Lugones's world-traveling is not about physical displacement but is rather an epistemic and hermeneutic shift, a traveling to "other worlds of sense."[27] Whereas Lugones speaks of multiplicitous *selves* (ontological pluralism) in which we can shift from one person to the next, Ortega appeals to a multiplicitous *self* (existential pluralism) in which there is still a unitary "I" that remains in between travel. While Lugones discusses the necessity of world-traveling for marginalized selves, where one must adopt dominant narratives in order to survive, she invites all of us to engage in a form of playful world-traveling where we grow to appreciate otherness. Drawing from Marilyn Frye's notion of arrogant perception, a manner in which we perceive otherness via a projection of assumed stereotypes, Lugones suggests an alternative way of perceiving, a loving perception. She describes such perception as a "cross-cultural and cross-racial travelling," where rather than consume the exotic other and appropriate them to fit into our world, we try to appreciate and empathize with differing ways of existence.[28]

Anzaldúa's Bridge and Anaximander's Apeiron

Such traveling in-between and "crossing" conjures the visual imagery of a bridge, an imagery that Anzaldúa evokes in her work on identity and difference. Anzaldúa's early work with Cherry Moraga *This Bridge Called My Back* speaks to the situatedness of living at the borderlands in a literal and figurative sense. The bridge represents being "in-between" worlds and the experience of marginalization. G. Sue Kasun highlights the epistemological importance of bridges in Anzaldúa's later work as the building and becoming of bridges comes to be essential for any understanding of knowledge production that resists totalization: "Anzaldúa (2002), at the end of her life's work, examined how the path toward "*conocimiento*," or knowing, included the complicated work of building and becoming bridges of understanding that span beyond current constructs of difference and identity."[29] Such building and becoming bridges entails resisting static categories of identity, where any solid "us versus them" binary constructs dissolve to form new collective identities. Anzaldúa doesn't downplay the importance of identities and their impact on our lived experiences, but as previously noted in discussing O'Byrne's work on genocide, identity politics can turn violent if it fails to empathize with and potentially learn from other worlds (*genera* not *genos*). We see this happen as Heidegger privileges the attunement of the German people and a single origin of dwelling.

Heidegger's "Building Dwelling Thinking" and his discussion of bridges in relation to dwelling best demonstrates his overemphasis on *words* to the detriment of *worlds*. In this text, he traces the etymological roots of building (*bauen*) to the Old High German *buan*, which means to dwell. He then says, "let us listen once more to what language says to us" and highlights the Old Saxan *wuon* and Gothic *wunian* to speak of peace in the sense of "to free" or "to safeguard" (*Friede*). What is freed is space (*Raum*) whose roots in German can be traced to the ancient meaning *rum*, indicating a place that is free for settlement. In other words, in building we free a space for settlement. In settling, we create boundaries (*peras*) within which to dwell. We *are* dwellers, and we build to dwell. Yet, not all building is dwelling. More specifically, Heidegger uses the example of the bridge to demonstrate a type of building that is not dwelling. Heidegger asserts, "We attain to dwelling, so it seems, only by means of building. The latter, building, has the former, dwelling, as its goal. Still, not every building is a dwelling. Bridges . . . are buildings but not dwellings."[30] Even though bridges are not proper places for dwelling, a locale that is "freed" for building only comes into existence by virtue of the bridge. Heidegger states, "The bridge is a locale. As such a thing, it allows a space into which earth and sky, divinities and mortals are admitted. The space allowed by the bridge contains many places variously near or far from the bridge."[31] The bridge allows a gathering of the fourfold, a gathering in which something is able to appear as a thing, as an enduring presence. I previously compared the fourfold of earth, sky, divinities, and mortals to Aristotle's four causes in that this quadrate is responsible for the coming into presence of a thing. In "The Question Concerning Technology," Heidegger references Aristotle's fourfold causality to show how *technē* is related to physis as *poiēsis* as a "bringing forth . . . Bringing forth brings out of concealment into unconcealment."[32] The bridge is a prerequisite for any "bringing forth" and for any determinate meaning, or solid ground. We are mortals by virtue of dwelling, but this capacity for dwelling is only possible via a bridge. Heidegger asserts, "For building brings the fourfold *hither* into a thing, the bridge, and brings *forth* the thing as a locale, out into which is already present, room for which is only now made *by* this locale."[33] This bridge appears to be the ontological difference in which beings and being are mutually reinforcing. The bridge is necessary to free a space for dwelling (what we must do in order *to be*), but the bridge only comes forth as a locale and a site for gathering the fourfold as an "in between" of (dwelling) spaces. In other words, the bridge cannot be thought without building, and building cannot be thought without the bridge. By thinking about the "in between" bridge of dwelling spaces, or worlds, Heidegger's thought may provide us with useful insights in regard to world-traveling. The bridge as apeiron, that concept of boundlessness that Heidegger interrogates in Anaximander's fragment, may be thought alongside the boundary, or *peras*, of worlds. The bridge is apeiron as it is symbolic of a manifold of possibilities prior to dwelling.

In "The Anaximander Fragment," Heidegger attempts a translation of Anaximander's fragment, the oldest passage in Western thinking that speaks of being. He moves beyond philological and historiological translating and asks that we set aside "familiar ways of representing things, as we ask ourselves in what the confusion of the contemporary world's fate consists."[34] Overall, Heidegger is not happy with previous translations that treat the fragment as an interpretation of the philosophy of nature. In such translations, being is reduced to actuality (*actualitas*), actuality is reduced to reality (*Wirklichkeit*), and reality becomes objectivity (*Objektivität*).[35] In other words, being is reduced to that which is present at hand *ousia* and not *physis*. It is the forgetting of being (*Seinsvergessenheit*) and its reduction to *ousia* that allows machinational thinking. In order to capture the potential of being to come forth in its presence (*physis*), Heidegger settles on the following translation of the fragment: "Along the lines of usage, for they let order and thereby also reck belong to one another (in the surmounting) of disorder."[36] Here, order and disorder belong to one another in the same way that the ontological difference comprises being and beings. A being only appears as an ordered gathering of the fourfold but contains within it the disorder (being) to presence as a different amalgamation of gathering.

For Heidegger, Anaximander's fragment "speaks of manifold being in totality."[37] Such a manifold of being is captured in the visual imagery of the bridge, as Heidegger asserts, "The space allowed by the bridge contains many places."[38] The bridge as apeiron and dwelling space as *peras* belong to one another. Apeiron, or limitless being, is also found in Heidegger's discussion of Neutral Dasein as the "potency of the essence" or the "not-yet of dispersion."[39] Heidegger's philosophy allows us to think the different possibilities of existence, different ways of being. And yet, instead of focusing on this *capacity* for dwelling, or the *bridge*, he ends BDT with an example of a farmhouse as dwelling space, one that invokes the same "childbed" of the peasant woman in his analysis of van Gogh's shoes, as he emphasizes the "*proper plight of dwelling*."[40] It is hard to think of this "plight" outside of a context of the *Black Notebooks*, where Germans must face this struggle and where Jews are worldless. Despite Heidegger's declarations that he searches for being outside of philological translations, his etymological efforts that aim at rediscovering the question of being culminate in one dwelling space (that is proper to Germans) and one historical destiny. Heidegger's emphasis is on *words* and not *worlds*. Heidegger asks us to engage in meditative thinking whereby we listen to the *saying* of language, of words, in order to reveal *one* particular *world* that is proper for dwelling.

In reading Heidegger against himself, can we think the bridge as a liminal space of possibilities, as a potential locale where different worlds are possible? Rather than focus on the dwelling of determinate meaning, can we emphasize the capacity for world-forming and the potential for world-traveling? In particular, how can we read Heidegger alongside other thinkers to emphasize different worlds of sexed/gendered being, and how can we world-travel to appreciate different potentialities for such being?

In *Nos/Otras: Gloria E. Anzaldúa, Multiplicitous Agency, and Resistance*, Andrea Pitts turns to Anzaldúa's work in order to expand a "critical trans politics" that seeks to resist the material means by which trans and gender-variant people are marginalized. Pitts states, "In her 1993 piece titled "Border Arte" and in her introduction to *This Bridge Called My Back* published in 2022, Anzaldúa appears to locate trans existence alongside other forms of liminal, border-crossing forms of experience and political significance."[41] In associating trans experience with border crossing and liminality, Pitts sees a way to view Anzaldúa's notion of multiplicitous agency as resistance. Such a reading of liminal experience as resistance is also present in Perry Zurn's trans poetics of dust, as he thinks dust poetically as an "in-between." Dust as the "in-between" is the bridge or apeiron of sexed/gendered experience.

By turning to a trans poetics of dust, I do not want to contribute to the "hypervisibility"[42] of trans existence, but nor do I want to ignore situated knowledges that contribute to a dismantling of dominant narratives. Ephraim Das Janssen asserts, "I aim to use Heidegger's theories to get at the heart of what gender is for *all* by examining those for whom gender just does not work out according to expectations."[43] For Janssen, while all bodies must perform and affirm gender according to a particular historical form or "style," an analysis of "transgressively gendering individuals can yield a greater understanding of how this ubiquitous phenomenon operates for all."[44] While we *all* perform and affirm gender, trans experience as liminality may function as Heidegger's hammer in that it breaks with dominant narratives of understanding and intelligibility. Such "breaking down" allows for new possibilities of understanding.

Zurn's Trans Poetics of Dust

In *How We Make Each Other: Trans Poetics in and at the Edge of the University*, Perry Zurn asks how trans poetics, that is, trans wisdom, creativity, and community, may transform higher education.[45] Like Heidegger, Zurn views a crisis at the university that cannot be solved through bureaucratic policy projects. Also, like Heidegger, Zurn turns to poetics to offer a response and to think about dwelling. However, unlike Heidegger, Zurn's trans poetics thinks decolonially, from the borderlands and with border-consciousness, as he thinks about the *bridging* of spaces, an in-between that is best captured in his poetics of dust.

The Creative Impotence of the University and Making Sense at the Margins

Heidegger is critical of the university for imposing a technical understanding of being where the act of learning becomes a lesson in utility. He laments how pedagogy is reduced to usefulness and lacks meditative or poetic thinking.

> One now fears the transition of the university into a trade school [. . . .] At bottom, however, one is only afraid of seeing what—in essence—already *is* [. . . .] One believes thereby that the university is slipping down into a mere trade school, that it is dissolving into a research institution which cuts itself off from "theory" and from "theoretical activity." Yet, it is not the exclusion of theory but precisely the "alignment" of theory to usefulness that conditions and justifies the existence of a trade school.[46]

This means a reduction of university to trade schools does not simply sever theory from practice and valorize the latter over the former; rather, such reduction signals a collapse whereby theory and thinking are always already practical. In other words, such reduction is indicative of a current technological ideology (*Gestell*) that thinks being in terms of optimization and future utility (which is not thinking, for Heidegger, in a proper sense).

According to Iain Thomson, such pedagogy *imposes* rather than *discloses*. Thomson asserts, "Such pedagogical approaches impose rather than disclose in that they require students to conform to a homogenizing external standard instead of helping them identify and cultivate their own distinctive talents and capacities."[47] Such cultivation is focused on what Thomson calls a "response-ability," where a key part of pedagogy for both teachers and learners includes a response, or engagement, that entails an "understanding of what it means for us to be."[48] A reduction of university to trade school presents the same ontological problem of standardized testing at any educational level in that students are not called on to think for themselves but are asked to memorize and regurgitate prefabricated universal understandings of being. Any deviation from the standard is seen as a sign of failure. The ontological significance of education, or the link between education and "what it means for us to be" is further highlighted in Thomson's article "Heidegger on Ontological Education, or: *How We Become What We Are*."[49] I emphasize the subtitle to accent the similarity in Zurn's title *How We Make Each Other*, for Zurn's concern regarding the university is also an ontological one, even if the "meaning making" he highlights takes place "at the edge" of the university, at its borders, not within its boundaries (*peras*). Realizing that university policies that focus on "inclusivity" are not enough, Zurn turns to the "borderlands of the academy" to imagine other ways "to dwell and to imagine."[50] Such imagining occurs as trans poetics.

Both Heidegger and Zurn emphasize the Ancient Greek root of poetics as *poiēsis*, as a process of making, or a coming forth into presence where such formation is not challenged forth via technological means but is allowed to let itself be.[51] However, whereas Heidegger's creative vision of the university entails a masculine ethos that overcomes its struggle to become *a people*, once again focusing on *one* world or *one* historical destiny, Zurn looks at the margins of the academy where "words are joined to materiality," where words represent the embodied worlds of trans existence. Unlike Heidegger's singular worldview, Zurn's trans poetics is a "cipher for 'moreness.'"[52]

Highlighting the masculine tone that Heidegger uses in his politico-poetic project to advance the destiny of the German people, Huntingon states,

The *Rektoratsrede*, for example, talks of the need for the "harshest self examination" (*härteste Selbstbesinnung*) and willful self assertion before the "creative impotence" of modern knowledge (SA, 29–31/SB, 9–11). His student address, invoking the hero Schlageter, calls German students to "let the strength of this hero's native mountains flow into your will!" (PS, 41). In another address during 1933, Heidegger emphatically proclaims, "*University study must become a risk* [*Wagnis*], not a refuge for the cowardly" (45). Rather than seek mere knowledge and information, students are called to face the unknown, the abysmal groundlessness of human existence, and thereby to preserve Germany's spiritual essence and secure its destiny. In this address, his employment of the term *Geschlecht*—which means at once race, nation, gender—transforms the academic schoolyard into a battlefield on which to forge a new manly humanity.[53]

By emphasizing the "creative impotence" of modern knowledge, Heidegger is referring to the previously mentioned vocationalization of universities, where learning becomes an activity of utility for the sake of some specialization. Proper thinking, in the sense of meditative or poetic thinking, where we are engaged in a way that we reckon with our own sense of how "to be" is lacking. The "abysmal groundlessness" that Heidegger mentions has the potential to open space for a myriad of possibilities, a variety of ways that we engage with our "response-ability." And yet, Heidegger's response is unidirectional with one (manly) destiny. Zurn, though also concerned with the utility-focused model of the university, highlights "counter *modes* of study," with an emphasis on this being plural. Zurn states,

> The university project is a capitalist venture with largely utilitarian procedures of production. An attention to poetics here means an attunement not to what gets produced in publication turnstiles, labs, and classrooms, but rather to what happens in the corridors, quads, study carrels, cafeterias, and cafes. It means tracing the creative commons, which is always under, beside, or just behind the knowledge production apparatus and its burgeoning administration systems. Here, counter modes of study and ways of knowing are inextricable from the ways we make things and make one another.[54]

Zurn makes clear the ontological significance of education as modes of study are inextricable from any form of sense making, but his "response-ability" is differently engaged. Whereas Heidegger turns to "one destiny," one space of dwelling that we previously discussed as being founded on the native soil of the German people, Zurn calls for a "return to the soil of sense, *through poetry*," but not with a focus on one space of dwelling; rather, Zurn conjures the border-consciousness of Anzaldúa and calls on Martinican theorist Édouard Glissant to create a poetics that is "latent, open, multilingual in intention, directly in contact with everything possible."[55]

In order to demonstrate the multifariousness and ongoing project of trans meaning-making at the edge of the university, Zurn goes to the Five College archives in Amherst, Massachusetts, to search for traces of trans existence and communal meaning-making and to explore uncovered survival writing as a form of trans poetics. Zurn states, trans poetics has historically referred to the "work and labor of transgender poets," but such poetics also has its roots "in the malleability of the trans body and the survival work of trans writing, underscoring the transformative materiality of words and worlds."[56] Like Ortega, Zurn accentuates *words and worlds*. Zurn looks to the archive to *gather* the words of former trans students and faculty in order to understand past worlds, their relation to the present, and the possible worlds of the future.

Breaking down *poiēsis,* Zurn highlights its "Proto Indo-European root *ci-,* meaning to collect or assemble; to pile, stow, or gather."[57] Essentially, when we gather, we make. Heidegger, too, is aware of the necessity of gathering for meaning making. As previously noted, Heidegger states a gathering of the fourfold is necessary in order for anything to be. Gathering (*Sammeln,* Sammlung) is "the power enacted through and as language, which brings human beings, things, and natural objects into relation with one another."[58] As Rebecca A. Longtin explains, "For both Heidegger and Dilthey, Hölderlin poetizes the fullness of time and the mysterious gathering of past and future in the present. This gathering is recollection (*Andenken*), which Hölderlin considers the task of poetry. For Hölderlin the vocation of the poet is to recollect, i.e., to gather what cannot be complete and to understand the unity of this gathering without dissolving difference."[59] Here, a gathering is essential in order to understand something in its presence, to understand something as being, yet this unity should not dissolve difference. Heidegger's philosophy provides many resources for thinking identity and difference and for thinking the possibility that groundlessness offers, which is why it is so disappointing to read the *Black Notebooks* and to see that difference is dissolved in favor of *a people.*

I see Zurn as offering a counterread to Heidegger, as forging a poetics that gathers in an effort to form words *and* worlds, to speak of a community of trans existence that doesn't dissolve difference. Several of Zurn's chapters are characterized as "attunements," an attunement is a manner in which we find ourselves in the world. For Heidegger, attunement (*Gestimmtheit*) or my being attuned indicates how a certain mood "brings Being to its 'there.' In having a mood, Dasein is always disclosed moodwise as that entity to which it has been delivered over in its Being."[60] Moods are thus disclosive of being. In chapter 2, "Anchoring: Attunements to History," Zurn recounts his visit to the archives and discloses a trans poetics of dust where dust becomes the world of trans existence. It should also be noted that "anchoring" refers to a solid grounding or rootedness. When someone anchors a ship, it is secured firmly in the water. Someone "solid" may serve as an "anchor" in that you can lean on them and count on them for support.

The "In-Between" and Border Consciousness of Dust

As Heidegger reminds us, for the most part, we go about our daily lives engaged in practical involvements that merit no further theoretical examination.[61] When a hammer serves its purpose, as when lodging a nail into a board, it is ready-to-hand (*zuhandenheit*). It's doing its job, so why would I stop to question it? Yet, when the hammer *doesn't* work, when it fails, it is laid before me as something present for scrutiny. It becomes present-at-hand (*vorhandenheit*) *as* hammer. What is this hammer that escapes intelligibility once it bypasses the realm of equipmental utility? Like any existential crisis, when something goes wrong, when something no longer runs smoothly, it is ripe for theoretical examination. Describing the ontological disclosiveness that accompanies the failed hammer, Andrew Royle states,

> Let us remain with our workman in his workshop, and now imagine that the workman reaches out for a hammer and finds instead an empty space. In now looking for his hammer, the workman starts to notice his workshop, which has been *there*, surrounding him, all the time. He casts an eye over the shelves, seeing dust; he spies a cracked window; becomes aware of a spider moving across the ceiling; he notices the detritus of uncompleted tasks and worries about deadlines. Heidegger says, in this 'looking around,' the referential context of Being is "lit up" (p. 74). By virtue of the space of the missing hammer it's

as if a light switches on and Dasein sees the world that has been *there* all along.⁶²

Royle describes surroundings that have been "there all along," yet remained unnoticed. It is only when the hammer fails to appear, and thus the worker is unable to function, that other aspects of his environment start to matter, such as dust. Royle's reference to dust may seem trivial, yet another scholar cites its accumulation in an effort to understand the bodily nature of Dasein. David Cerbone tries to locate aspects of Heidegger's philosophy that may offer hints at how embodiment figures into Dasein's way of being. Cerbone refers to *The Fundamental Concepts of Metaphysics* to make a distinction between the "readiness-to-hand" of equipment and the "capacity" of bodily organs. He states, "Equipment is always ready for something, and an organ has a capacity for something, but equipment is ready for use regardless of whether it's actively being taken hold of or gathering dust in the back of the workshop; organs, by contrast, have the capacities they have, to see, to grip, to pump blood, and so forth, only insofar as they are integrated into a living organism."⁶³ Essentially, Dasein's embodied way of being is not analogous to the equipmental nature of objects that are "ready-to-hand," but what is intriguing about this example is the reference to dust because of its seemingly benign nature. Something that gathers dust is, in a way, forgotten and out of use. Things gather dust, collect dust. So what? Both Royle and Cerbone reference dust in thinking about the intelligibility of Dasein as a nod to how little dust matters. Care is the being of Dasein in that it is the basis on which we understand the phenomenological relations that allow for being. My structure of care can be negatively or positively enacted in that entities/others can show up and authentically matter or they can "pass me by."⁶⁴ Dust doesn't matter, not unless something else in our environment doesn't work or is under theoretical examination. Only then do we notice its accumulation.

Zurn's trans poetics of dust takes note of what seemingly "passes us by" and speaks to the power and community of accumulation. He states, "I want to propose dust as an analytic for trans archival praxis—that is, as a frame for analyzing the poetics of trans story in and at the edge of the archive."⁶⁵ As an analytic, dust is liminal as it teeters between life and death, visible and invisible. For Zurn, dust, like the history of trans life is peripheral, largely left unnoticed, except when "they clump together like dust bunnies, showing the agglomeration of trans concerns, trans resistance habits, and the tireless efforts of individual trans people to make room."⁶⁶

Zurn notes, while the internet may provide trans folk with a sense of community today, trans history remains fractured. His research at the Five College archives recounts stories of both isolation and resistance, but paramount to his archival research is an emphasis on the *making* of history, of becoming.

Dust, as liminal, is the *apeiron* or bridge of sexed/gendered existence in that it highlights the continuous making of sexed/gendered worlds. For Zurn, "Dust 'vascillates between invisibility and those discrete instances when it appears in the spotlight,' drawing attention to space itself, to the air that hangs between things. Trans folk, too, seem to be invisibilized and spotlighted by turns, never wholly here nor wholly hidden, but when we do surface, we bare the space of gender in all its grainy, and convoluted detail. Dust—and certainly transness—does this deconstructive work."[67] Spotlighting transness makes gender itself visible. As previously stated, for Heidegger, the bridge allows a gathering of the fourfold, the gathering required for a space to appear as an enduring presence. Dust, transness, as the bridge, opens a space for gender to appear as an enduring presence. Yet, that presence is never total, because a different source of gathering is possible. Trans life shows gender in all its "grainy and convoluted detail," hence the popular need for dust mops.

While queer visibility and the recounting of situated knowledges is important, there is the aforementioned risk of hypervisibility. A spotlight on trans life makes trans bodies more visible and thus more vulnerable to violence. Dust remains largely invisible until it accumulates in dust traps or bothers those with allergies, in which case it must be eliminated for propriety's sake. Zurn speaks of "cis allergies," in which "cisgender is an illusion of dust-less, generation- and degeneration-free gendered existence."[68] Trans folk must be swept under the rug, but like dust, they linger. There is always a residue or trace that upsets neatly packed or totalized categories. Zurn muses, "What if gender expression as we know it were always the residual effects of some more organic, fundamental force? And what if transing gender simply illuminated that dusty-ness? Imagine trans particulates as the residue of gender as lived, which is always more than cis veneer would have us believe."[69] Under that boundary (*peras*) of veneer, that gathers as a solid presence, lies the potential for "moreness," or limitless possibilities (apeiron). Heidegger understands that bridge and space are mutually reinforcing, and yet he focuses on a single origin of dwelling, a boundary that border-consciousness is not capable of occupying.

Heidegger's philosophy provides us with resources to think the potentiality of becoming, yet his identity politics lead to a foreclosing of worlds.

We cannot remain in-between worlds forever, nor is it always a desirable place to be, as we need anchors to support our sense of self and our sense of world-forming. Yet such liminal thinking acts as a resistance to totalized systems of meaning making, systems built around politics of exclusion. Though we must "ground the ground," we must not lose sight of the bridge as possibility or as "moreness." Without the ability to world-travel, identity politics turn genocidal. Or, in responding to the problem, "what is woman?" in any definitive sense, we're merely sweeping dust under the rug.

Notes

Acknowledgments

1. Robyn Ferrell, *Copula: Sexual Technologies, Reproductive Powers* (Albany: SUNY Press, 2006).

Introduction

1. Beauvoir demonstrates how woman is viewed as "Other" in relation to "man." She states, to men "she is sex—absolute sex, no less. She is defined and differentiated with reference to man and not with reference to her; she is the incidental, the inessential as opposed to the essential. He is the Subject, he is Absolute—she is the Other." See Simone de Beauvoir, *The Second* Sex (New York: Random House, 1991), xxii. A practical example of man as "standard" and woman as "Other" is seen in biology texts where the human body has historically been represented through male anatomy. Furthermore, women have been historically excluded from participation in research trials. Their monthly hormonal cycles have categorized them as deviant bodies in contrast to the neutral male body. In chapter 2, I will further explore how "woman" is marked by sexual difference according to Judeo-Christian origin stories and how Heidegger resists this assumed difference prior to ontological investigation.

2. Heidegger makes a distinction between the ontic and the ontological with this contrast being described as the ontological difference. Ontic concerns detail our preoccupation and questioning of beings or entities and their properties/behaviors whereas ontological dealings scrutinize our relation to being. What being "is" is debatable in Heidegger, though he realized that just by saying "Being is," we turn Being into a being by uttering the copula "is." What is certain is that Heidegger does not want to characterize being as mere presence (as *ousia*), as if it is something that can be given and susceptible to empirical scrutiny. I speak of being as a historical

becoming; that is, as a temporal constitution that includes the historical awareness according to which beings come to presence at all. Despite the ontic/ontological distinction being cannot be thought without beings.

3. See Judith Butler, *Gender Trouble* (New York: Routledge, 1999), 10–11 and Gayle Rubin, "The Traffic in Women: Notes on the 'Political Economy' of Sex," *Toward an Anthropology of Women*, ed. Rayna R. Reiter (New York: Monthly Review Press, 1975).

4. Gayle Rubin, "The Traffic in Women: Notes on the 'Political Economy' of Sex," 165.

5. Paisley Currah, *Sex Is as Sex Does: Governing Transgender Identity* (New York: NYU Press, 2022), 39.

6. A set of universal, unchanging criteria does not decide legal sex recognition; rather, such decisions are made in view of certain political/economic motivations. As Currah demonstrates, it's in a state's best interest, in terms of national security, to allow a change from M to F on a person's driver's license if that person is feminine presenting. It is not, however, in a state's best interest to allow sex reclassification on a birth certificate when questions of inheritance are in tow. Currah notes that whereas "sex" on a driver's license may be an issue of spatial logics (we must be able to track people), "sex" on a birth certificate is a question of temporal logic and distribution of property. See Currah, *Sex Is as Sex Does: Governing Transgender Identity*, 103.

7. I will say more about the they (*das Man*) as it pertains to Heidegger's philosophy, but for those unfamiliar with the term, I will briefly define it here as social convention and popular opinion. To say that we do as they do is to highlight how we are influenced by our being with others and how we tend to adopt their same viewpoints and habits.

8. Jules Gill-Peterson, *Histories of the Transgender Child* (Minneapolis: University of Minnesota Press, 2018).

9. See Martin Heidegger, GA 2. *Sein und Zeit* (1927). Ed. Friedrich Wilhelm von Herrmann, 1977/*Being and Time*, trans. John Macquarrie and Edward Robinson (Oxford, UK: Blackwell, 1962), 146 and Martin Heidegger, N3 *Nietzsche*, vol. 3, *The Will to Power as Knowledge and Metaphysics*, ed. and trans. by Joan Stambaugh, David Farrell Krell, and Frank A. Capuzzi (San Francisco, CA: Harper, 1991), 231.

10. For Heidegger, each era is characterized by a certain worldview or historical awareness in relation to how it understands being. Heidegger refers to our current technological age as *Gestell* or enframing where we approach the world as an amalgam of resources ready to be calculated, exploited, and stockpiled for future use.

11. Heidegger prioritized ontology over ethics, separating being from the question of value; however, there has been scholarly debate about whether a normative ethics can be found in Heidegger's thought. While Heidegger doesn't provide any rule-based accounts on how to act, he does prescribe conditions under which Dasein can live authentically or under which Dasein can attain a certain spiritual

attunement to "beyng." Such conditions are viewed as more valuable than others and so it could be argued that claims regarding "what is" are necessarily tied to questions of "what ought to be." I have considered the extent to which I should engage with questions regarding Heidegger and ethics but ultimately decided that a more exhaustive treatment of the matter would detract from the central tenets of this project. For further discussion regarding Heidegger and ethics, see Eric Sean Nelson, "Heidegger and the Questionability of the Ethical," *Studia Phenomenologica* VIII (2008): 411–35; Frederick Olafson, *Heidegger and the Ground of Ethics* (Cambridge, UK: Cambridge University Press, 1998); and Lawrence Hatab, *Ethics and Finitude* (Lanham, MD: Rowman & Littlefield, 2000).

12. Martin Heidegger, GA 26. *Metaphysische Anfangsgründe der Logik im Ausgang von Leibniz* (1928), ed. Klaus Held, 1978, 1990 (2nd rev. ed.), 2007 (3d rev. ed.); *The Metaphysical Foundations of Logic*, trans. Michael Heim (Bloomington: Indiana University Press, 1984).

13. Meyer Shapiro, "The Still Life as a Personal Object: A note on Heidegger and van Gogh," *Bloomsbury Anthology of Aesthetics* (New York: Bloomsbury, 2012), 403–7.

14. See Theodore Kisiel, "Heidegger's *Gesamtausgabe:* An International Scandal of Scholarship," *Philosophy Today* 39, no. 1 (1995): 3–15; and Richard Wolin, *Heidegger in Ruins: Between Philosophy and Ideology* (New Haven, CT: Yale University Press, 2023).

15. See Victor Farías, *Heidegger and Nazism* (Philadelphia: Temple University. Press, 1989) and Emmanuel Faye, *Heidegger: The Introduction of Nazism into Philosophy in Light of the Unpublished Seminars of 1933–1935*, trans. Michael B. Smith (New Haven, CT: Yale University Press, 2011).

16. Given this nonlinear and stand-alone structure, certain explanations of Heidegger's philosophy may be repeated for clarity.

17. Pearl Cleage, *Mad at Miles: A Blackwoman's Guide to Truth* (Detroit, MI: Cleage Group, 1990).

18. In reference to Aristotle, Heidegger said, "regarding the personality of a philosopher, our only interest is that he was born at a certain time, that he worked, and that he died." Scholars have referred to this quote to demonstrate how the biography of a philosopher doesn't matter; that is, a philosopher's life story is inconsequential to the work produced. It is strange to think that Heidegger would request that we dismiss Aristotle's character and that we only deal with his philosophical concepts—Aristotle, a thinker touted as the father of virtue ethics, whose work could not be separated from the concerns of the *polis*. See GA 18 *Grundbegriffe der aristotelischen Philosophie* (1924), ed. Mark Michalski, 2002; *Basic Concepts of Aristotelian Philosophy*, trans. Robert D. Metcalf and Mark Basil Tanzer (Bloomington: Indiana University Press, 2009), 4.

19. Patricia Huntington, *Ecstatic Subjects, Utopia, and Recognition: Kristeva, Heidegger, Irigaray* (Albany: SUNY Press, 1998), xiii.

20. Huntington, *Ecstatic Subjects, Utopia, and Recognition*, xvii.

21. Gregory Fried, *Towards a Polemical Ethics: Between Heidegger and Plato* (Lantham, MD: Rowman & Littlefield, 2021), 265. *Phronēsis* is a Greek term that can roughly be translated as practical wisdom.

22. Here, *polemos* signifies struggle or confrontation. In Greek mythology, Polemos is an embodiment of war, but *polemos* need not refer to any physical struggle. Fried sketches out many definitions of *polemos* and polemical thinking in Heidegger, including *polemos* as an ontological concept and strife between Dasein and being. See Gregory Fried, *Heidegger's Polemos: From Being to Politics* (New Haven, CT and London: Yale University Press, 2000).

23. Fried, *Heidegger's Polemos: From Being to Politics*, 2.

24. Günther Anders, "Pseudo-concreteness of Heidegger's Philosophy," *Philosophy and Phenomenological Research* 8, no. 3 (1948): 349.

25. See Richard R. Askay, "Heidegger, the Body, and the French Philosophers," *Continental Philosophy Review* 32 (1999): 29–35; Kevin A. Aho, *Heidegger's Neglect of the Body* (Albany: SUNY Press, 2009); Frank Schalow, *The Incarnality of Being: The Earth, Animals, and the Body in Heidegger's Thought* (Albany: SUNY Press, 2006); Daniela Vallega-Neu, *The Bodily Dimension in Thinking* (Albany: SUNY Press, 2005).

26. Jacques Derrida, *Margins of Philosophy* trans. Alan Bass (Chicago, IL: University of Chicago, 1972).

27. Gayatri Spivak, "Can the Subaltern Speak?" in *Marxism and the Interpretation of Culture*, ed. Cary Nelson and Lawrence Grossberg (London: Macmillan, 1988).

28. Patricia Hill Collins, *Black Feminist Thought: Knowledge, Consciousness, and the Politics of Empowerment* (Abingdon, UK: Routledge, 1990), 35–36.

29. There is no single "feminist method" or "feminist standpoint," but the indicated bullet points suggest distinctive features of feminist research. These points are taken from Sandra Harding, "Introduction: Is There a Feminist Method?" in *Feminism and Methodology*, ed. Sandra Harding (Bloomington: Indiana University Press, 1988) and Sandra Harding, "Rethinking Standpoint Epistemology: What Is Strong Objectivity?" in *Feminist Epistemologies*, ed. L. Alcoff and E. Potter (New York: Routledge, 1993).

30. Heidegger references *alētheia* as the truth of unconcealment in several of his works. In "The Question Concerning Technology," he states, "Technology comes to presence in the realm where revealing and unconcealment take place, where *alētheia*, truth, happens." Martin Heidegger, GA 7. *Vorträge und Aufsätze* (1936–1953), ed. Friedrich-Wilhelm von Herrmann, 2000; "The Question Concerning Technology," trans. William Lovitt, in David Farrell Krell, ed., *Basic Writings* (San Francisco, CA: Harper Collins, 1993), 319. In "The End of Philosophy and the Task of Thinking," he asserts, "It is not for the sake of etymology that I stubbornly translate the name *alētheia* as unconcealment, but for the sake of the matter that must be considered when we think adequately that which is called Being and thinking." Martin Heidegger, *Zur Sache des Denken* (Tübingen, Germany: Max Niemeyer Verlag, 1969), 61–80;

"The End of Philosophy and the Task of Thinking," trans. Joan Stambaugh, in David Farrell Krell, ed., *Basic Writings* (San Francisco, CA: Harper Collins, 1993), 445.

31. Donna Haraway, "Situated Knowledges: The Science Question in Feminism and the Privilege of Partial Perspective," *Feminist Studies* 14, no. 3 (1988), 575–99.

32. Trish Glazebrook, *Heidegger on Science* (Albany: SUNY Press, 2012), 18.

33. Martin Heidegger, *Being and Time*, 143. Heidegger notes, "This 'bodily nature' hides a whole problematic of its own, though we shall not treat it here."

34. See Karen Barad, "Posthumanist Performativity: Toward an Understanding of How Matter Comes to Matter," *Signs: Journal of Women in Society and Culture* 28, no. 3 (2003): 801–31. Barad criticizes how language has been given too much power, while looking at the "intra-active" quality of materiality. See also Elizabeth Grosz, *Becoming Undone: Darwinian Reflections on Life, Politics, and Art* (Durham, NC: Duke University Press, 2011), where she challenges nature as passive matter.

35. As Talia Mae Bettcher notes, Harold Garfinkel's "naturalist attitude" view about sex draws from Husserl's phenomenology in that it presupposes a "common-sense" view according to which the natural world exists independently of our minds. Such a "naturalist attitude" supposes the following "common-sense" view regarding the nature of sex: "First, there is a commitment to natural sexual dichotomy: exactly two (mutually exclusive) sexes exist, every human being is 'naturally' one or the other, and exceptions to this division may be dismissed as 'unnatural.' Second, there is a commitment to the natural invariance of sex: a human being can never change sex, and any sex transfers are merely ceremonial. Finally, there is an almost exclusive appeal to genitalia: genitals essentially determine sex membership" (Garfinkel, 1967). Bettcher analyzes the moral presumptions at play when we try to guess the "private" genitalia of persons based on their "public" gender presentation. See Talia Mae Bettcher, "Full-Frontal Morality: The Naked Truth about Gender," *Hypatia* 27, no. 2 (2012): 319–37 and Harold Garfinkel, *Studies in Ethnomethodology* (Englewood Cliffs, NJ: Prentice Hall, 1967).

36. Martin Heidegger, GA 51. *Grundbegriffe* (1941). Ed. Petra Jaeger, 1981, 1991 (rev. ed.); *Basic Concepts*, trans. Gary E. Aylesworth. Bloomington and Indianapolis: Indiana University Press, 1993, 51–53.

37. Martin Heidegger, *Der Ursprung des Kunstwerkes*, ed. H. G. Gadamer (Stuttgart, Germany: P. Reclam, 1960); "The Origin of the Work of Art," trans. Albert Hofstadter, in David Farrell Krell ed., *Basic Writings* (San Francisco, CA: Harper Collins, 1993), 203.

38. See Kevin Aho, *Existential Medicine: Essays on Health and Illness* (Lantham, MD: Rowman & Littlefield, 2018); Havi Carel, *Phenomenology of Illness* (Oxford, UK: Oxford University Press, 2017); Fredrik Svenaeus, *Phenomenological Bioethics: Medical Technologies, Human Suffering, and the Meaning of Being Alive* (New York: Routledge, 2017).

39. See Iris Marion Young, "Pregnant Embodiment: Subjectivity and Alienation," *Journal of Medicine and Philosophy* 9 (1984), 45–62; Dana S. Belu, *Heidegger,*

Reproductive Technology, and the Motherless Age (Cham, Switzerland: Palgrave Macmillan, 2017); and Lanei Rodemeyer, "Dasein Gets Pregnant," *Philosophy Today* 42 (1998): 76–84.

40. Harding, "Introduction: Is There a Feminist Method?" 6.

41. See Luce Irigaray, *The Forgetting of Air in Martin Heidegger*, trans. Mary Beth Mader (Austin, TX: University of Texas Press, 1999); Anne O'Byrne, *Natality and Finitude* (Bloomington: Indiana University Press, 2010); Alison Stone, *Being Born: Birth and Philosophy* (Oxford, UK: Oxford University Press, 2019); Leslie MacAvoy, "The Heideggerian Bias toward Death: A Critique of the Role of Being-towards-Death in the Disclosure of Human Finitude," *Metaphilosophy* 27 (1996): 63–77; Lisa Guenther, "Being-from-others: Reading Heidegger After Cavarero," *Hypatia* 23, no. 1 (2008), 99–118.

42. Adriana Cavarero, *In Spite of Plato: A Feminist Rewriting of Ancient Philosophy* trans. Serena Anderlini-D'Onofrio and Aine O'Healy (Cambridge, UK: Polity Press, 1995) and Adriana Cavarero, *Relating Narratives: Storytelling and Selfhood*, trans Paul Kottman (New York: Routledge, 2000).

43. Deborah Orr, "Thinking through the Body: An Introduction to *Beliefs, Bodies, and Being*," *Belief, Bodies, and Being: Feminist Reflections on Embodiment*, ed. Deborah Orr, Linda López Mcallister, Eileen Kahl, and Kathleen Earle (Lanham: Rowman & Littlefield, 2006), 1–10.

44. Carol Bigwood, *Earth Muse: Feminism, Nature, and Art* (Philadelphia: Temple University Press, 1993).

45. Plato, *Symposium*, trans. Alexander Nehamas and Paul Woodruff (Indianapolis, IN: Hackett, 1989). While Diotima, a woman, teaches Socrates the truth about *eros* (and in chapter 5, I reference how women as educators are often mediators of the "law of the father"), she emphasizes that the higher form of "giving birth in beauty" is for "boys." She asserts, "To seek to give birth to such ideas as will make young men better" (58, 211c), and, "When someone rises by these stages, through loving boys correctly, and begins to see this beauty, he has almost grasped his goal" (59, 208b–9b). She also notes that those who are "pregnant in body" turn to women, while those who are "pregnant in soul" turn to men (56).

46. Gayle Rubin, "The Traffic in Women: Notes on the 'Political Economy' of Sex." *Toward an Anthropology of Women*, ed. Rayna R. Reiter (New York: Monthly Review Press, 1975), 157–210; Mary Rawlinson, *Just Life: Bioethics and the Future of Sexual Difference* (New York: Columbia University Press, 2016); Dana S. Belu, *Heidegger, Reproductive Technology, and the Motherless Age* (Cham, Switzerland: Palgrave Macmillan, 2017).

47. Brittany Cooper, "God Help My Friendship with White Evangelicals after *Dobbs*," *The Cut*, June 24, 2022, accessed at https://www.thecut.com/2022/06/white-evangelicals-dobbs-scotus-decision.html.

48. Irigaray, *Forgetting of Air in Martin Heidegger* and Ewa Ziarek, "Toward a Radical Female Imaginary: Temporality and Embodiment in Irigaray's Ethics," *Diacritics* 28, no. 1 (1998): 59–75.

49. Heidegger, *Ontology—The Hermeneutics of Facticity*, 24.

50. Tao Leigh Goffe, "Stolen Life, Stolen Time: Black Temporality, Speculation, and Racial Capital," *South Atlantic Quarterly* 121, no. 1 (2022): 109–30; Jack Halberstam, *In a Queer Time and Place: Transgender Bodies, Subcultural Lives* (New York: NYU Press, 2005); Alison Kafer, *Feminist, Queer, Crip* (Bloomington: Indiana University Press, 2013).

51. Jacob Hale, "Suggested Rules for Non-Transsexuals Writing about Transsexuals, Transsexuality, Transsexualism, or Trans__" (1997), last updated November 18, 2009, https://sandystone.com/hale.rules.html and Talia Mae Bettcher " 'When Tables Speak': On the Existence of Trans Philosophy," *Daily Nous* (2018) http://dailynous.com/2018/05/30/tables-speak-existence-trans-philosophy-guest-talia-mae-bettcher/.

52. Megan Burke, "Cis Sense and the Habit of Gender Assignment," *Journal of Speculative Philosophy* 36, no. 2 (2022): 206–18.

53. Robin Dembroff, "Cisgender Commonsense and Philosophy's Transgender Trouble," *TSQ: Transgender Studies Quarterly* 7, no. 3 (2020): 399–406.

54. Kevin Aho, "Gender and Time: Revisiting the Question of Dasein's Neutrality," *Epoché*, 12, no. 1 (2007): 138.

55. Heidegger, *Being and Time*, 38.

56. Aho, "Gender and Time: Revisiting the Question of Dasein's Neutrality," 138.

57. Heidegger, *Being and Time*, 98.

58. Heidegger, *Being and Time*, 374.

59. Heidegger, *Being and Time*, 393–95.

60. Martin Heidegger, GA 65, *Beiträge zur Philosophie (Vom Ereignis)* (1936–1938). Ed. Friedrich-Wilhelm von Herrmann, 1989, 1994 (rev. ed.); *Contributions to Philosophy (Of the Event)*, trans. Richard Rojcewicz and Daniela Vallega-Neu (Bloomington: Indiana University Press, 2012), 44. Heidegger states, "The beginning is what grounds itself and what reaches ahead; it is self-grounding in the ground which is fathomed and opened up through the beginning [. . .] Because every beginning is unsurpassable, it must constantly be repeated and must be placed through confrontation into the uniqueness of its incipience [*Anfänglichkeit*] and thus of its ineluctable reaching ahead. This confrontation is original when it itself is inceptual, but this necessarily as *another* beginning."

61. Susan J. Brison, *Aftermath Violence and the Remaking of a Self* (Princeton, NJ: Princeton University Press, 2022), xi–xii.

Chapter 1

1. John Haugeland, Dasein *Disclosed*, ed. Joseph Rouse (Cambridge, MA and London: Harvard University Press, 2013), 30.

2. Martin Heidegger, GA 7. *Vorträge und Aufsätze* (1936 to 1953), ed. Friedrich-Wilhelm von Herrmann, 2000; "The Question Concerning Technology,"

trans. William Lovitt, in David Farrell Krell, ed., *Basic Writings* (San Francisco, CA: Harper Collins, 1993), 311–41.

3. I have tried to speak of "laboring Dasein" and "laboring subject" rather than "laboring woman" to account for the experiences of trans (including nonbinary) persons, who become pregnant; though, as I engage with existing literature, sensitivity to such language is not always possible. This may be due to directly quoting scholars who discuss female pregnancy or due to examining "woman" as a feminine trope. For example, Belu is primarily concerned with how "women's bodies" figure among the standing reserve, and she is concerned with a possible future where reproductive technology may lead us into a "motherless" age where such bodies are no longer required for procreation. See Dana S. Belu, *Heidegger, Reproductive Technology, and the Motherless Age* (Cham, Switzerland: Palgrave Macmillan, 2017).

4. Corine Pelluchon, *Nourishment: Philosophy of the Political Body*, trans. Justin E. H. Smith (London and New York: Bloomsbury, 2019), 35.

5. Corine Pelluchon, *Nourishment: Philosophy of the Political Body*, 35.

6. Medicaid is health insurance for Americans who fall in the lower-income bracket.

7. I am a white cisgender bisexual woman. That my narrative doesn't explicitly touch more on concerns of racial injustice and the largely heteronormative framework of reproductive health-care in the United States speaks volumes to my privilege.

8. For work that addresses a phenomenology of miscarriage, see Jennifer Scuro, *The Pregnancy [does-not-equal] Childbearing Project: A Phenomenology of Miscarriage* (Lanham, MD: Rowman & Littlefield, 2017).

9. Lanei Rodemeyer, "Applying Time to Feminist Philosophy of the Body," in *Belief, Bodies, and Being: Feminist Reflections on Embodiment*, ed. Deborah Orr, Linda López McAllister, Eileen Kahl, and Kathleen Earle (Lanham, MD: Rowman & Littlefield, 2006), 206.

10. Lanei Rodemeyer, "Applying Time to Feminist Philosophy of the Body," 206.

11. Lanei Rodemeyer, "Applying Time to Feminist Philosophy of the Body," 206.

12. Martin Heidegger, GA 2. *Sein und Zeit* (1927). Ed. Friedrich Wilhelm von Herrmann, 1977; *Being and Time*, trans. John Macquarrie and Edward Robinson (Oxford, UK: Blackwell, 1962), 68.

13. Lanei Rodemeyer, "Dasein Gets Pregnant," *Philosophy Today* 42 (1998): 76–84. It should be noted that Rodemeyer's account of the pregnant subject, along with Iris Marion Young's, explicitly speaks about the woman who chooses to give birth and who approaches pregnancy as a positive experience.

14. Rodemeyer, "Dasein Gets Pregnant," 80–81.

15. Heidegger, *Being and Time*, 474.

16. Heidegger, *Being and Time*, 419.

17. Heidegger states, "The character of Dasein's being—this 'that it is'—is veiled in its 'whence' and 'wither,' yet disclosed in itself all the more unveiledly;

we call it the '*thrownness*' *[Geworfenheit]* of this entity into its 'there'; indeed, it is thrown in such a way that, as Being-in-the-world, it is the 'there' " (1962, 174). See also *Being and Time*, 236–67.

18. Heidegger, *Being and Time*, 479.

19. Adriana Cavarero critiques this view that we are *thrown* into existence from nowhere. While Heidegger's notion of thrownness and being born on the basis of a nullity speaks of an existential state that allows for different possibilities of existence, rather than any literal bodily projection into existence, he never acknowledges the facticity of our being born from a body, let alone examine how it may hold ontological significance. Cavarero puts accent on how our being born is "a coming from the mother's womb." Adriana Cavarero, *In Spite of Plato: A Feminist Rewriting of Ancient Philosophy*, trans. Serena Anderlini-D'Onofrio and Aine O'Healy (Cambridge, UK: Polity Press, 1995), 6.

20. Anne O'Byrne, *Natality and Finitude* (Bloomington: Indianapolis University Press, 2010), 6.

21. Leslie MacAvoy, "The Heideggerian Bias toward Death: A Critique of the Role of Being-toward-Death in the Disclosure of Human Finitude," *Metaphilosophy* 27 (1996): 76.

22. Alison Stone, *Being Born: Birth and Philosophy* (Oxford, UK: Oxford University Press, 2019), 213.

23. Rodemeyer, "Dasein Gets Pregnant," 82.

24. Rodemeyer, "Dasein Gets Pregnant," 80. See also, Iris Marion Young, "Pregnant Embodiment: Subjectivity and Alienation," *Journal of Medicine and Philosophy* 9 (1984), 45–62 and Iris Marion Young, *On Female Body Experience: 'Throwing Like a Girl' and Other Essays* (Oxford, UK: Oxford University Press, 2005).

25. Haugeland, Dasein *Disclosed*, 5.

26. Heidegger, *Being and Time*, 477.

27. See Sara Gavrell "Obstetrics' Security Blanket: The Case of Continuous Electronic Fetal Monitoring in Healthy Births." *APA Women in Philosophy Blog*, July 14, 2021.

28. See, for example, Anthony Vincent Fernandez, "Embodiment and Objectification in Illness and Healthcare: Taking Phenomenology from Theory to Practice," *Journal of Clinical Nursing* 29, no. 21–22 (2020): 4403–12.

29. Martin Heidegger, GA 89. *Zollikoner Seminare* (1959–1969), ed. Peter Trawny, 2017; *Zollikon Seminars: Protocols—Conversations—Letters*, trans. Franz Mayr and Richard Askay (Evanston, IL: Northwestern University Press, 2001).

30. Dana S. Belu, *Heidegger, Reproductive Technology*, 103–19.

31. Belu, *Heidegger, Reproductive Technology*, 1–2.

32. See, for example, Elsa Lena Ryding, Klaas Wijma, and Barbro Wijma, "Experiences of Emergency Cesarean Section: A Phenomenological Study of 53 Women," *Birth* 25, no. 4 (1998): 246–51.

33. Sandra Lee Bartky, *Femininity and Domination: Studies in the Phenomenology of Oppression* (New York & London: Routledge, 1990), 83.

34. Belu, *Heidegger, Reproductive Technology*, 38.

35. Belu, *Heidegger, Reproductive Technology*, 115.

36. Belu, *Heidegger, Reproductive Technology*, 115.

37. Dana S. Belu, "Nature and Technology in Modern Childbirth: A Phenomenological Interpretation," *Techné* 16 (2012): 3.

38. Heidegger, "The Question Concerning Technology."

39. See NCHS Data Brief, no. 387, October 2020. https://www.cdc.gov/nchs/data/databriefs/db387-H.pdf.

40. Sara Ruddick, *Maternal Thinking: Toward a Politics of Peace* (Boston, MA: Beacon Press, 1989).

41. Heidegger, "The Question Concerning Technology," 114.

42. I presented a portion of this text at the American Philosophical Association Central Division Meeting in Chicago, February 24, 2022. Antoine Pageau-St-Hilaire was in the audience and raised this issue.

43. See section 56, "The Character of Conscience as a Call" and section 57, "Conscience as the Call of Care in Heidegger," *Being and Time*, 317–25.

Chapter 2

1. Jacques Derrida, "*Geschlect: différence sexuelle, différence ontologique,*" *Cahier de l'Herne*, ed. Michel Haar (1983): 419–30; translated as "*Geschlect*: Sexual Difference, Ontological Difference," *Research in Phenomenology* 13, no. 1 (1983): 65–83.

2. Martin Heidegger, GA 26. *Metaphysische Anfangsgründe der Logik im Ausgang von Leibniz* (1928), ed. Klaus Held (1978) 1990 (2nd rev. ed.), 2007 (3d rev. ed.); *The Metaphysical Foundations of Logic* trans. Michael Heim (Bloomington: Indiana University Press, 1984).

3. Martin Heidegger, GA 63. *Ontologie. Hermeneutik der Faktizität* (1923), ed. Käte Bröcker-Oltmanns, 1988; *Ontology—The Hermeneutics of Facticity*, trans. John Van Buren (Bloomington: Indiana University Press, 1999).

4. Heidegger, *Ontology—The Hermeneutics of Facticity*, 18.

5. Heidegger, *Ontology—The Hermeneutics of Facticity*, 16.

6. I understand sex/gender as a composite of sexual difference, a difference that is at once ontological and political, where "sex is always already gender" and where "sex is whatever an entity whose decisions are backed by the force of the law says it is." See Judith Butler, *Gender Trouble* (New York: Routledge, 1999), 10–11 and Paisley Currah, *Sex Is as Sex Does: Governing Transgender Identity* (New York: NYU Press, 2022), 9. See the "Introduction" for a further clarification of what I intend by sex/gender.

7. Heidegger, *Ontology—The Hermeneutics of Facticity*, 18.

8. Heidegger, *Ontologie: Hermeneutik der Faktizität*, 22. Thanks to Jeffrey Gower for confirming this translation for me.

9. According to Genesis, "Man ought not cover his head," because he was made in the glory and likeness of God. Woman, however, was made in the glory of man. She must cover her head to show submission to him. Hair has also been a symbol of seduction, so woman must cover her head lest she shame herself by attracting men.

10. Heidegger, *Ontology—The Hermeneutics of Facticity*, 35.

11. Heidegger, *Ontology—The Hermeneutics of Facticity*, 86.

12. Heidegger, *Ontology—The Hermeneutics of Facticity*, 9.

13. Saint Augustin. "La Trinité, Livre XII, 10," trad. par Sophie Dupuy-Trudelle dans *Philosophie, Catéchèse, Polémique, Œuvres III*, ed. publiée sous la direction de Lucien Jerphagnon (Paris: Gallimard, 2002).

14. See Martin Heidegger, GA 2. *Sein und Zeit* (1927), ed. Friedrich Wilhelm von Herrmann, 1977; *Being and Time*, trans. John Macquarrie and Edward Robinson (Oxford, UK: Blackwell, 1962), 284.

15. Interestingly, Arendt further notes that, according to Genesis, "the multitude of human beings becomes the result of multiplication." In GA 26, when Heidegger argues for a certain sexed/gendered neutrality of Dasein, he highlights how the dispersion of Dasein into sex/gender is the affair of "multiplication" rather than "multiplicity." See Hannah Arendt, *The Human Condition* (Chicago, IL: University of Chicago Press, 1998), 8.

16. I previously discussed Heidegger's question "Problem: What is Woman" in "Heidegger's Sexless Community: *Ni homme ni femme—c'est un Dasein*," Heidegger Circle Proceedings, Goucher College (2018) and "Heidegger on Being a Sexed or Gendered Human Being," Invited Symposium in *Gatherings: The Heidegger Circle Annual* 12 (2022).

17. Kevin Aho, "Gender and Time: Revisiting the Question of Dasein's Neutrality," *Epoché* 12, no. 1 (Fall 2007): 137–55.

18. Heidegger, *Being and Time*, 374.

19. John Haugeland, Dasein *Disclosed: John Haugeland's Heidegger*, ed. Joseph Rouse (Cambridge, MA: Harvard University Press, 2013).

20. Trish Glazebrook, "Heidegger and Ecofeminism," in *Feminist Interpretations of Martin Heidegger*, ed. Nancy J. Holland and Patricia Huntington (University Park: Penn State University Press, 2001), 233.

21. Kevin Aho, "Gender and Time: Revisiting the Question of Dasein's Neutrality," 144.

22. The "second sex" is a reference to Simone de Beauvoir and her insight that "man" is defined as the neutral standard, whereas "woman" as the "second sex" is always defined as other in relation to man. Feminist scholars have critiqued Heidegger for passing off his masculine viewpoint as one of "neutrality." Here are a few examples: Luce Irigaray argues that Heidegger's philosophy is one of phallogocentrism that forgets the feminine. Carol Bigwood also highlights the suppression of the "feminine" by technology and Western culture, in general—though Bigwood does

find paths in Heidegger's later thought that opens up the question of the "feminine." Tina Chanter accuses Heidegger of focusing on work-oriented tasks at the expense of issues such as sexuality and eroticism. Nancy J. Holland and Patricia Huntington edited a volume, *Feminist Interpretations of Martin* Heidegger, that provides a range of chapters that explore "the feminine" in Heidegger's work. Huntington also wrote a monograph, *Ecstatic Subjects, Utopia, and Recognition: Kristeva, Heidegger, Irigaray*, where she undergirds his masculine ethos. Anne O'Byrne illuminates Heidegger's inability to address the significance of natality and birth in his discussion of finitude. Simone de Beauvoir, *The Second Sex* (New York: Random House, 1991); Luce Irigaray, *The Forgetting of Air in Martin Heidegger*, trans. Mary Beth Mader (Austin, TX: University of Texas Press, 1999); Carol Bigwood, *Earth Muse: Feminism, Nature, and Art* (Philadelphia: Temple University Press, 1993); Tina Chanter, "The Problematic Normatives Assumptions of Heidegger's Ontology," *Feminist Interpretations of Martin Heidegger*, ed. Nancy J. Holland and Patricia Huntington (University Park: Penn State University Press, 2001): 73–108; Patricia Huntington, *Ecstatic Subjects, Utopia, and Recognition: Kristeva, Heidegger, Irigaray* (Albany: SUNY Press, 1998); and Anne O'Byrne, *Natality and Finitude* (Bloomington and Indianapolis: Indiana University Press, 2010).

23. Heidegger, *Metaphysical Foundations of Logic*, 18–21.

24. Heidegger, *Metaphysical Foundations of Logic*, 135–36.

25. Heidegger, *Metaphysical Foundations of Logic*, 166.

26. Heidegger, *Being and Time*, 184–85.

27. Martin Heidegger, GA 9. *Wegmarken* (1919–1961). Ed. Friedrich-Wilhelm von Herrmann (1976) 1996 (rev. ed.); "On the Essence of Ground," in *Pathmarks*, ed. William McNeill (Cambridge, UK: Cambridge University Press, 1998), 123.

28. In a mode of circumspective concern, I am engaged with my surroundings via a practical involvement where things are "ready-to-hand" or via a theoretical examination where things become "present-at-hand." Heidegger uses the example of a hammer to demonstrate how we typically deal with objects in our environment (that form our world). For the most part, we view objects in the world in terms of their equipmental being, as having some sort of significance in terms of the purpose they serve; they are viewed as things that are "ready-to-hand." A hammer is "ready-to-hand" in my practical involvement with it, as I use it to drive a nail into a board as part of a larger project of, say, building a birdhouse. As "ready-to-hand" the hammer *as* hammer escapes any theoretical understanding of what this thing actually is in terms of what it has the potential to be. However, if the head were to fall off the hammer, and I were no longer able to use it within the context of my larger project, the hammer is "there" before me *as* a hammer. The hammer becomes "present-at-hand." When things are "present-at-hand" they pose a theoretical problem in that they do not automatically appear as intelligible within my world. There is something positive about this bare existent state of "present-at-handness" in that meaning is not yet determined. In this moment, I am in the process of world-forming as I try to understand a nexus

of relations within which to incorporate it into my world. Heidegger describes our relations to others, in terms of how they matter, as one of solicitude. Such relations can be governed by an inauthentic enaction or authentic enaction of care. In chapter 1, I discuss the distinction between authentic ("leaping ahead") and inauthentic ("leaping in") modes of caring within the context of giving birth. These forms of solicitude are "positive" in that the others with whom I am engaging are not "passed by." Heidegger states, "Being for, or against, or without one another, passing one another by, not 'mattering' to one another—these are possible ways of solicitude [. . . .] With regard to its positive modes, solicitude has two extreme possibilities. It can, as it were, take away 'care' from the Other and put itself in his position in concern: it can *leap in* for him. This kind of solicitude takes over for the Other that with which he is to concern himself [. . . .] In contrast to this, there is also the possibility of a kind of solicitude which does not so much leap in for the Other as *leap ahead* of him [*ihm vorausspringt*] in his existentiell potentiality-for-Being, not in order to take away his 'care' but rather to give it back to him authentically as such for the first time." See Heidegger, *Being and Time*, 158–59.

29. Heidegger states, "In being governed by nature, mythic Dasein has the peculiarity of not being conscious of itself with regard to its mode of being (which is not to say that mythic Dasein lacks self-awareness). But it also belongs essentially to factical dissemination that thrownness and captivation remain deeply hidden from it, and in this way the simplicity and 'carelessness' of an absolute sustenance from nature arise in Dasein." Thus, it is not that mythic Dasein lacks care (that temporal affective structure is present) but that it lacks the ability to engage with and enact its structure of care positively and authentically. Heidegger, *The Metaphysical Foundations of Logic*, 138.

30. Heidegger, "On the Essence of Ground," 122.
31. Heidegger, *Being and Time*, 114–19.
32. Derrida, "*Geschlect*: Sexual Difference, Ontological Difference," 73.
33. Heidegger, *The Metaphysical Foundations of Logic*, 136–37.
34. Derrida, "*Geschlect*: Sexual Difference, Ontological Difference," 71.
35. Glazebrook, "Heidegger and Ecofeminism," 231.
36. Derrida, "*Geschlect*: Sexual Difference, Ontological Difference," 69.
37. Judith Butler, *Gender Trouble* (New York and London: Routledge, 1990): 10–11.
38. Ephraim Das Janssen, *Phenomenal Gender: What Transgender Experience Discloses* (Bloomington: Indiana University Press, 2017), 73.
39. Heidegger, "Language in the Poem: A Discussion on Georg Trakl's Poetic Work," 195.
40. Heidegger, *The Metaphysical Foundations of Logic*, 137.
41. Heidegger, *The Metaphysical Foundations of Logic*, 139.
42. Heath Massey, *The Origin of Time: Heidegger and Bergson* (Albany: SUNY Press, 2015).

43. Charles Darwin, *The Descent of Man, and Selection in Relation to Sex* (Westminster, UK: Penguin, 2004).

44. Martin Heidegger, GA 29/30. *Die Grundbegriffe der Metaphysik: Welt—Endlichkeit—Einsamkeit* (1929–30), ed. Friedrich-Wilhelm von Herrmann, 1983; *The Fundamental Concepts of Metaphysics: World, Finitude, Solitude*, trans. William McNeill and Nicholas Walker (Bloomington: Indiana University Press, 1995), 285.

45. Michael E. Zimmerman, "Ontical Craving versus Ontological Desire," *From Phenomenology to Thought, Errancy, and Desire*, ed. Babette Babich (Dordrecht, Germany: Springer, 1995): 501–523.

46. Heidegger, "On the Essence of Ground," 135.

47. As Brett Buchanan highlights, Levinas associates Heidegger's notion of Dasein and the struggle for being with Darwin and an animal's struggle for life. Levinas asserts, "I do not know at what moment the human appears, but what I want to emphasize is that the human breaks with pure being. A being is something that is attached to being, to its own being. That is Darwin's idea. The being of animals is a struggle for life. A struggle for life without ethics. It is a question of might. Heidegger says at the beginning of Being and Time that Dasein is a being who in his being is concerned for this being itself. That's Darwin's idea: the living being struggles for life. The aim of being is being itself." Emmanuel Levinas, "The Paradox of Morality: An Interview with Emmanuel Levinas," interview by Tamra Wright, Peter Hughes, and Alison Ainley, trans. Andrew Benjamin and Tamra Wright, *The Provocation of Levinas: Rethinking the Other*, ed. Robert Bernasconi and David Wood (New York: Routledge, 1988), 172. As cited by, Brett Buchanan, *Onto-Ethologies: The Animal Environments of Uexkull, Heidegger, Merleau-Ponty, and Deleuze* (Albany: SUNY Press, 2008), 49.

48. Heidegger, *Being and Time*, 71.

49. Heidegger, *Being and Time*, 225.

50. Heidegger, *Being and Time*, 73.

51. Heidegger, *Being and Time*, 84.

52. Heidegger, *The Fundamental Concepts of Metaphysics: World, Finitude, Solitude*, 378. As cited by Buchanan, *Onto-Ethologies: The Animal Environments of Uexkull, Heidegger, Merleau-Ponty, and Deleuze*, 46.

53. Heidegger, *Being and Time*, 71.

54. Heidegger, "On the Essence of Ground," 135.

55. Martin Heidegger, *Der Ursprung des Kunstwerkes*, ed. H. G. Gadamer (Stuttgart, Germany: P. Reclam, 1960); "The Origin of the Work of Art," trans. Albert Hofstadter in David Farrell Krell, ed., *Basic Writings* (San Francisco, CA: Harper Collins, 1993), 202.

56. François Jacob, "Heidegger and Darwin: The As-Structure and Variability Per Se," in *The Possible and the Actual* (New York: Pantheon, 1982), 35. Charles Darwin, *On the Origin of Species by Means of Natural Selection, or the Preservation of Favoured Races in the Struggle for Life* (1859), 194.

57. Heidegger, "Origin of the Work of Art," 187.
58. Heidegger, "Origin of the Work of Art," 142.
59. Heidegger, "Origin of the Work of Art," 203.
60. Derrida, "*Geschlect:* Sexual difference, Ontological difference," 74.
61. Heidegger, *The Metaphysical Foundations of Logic*, 137.
62. Heidegger, *The Metaphysical Foundations of Logic*, 137.
63. See Elizabeth Grosz, *Becoming Undone: Darwinian Reflections on Life, Politics, and Art* (Durham, NC: Duke University Press, 2011); Stephen Seely, "Does Life Have (a) Sex? Thinking Ontology and Sexual Difference with Irigaray and Simondon," in *Feminist Philosophies of Life* (Montreal. QC, and Kingston, ON: McGill-Queen's University Press, 2016), and Gibert Simondon, *L'individuation à la lumiere des notions de forme et d'information* (Grenoble, France: Jérôme Millon, 2017.
64. Grosz, *Becoming Undone: Darwinian Reflections*, 69.
65. Grosz, *Becoming Undone: Darwinian Reflections*, 146.
66. Heidegger, *Metaphysical Foundations of Logic*, 137.
67. Ernst Cassirer and Martin Heidegger, *Débat sur le Kantisme et la philosophie (Davos, mars 1929) et Autres textes de 1929–1931*, présentés par Pierre Aubenque, trad. de l'allemand par P. Aubenque, J. M. Fataud, and P. Quillet (Paris: Beauchesne, 1972), 44.
68. See Richard R. Askay, "Heidegger, the Body, and the French Philosophers," *Continental Philosophy Review* 32 (1999): 29–35.
69. Heidegger, *Being and Time*, 109. Heidegger states, "Bodiliness hides a whole problematic of its own, though we will not deal with it here."
70. Martin Heidegger, GA 89. Zollikoner *Seminare* (1959–1969), ed. Peter Trawny, 2017; *Zollikon Seminars: Protocols—Conversations—Letters*, trans. Franz Mayr and Richard Askay (Evanston, IL: Northwestern University Press, 2001), 87.
71. Derrida, "*Geschlect:* Sexual Difference, Ontological Difference," 75.
72. Derrida, "*Geschlect:* Sexual Difference, Ontological Difference," 75.

Chapter 3

1. Maggie Nelson states, "One of the most annoying things about hearing the refrain "same-sex marriage" over and over again is that I don't know many—if any—queers who think of their desire's main feature as being "same-sex." Maggie Nelson, *The Argonauts* (Minneapolis, MN: Graywolf Press, 2015).
2. Before the passage of this law, access to assisted reproductive technology was reserved for married heterosexual couples or heterosexual couples who could prove a cohabitation of at least two years. Access was only permitted on the grounds of infertility, or in the case of medical conditions whereby technology could prevent the transmission of certain genetic predispositions. In France, surrogacy is illegal. This is why the ART extension is permitted to single women and lesbians and not gay couples.

3. The first two sections of this chapter, "Framing" and "Reproductive Enframing," were previously published as "Queering Gestell: Thinking outside Butler's Frames and inside Belu's Reproductive Enframing," in *Journal of Speculative Philosophy*, SPEP Issue, 36, no. 3 (2022): 194–205, https://doi.org/10.5325/jspecphil.36.2.0194. Due to space constraints, I was unable to offer a detailed account of the way that race figures into discussions of reproductive enframing and assisted reproductive technology. In section 3, "Coda: Race as Technology in Reproductive Enframing," I provide such an analysis. Adding a coda rather than integrating a discussion of race into the previous article may be problematic in that it may suggest that race is separate from concerns of sex/gender. This is not my intention. I decided to add a coda as a means to preserve the original text as it had previously been published.

4. Manon Beury, "En couple aves une femme trans, je suis exclue de la 'PMA pour toutes'" *Libération* (August 4, 2020). Last accessed April 19, 2021, https://www.liberation.fr/debats/2020/08/04/en-couple-avec-une-femme-trans-je-suis-exclue-de-la-pma-pour-toutes_1795938/.

5. Sylviane Agacinski, "Deux mères = un père?" *Le Monde*, February 3, 2013.

6. I usually dislike it when women are associated with famous men, as it discredits their existence as beings in themselves. However, I reference Agacinski's link to Jospin here to highlight her political sway. Agacinski is a public intellectual who is given powerful platforms.

7. "Heidegger, une pensée brûlante," *Cinéma Étoile Saint-Germain-des-Prés*, December 8, 2013.

8. Sylviane Agacinski, *Corps en Miettes* (Paris: Flammarion, 2013). This notion of "not being behind" is intriguing as the linear progression of the French enlightenment has been used elsewhere to declare the "backwardness" of Muslim women who choose to veil in opposition to liberated French women. Judith Butler references how a collective "modern" mentality works to exclude those not living in the "progressive" time of the "now" in "Sexual Politics, Torture, and Secular Time," *Frames of War* (London: Verso Books, 2009), 115.

9. Sylviane Agacinski, *Politique des sexes* (Paris: Éditions du Seuil, 2001), 13.

10. Judith Butler, *Frames of War: When Is Life Grievable?* (London and New York: Verso, 2009), 112.

11. Sara Ahmed, *Queer Phenomenology: Orientations, Objects, Others* (Durham, NC and London: Duke University Press, 2006), 2.

12. Martin Heidegger, GA 2. *Sein und Zeit* (1927), ed. Friedrich Wilhelm von Herrmann, 1977; *Being and Time* trans. John Macquarrie and Edward Robinson (Oxford, UK: Blackwell, 1962).

13. See Emily Martin, "The Egg and the Sperm: How Science Has Constructed a Romance Based on Stereotypical Male-Female Roles," *Signs* 16, no. 3 (1991): 485–501; and Nancy Tuana, "The Weaker Seed: The Sexist Bias of Reproductive Theory," *Hypatia* 3, no. 1 (1988): 35–59.

14. Lisa Duggan, *The New Homonormativity: The Sexual Politics of Neoliberalism* (Durham, NC and London: Duke University Press, 2002).

15. Benjamin T. Singer, "From the Medical Gaze to Sublime Mutations: The Ethics of (Re)Viewing Non-Normative Body Images," *The Transgender Studies Reader*, ed. Susan Stryker and Stephen Whittle (New York: Routledge, 2006), 601–20.

16. Martin Heidegger, GA 7. *Vorträge und Aufsätze* (1936–1953), ed. Friedrich-Wilhelm von Herrmann, 2000; "The Question Concerning Technology," trans. William Lovitt, in David Farrell Krell, ed., *Basic Writings* (San Francisco, CA: Harper Collins, 1993), 311–41.

17. Dana S. Belu, *Heidegger, Reproductive Technology, and the Motherless Age* (Cham, Switzerland: Palgrave Macmillan, 2017).

18. Belu, *Heidegger, Reproductive Technology, and the Motherless Age*, 62.

19. *In vitro gametogenesis* is an example of how our genetic material can be other than what it is, as this process allows scientists to create egglike and spermlike cells from adult stem cells. Such cells can come from one person regardless of sex/gender and upsets any strict correlation between sexual difference and reproductive difference.

20. Belu, *Heidegger, Reproductive Technology, and the Motherless Age*, 65.

21. Belu, *Heidegger, Reproductive Technology, and the Motherless Age*, 7.

22. This is not to say that all forms of assisted reproductive technology should be permitted. I do not think that all forms of technology, simply by virtue of their being thought into existence, have the right to exist. I am, however, emphasizing the complexity of technology as something other than "human activity" or "mere instrumentality." Technology as ideology goes beyond mere regulation of technological apparatuses.

23. Martin Heidegger, *Der Ursprung des Kunstwerkes*, ed. H. G. Gadamer (Stuttgart, Germany: P. Reclam, 1960); "The Origin of the Work of Art," trans. Albert Hofstadter, in David Farrell Krell, ed., *Basic Writings* (San Francisco, CA: Harper Collins, 1993), 333.

24. Heidegger, "The Origin of the Work of Art."

25. Robyn Ferrell, *Copula: Sexual Technologies, Reproductive Powers* (Albany: SUNY Press, 2006).

26. Rachel Epstein, "Space invaders: Queer and Trans Bodies in Fertility Clinics," *Sexualities* 21, no. 7 (2018): 1039–58. Nirmal Puwar, *Space Invaders: Race, Gender, and Bodies Out of Place* (London: Bloomsbury, 2004).

27. Shannon Winnubst, *Queering Freedom* (Bloomington: Indiana University. Press, 2006).

28. Heidegger uses the example of a hammer to demonstrate how we typically deal with objects in our environment/in our world. For the most part, we view objects in the world in terms of their equipmental being, as having some sort of significance in terms of the purpose they serve; they are viewed as things that are "ready-to-hand." A hammer is "ready-to-hand" in my practical involvement with it, as I use it to drive a nail into a board as part of a larger project of, say, building a birdhouse. As "ready-to-hand" the hammer *as* hammer escapes any theoretical understanding of what this thing actually is (or has the potential to be). However,

if the head were to fall off the hammer, and I were no longer able to use it within the context of my larger project, the hammer is "there" before me *as* a hammer. The hammer becomes "present-at-hand." When things are "present-at-hand" they pose a theoretical problem in that they do not automatically appear as intelligible within my world. There is something positive about this bare existent state of "present-at-handness," in that meaning is not yet predetermined. For a discussion of the distinction between "ready-to-hand" and "present-at-hand," see Heidegger, *Being and Time*, 70–74.

29. Michel Foucault, *The History of Sexuality, Vol. I: An Introduction* (New York: Vintage, 1990).

30. Heidegger, "The Question Concerning Technology," 313.

31. Heidegger, "The Question Concerning Technology," 319.

32. Heidegger, "The Question Concerning Technology," 329.

33. Camisha A. Russell, *The Assisted Reproduction of Race*, 73.

34. Camisha A. Russell, *The Assisted Reproduction of Race*, 96. Russell references Miguel De Beistegui, *The New Heidegger* (London: Continuum, 2005), 98.

35. For example, Heidegger asserts, "Only someone who is German can in an originary new way poetize being and say being—he alone will conquer anew the essence of θεωρία [theory, beholding] and finally create *logic*." Martin Heidegger, GA 94. *Überlegungen II–VI (Schwarze Hefte 1931–1938)*, ed. Peter Trawny, 2014; *Ponderings II–VI, Black Notebooks 1931–1938*, trans. Richard Rojcewicz (Bloomington and Indianapolis: Indiana University Press, 2016), 21.

36. Heidegger, *Ponderings II–VI Black Notebooks 1931–1938*, 342.

37. Heidegger asserts, "As soon as what is unconcealed no longer concerns man even as object, but exclusively as standing-reserve, and man in the midst of objectlessness is nothing but the orderer of the standing-reserve, then he comes to the very brink of a precipitous fall; that is, he comes to the point where he himself will have to be taken as standing-reserve." Heidegger, "The Question Concerning Technology," 332.

38. Tina Chanter, "The Problematic Normatives Assumptions of Heidegger's Ontology," *Feminist Interpretations of Martin Heidegger*, ed. Nancy J. Holland and Patricia Huntington (University Park: Penn State University Press, 2001), 82.

39. Holland cites "sexuality" and "eroticism" as issues that Heidegger neglects. She asserts that by focusing on interactions that are task-oriented, he fails to account for things done out of pleasure. By referencing "sexuality" and "eroticism," I do not wish to conflate sexuality with acts of sex that lead to reproduction, but nor do I want to completely distinguish the two. For example, Agacinski sets up such a distinction when she defines sexuality as a matter of desire and sexual difference as a question of generation. Such a contrast works to create a separation between heteronormative reproductive bodies and queer nonreproductive bodies.

40. Martin Heidegger, N3 *Nietzsche*, vol. 3, *The Will to Power as Knowledge and Metaphysics*, ed. and trans. Joan Stambaugh, David Farrell Krell, and Frank A. Capuzzi (San Francisco, CA: Harper, 1991), 231.

41. For a fuller discussion of how philosophers, including Heidegger, tend to privilege finitude at the expense of our birth, see Anne O'Byrne, *Natality and Finitude* (Bloomington and Indianapolis: Indiana University Press, 2010).
42. Heidegger, *Being and Time*, 48.
43. Heidegger, "The Question Concerning Technology," 313–17.
44. Lorraine Markotic, "Paternity, Enframing, and a New Revealing: O'Brien's Philosophy of Reproduction and Heidegger's Critique of Technology," *Hypatia* 31, no. 1 (2016): 123–24.
45. Heidegger, "The Question Concerning Technology," 317.
46. See Plato, *Republic*, trans. Paul Shorey, book V, section I, in *The Collected Dialogues*, ed. Edith Hamilton and Huntington Cairns (Princeton, NJ: Princeton University. Press, 2005).
47. Heidegger states, "Uncovering is a way of Being for Being-in-the-world. Circumspective concern, or even that concern in which we tarry and look at something, uncovers entities within-the-world." Heidegger, *Being and Time*, 263.
48. Robert Bernasconi, "Who Invented the Concept of Race," in *Theories of Race and Racism: A Reader*, 2nd ed. (Milton Park: Taylor & Francis, 2020), 84.
49. Sylvia Wynter, "Unsettling the Coloniality of Being/Power/Truth/Freedom: Towards the Human, after Man, Its Overrepresentation—An Argument," *New Centennial Review* 3, mo. 3 (2003): 264.
50. Wynter, "Unsettling the Coloniality," 264. Aníbal Quijano, "Qué tal Raza!" Paper presented at the Conference of Coloniality Working Group, at SUNY-Binghamton, 2000.
51. Quijano asserts that gender has a "biogenetically determined anatomical differential correlate." Presumably, Quijano views gender as "social sex" where sex is defined by determined anatomical criteria. In chapter 2, "Problem: What Is Woman? The Hermeneutics of Sex/Gender Facticity," I speak of sex/gender as collapsible terms, following Butler's argument that "sex is always already gender." In this book, I am not interested in "grounding" definitions of sex or gender, and I speak of them as related terms insofar as I view them both as historically contingent.
52. Ann Laura Stoler, *Race and the Education of Desire: Foucault's History of Sexuality and the Colonial Order of Things* (Durham, NC: Duke University Press, 1995), 184.
53. Dorothy Roberts, *Killing the Black Body: Race, Reproduction, and the Meaning of Liberty* (New York: Vintage, 1999).
54. Dorothy Roberts, *Killing the Black Body: Race, Reproduction, and the Meaning of Liberty*, 10–19.
55. Camisha A. Russell, *The Assisted Reproduction of Race*, 39.
56. Laurence Brunet, "Procréations médicalement assistées et catégories 'ethno-raciales': l'enjeu de la ressemblance," *Les catégories ethno-raciales à l'ère des biotechnologies* (Paris: Société de législation compare, 2011), 135–54.
57. Camisha A. Russell, *The Assisted Reproduction of Race*, 42.

58. Camisha A. Russell, *The Assisted Reproduction of Race*, 43.
59. Kimberlé Crenshaw, "The Urgency of Intersectionality," *TEDWomen* 2016.
60. Camisha A. Russell, *The Assisted Reproduction of Race*, 12.
61. International Fertility Law Group, "Why Is There a Shortage of Black Egg Donors and Black Sperm Donors," March 12, 2021, last accessed, April 14, 2022, https://www.iflg.net/black-egg-donor-sperm-donor-shortage/.
62. Jasbir K. Puar, "Homonationalism as Assemblage: Viral Travels, Affective Sexualities," *Jindal Global Law Review* 4, no. 2 (2003): 34.
63. Jasbir K. Puar, "Homonationalism as Assemblage: Viral Travels, Affective Sexualities," 35.
64. The Napoleon Series Archive, "French Civil Code," trans. George Spence. London: William Benning, 1827, https://www.napoleonseries.org/research/government/code/book1/c_title05.html, last accessed August 15, 2023.
65. The following message was placed under the section "Who We Are?" in a now defunct *Manif pour tous* webpage https://www.lamanifpourtous.fr/fr/qui-sommes-nous/notre-message: "Le projet de loi 'Mariage pour tous' bouleverse le Code civil en supprimant systématiquement les mots de 'mari' et de 'femme,' de 'père' et de 'mère,' au profit de termes asexués, indifférenciés (notamment 'parents'). Ce projet entend ainsi supprimer légalement l'altérité sexuelle et remettre en cause le fondement de l'identité humaine: la différence sexuelle et la filiation en résultant. Il ouvre la voie à une nouvelle filiation 'sociale,' sans rapport avec la réalité humaine. Il crée le cadre d'un nouvel ordre anthropologique, fondé non plus sur le sexe mais sur le genre, la préférence sexuelle." The current "Who We Are?" section of their new webpage reiterates this emphasis on sexual difference, indicating "La Manif Pour Tous défend le mariage homme-femme, le couple homme-femme étant le seul susceptible de concevoir un enfant, celui-ci ayant profondément besoin de connaître ceux qui ont lui donné la vie et, dans la mesure du possible, d'être élevé par eux (art. 7 de la CIDE)." Manif pour tous, "Qui sommes-nous?," https://www.lamanifpourtous.fr/qui-sommes-nous/le-mouvement, last accessed August 15, 2023.
66. Bruno Perreau, *Queer Theory The French Response* (Stanford, CA: Stanford University Press, 2016), 4–5.
67. Bruno Perreau, *Queer Theory The French Response*, 124–25.
68. Bruno Perreau, *Queer Theory The French Response*, 124.
69. While I understand there are several different forms of veiling (burqa, hijab, niqab), I use the general term *veiled woman* as a trope. Political debates do not often take these differences into account, and "the veil" has come to represent a univocal symbol of oppression.
70. Joan W. Scott, *The Politics of the Veil* (Princeton, NJ: Princeton University Press, 2007).
71. Michel Mercier, *Colette au Temps de Claudine* (Paris: Livre de Poche, 2004), 15.

72. "Hungary to Provide Free Fertility Treatment to Boost Population," *BBC News*, January 10, 2020, last accessed April 24, 2022, https://www.bbc.com/news/world-europe-51061499.

73. Camisha A. Russell, *The Assisted Reproduction of Race*, 69.

74. Andrew J. Mitchell, *The Fourfold: Reading the Late* Heidegger (Evanston, IL: Northwestern University Press, 2015), 50.

75. Michel Foucault, *The History of Sexuality Vol. I: An Introduction* (New York: Vintage, 1990).

76. Martin Heidegger, "The Way to Language," trans. Peter Hertz (revised by David Farrell Krell), *Basic Writings*, ed. David Farrell Krell (San Francisco, CA: Harper Collins, 1993), 408–9.

77. Martin Heidegger, "The Way to Language," 420–42.

78. Heidegger, "The Origin of the Work of Art," 202.

79. Heidegger, "The Origin of the Work of Art," 203.

80. Heidegger, "The Question Concerning Technology," 311.

81. Camisha A. Russell, *The Assisted Reproduction of Race*, 51.

Chapter 4

1. Grumet, *Bitter Milk: Women and Teaching*, 132.

2. Madeleine R. Grumet, *Bitter Milk: Women and Teaching* (Amherst: University of Massachusetts Press, 1988), xvi.

3. Martin Heidegger, GA 12, *Unterwegs zur Sprache* (1950–1959), ed. Friedrich-Wilhelm von Herrmann, 1985; *On the Way to Language*, trans. Peter D. Hertz (San Francisco, CA: Harper & Row, 1982), 29.

4. John D. Caputo, *Hermeneutics: Facts and Interpretation in the Age of Information* (London: Penguin, 2018), 16.

5. Hermes fostered and saved many children, including Dionysus (see Pseudo-Apollodorus, *Bibliotheca* 3, 28–29, trans. Aldrich Greek, mythographer, second century AD); Asklepios (see Pausanias, *Description of Greece* 2. 26. 6, trans. Jones, Greek travelogue, second century AD); Aristaios (see Pindar, *Pythian* Ode 9, ant 3, trans. Conway, Greek lyric, fifth century BC); Dioskouroi (see Pausanias, *Description of Greece* 3. 26. 2, trans. Jones, Greek travelogue, second century AD); and Helene (see Pseudo-Hyginus, *Astronomica* 2. 7, trans. Grant, Roman mythographer, second century AD). Also, see the Theoi Project, 2000–2019, https://www.theoi.com/Olympios/HermesMyths3.html#Fostering, last accessed October 15, 2020.

6. Marion Grau, "Putting Hermes Back into Hermeneutics" *Refiguring Theological Hermeneutics: Hermes, Trickster, Fool* (New York: Palgrave Macmillan, 2014), 81 and Vincent Crapanzano, *Hermes' Dilemma and Hamlet's Desire: On the Epistemology of Interpretation* (Cambridge, MA: Harvard University Press, 1992), 44.

7. Martin Heidegger, "Brief über den Humanismus," *Wegmarken* (Frankfurt am Main, Germany: Vittorio Klostermann Verlag, 1967), 145–94; "Letter on Humanism," *Basic Writings*, ed. David Farrell Krell (San Francisco, CA: Harper Collins, 1993), 245.

8. French thinkers such as Sartre, De Waelhens, Merleau-Ponty, Ricœur, and Levinas have reproached Heidegger for his neglect of the body.

9. When I refer to "banking systems of education," I am thinking about bell hooks's *Teaching to Transgress: Education as the Practice of Freedom*. Here, hooks borrows Paolo Freire's "banking concept of education." See bell hooks, *Teaching to Transgress: Education as the Practice of Freedom* (New York and London: Routledge, 1994).

10. Martin Heidegger, GA 63. *Ontologie. Hermeneutik der Faktizität* (1923), ed. Käte Bröcker-Oltmanns, 1988; *Ontology—The Hermeneutics of Facticity*, trans. John van Buren (Bloomington: Indiana University Press, 2008), 18.

11. Saint Augustin, "La Trinité, Livre XII, 10," trad. par Sophie Dupuy-Trudelle dans *Philosophie, Catéchèse, Polémique, Œuvres III*, ed. publiée sous la direction de Lucien Jerphagnon (Paris: Gallimard, 2002).

12. Simone de Beauvoir, *The Second Sex*, trans. H. M. Parshley (New York: Random House, 1974).

13. Plato, *Symposium*, trans. Alexander Nehamas and Paul Woodruff (Indianapolis, IN and Cambridge, UK: Hackett, 1989).

14. Grumet, *Bitter Milk: Women and Teaching*, 84.

15. Nonnus, *Dionysiaca*, book 9.28, trans. W. H. D. Rouse (Greek epic fifth century AD)., https://www.theoi.com/Text/NonnusDionysiaca9.html.

16. Apollonius Rhodius, *Argonautica*, book 4, trans. E. V. Rieu (Greek epic, third century BC), https://www.theoi.com/Olympios/HermesMyths3.html#Fostering.

17. Nonnus, *Dionysiaca*, Book 9.28, trans. W. H. D. Rouse (Greek epic fifth century AD), https://www.theoi.com/Text/NonnusDionysiaca9.html.

18. Mathias Warnes, "Heidegger and the Festival of Being: From the Bridal Festival to the Round Dance," PhD diss., University of British Columbia (2012), 16.

19. Martin Heidegger, N1 *Nietzsche*, vol. 1: *The Will to Power as Art*, ed. and trans. Joan Stambaugh, David Farrell Krell, and Frank A. Capuzzi (San Francisco, CA: Harper, 1991), 88.

20. Sara Carrigan Wooten, "Whispers in the Halls: Exploring the Mother/Teacher in Madeleine Grumet's *Bitter Milk: Women and Teaching*," *Journal of Curriculum Theorizing* 27, no. 3 (2011).

21. Grumet, *Bitter Milk: Women and Teaching*, 133.

22. When I refer to "mother tongue," I am referencing Julia Kristeva's notion of the semiotic, the prelinguistic stage associated with the maternal. Grumet makes note of Kristeva and takes care to highlight that both authors, while accenting the importance of the maternal, are not advocating for a return to the private realm at the expense of the public and political. See Julia Kristeva, *Revolution in Poetic Language*, trans. Margaret Waller (New York: Columbia University Press, 1984).

23. Martin Heidegger, "The Way to Language," trans. Peter Hertz (revised by David Farrell Krell), *Basic Writings* ed. David Farrell Krell (San Francisco, CA: Harper Collins, 1993), 404.

24. Heidegger, "Letter on Humanism," 237.

25. Carol Hay, "Girlfriend, Mother, Professor," in *The Stone, New York Times Opinionator* (January 25, 2016).

26. Ben Schmidt, "Gendered Language in Teaching Reviews: Interactive Chart," https://benschmidt.org/profGender.

27. Schmidt, "Gendered Language in Teaching Reviews: Interactive Chart."

28. bell hooks, *Teaching to Transgress: Education as the Practice of Freedom* (New York and London: Routledge, 1994).

29. Martin Heidegger, GA 7. *Vorträge und Aufsätze* (1936–1953), ed. Friedrich-Wilhelm von Herrmann, 2000; "The Question Concerning Technology," trans. William Lovitt in David Farrell Krell, ed., *Basic Writings* (San Francisco, CA: Harper Collins, 1993), 323.

30. Ian Thomson, "Heidegger on Ontological Education, or: How We Become What We Are," *Inquiry* 44 (2001): 243–68.

31. Grumet, *Bitter Milk: Women and Teaching*, 62.

32. Martin Heidegger, GA 89. *Zollikoner Seminare* (1959–1969), ed. Peter Trawny, 2017; *Zollikon Seminars: Protocols—Conversations—Letters*, trans. Franz Mayr and Richard Askay (Evanston, IL: Northwestern University Press, 2001), 86–87.

33. Heidegger, *Zollikon Seminars: Protocols, Conversations, Letters*, 90–91.

34. Heidegger, *Zollikon Seminars: Protocols, Conversations, Letters*, 91.

35. Stephan Käufer, "Jaspers, Limit-Situations, and the Methodological Function of Authenticity," *Heidegger, Authenticity and the Self: Themes from Division Two of Being and Time*, ed. Denis McManus (London and New York: Routledge, 2015), 102.

36. John Haugeland, *Dasein Disclosed: John Haugeland's Heidegger*, ed. Joseph Rouse (Cambridge, MA: Harvard University Press, 2013).

37. Lauren Freeman, "Reconsidering Relational Autonomy: A Feminist Approach to Selfhood and the Other in the Thinking of Martin Heidegger," *Inquiry* 54, no. 4 (2011), 375. Freeman takes this quote from Martin Heidegger, *Kant and the Problem of Metaphyics*, trans. Richard Taft, 5th ed. (Bloomington: Indiana University Press, 1990), 165.

38. Anne O'Byrne, *Natality and Finitude* (Bloomington: Indiana University Press, 2010), 49.

Chapter 5

1. Throughout the *Black Notebooks*, Heidegger spells *being"* with a *y* (*beyng*).

2. In chapter 2, "Queering Gestell: Partial Enframing, Racial Breeding, and Assisted Reproductive Technology," I explore how breeding becomes ontologically

significant when race becomes a "self-conscious thought" rather than something that naturally evolves. I am re-referencing parts of the following quote:

> The breeding of human beings is not a taming in the sense of a suppression and hobbling of sensuality; rather, breeding is the accumulation and purification of energies in the univocity of the strictly controllable "automatism" of every activity. Only where the absolute subjectivity of will to power comes to be the truth of beings as a whole is the principle of a program of racial breeding possible; possible, that is, not merely on the basis of naturally evolving races, but in terms of the self-conscious thought of race. That is to say, the principle is metaphysically necessary. Just as Nietzsche's thought of will to power was ontological rather than biological, even more was his racial thought metaphysical rather than biological in meaning.

Martin Heidegger, N3 *Nietzsche*, vol. 3, *The Will to Power as Knowledge and Metaphysics*, ed. and trans. Joan Stambaugh, David Farrell Krell, and Frank A. Capuzzi (San Francisco, CA: Harper, 1991), 231.

3. Heidegger, *Ponderings II–VI: Black Notebooks 1931–1938*, 246.

4. Martin Heidegger, GA 26. *Metaphysische Anfangsgründe der Logik im Ausgang von Leibniz* (1928), ed. Klaus Held, 1978, 1990 (2nd rev. ed.), 2007 (3d rev. ed.); *The Metaphysical Foundations of Logic*, trans. Michael Heim (Bloomington: Indiana University Press, 1984), 139.

5. Marting Heidegger, GA 95. *Überlegungen VII–XI (Schwarze Hefte 1938–1939)*, ed. Peter Trawny, 2014; *Ponderings VII–XI: Black Notebooks 1938–1939*, trans. Richard Rojcewicz (Bloomington: Indiana University Press, 2017), 28. I argue that the "leap" Heidegger refers to here is in direct contestation of Darwin. Quoting Darwin, François Jacob notes, "for natural selection can act only by taking advantage of slight successive variations; she can never take a leap but must advance by the shortest and slowest steps." François Jacob, "Heidegger and Darwin: The As-Structure and Variability *Per Se*," *The Possible and the Actual* (New York: Pantheon, 1982), 35. Charles Darwin, *On the Origin of Species by Means of Natural Selection, or the Preservation of Favoured Races in the Struggle for Life* (London: John Murray, 1859), 194.

6. Heidegger, *Ponderings II–VI: Black Notebooks 1931–1938*, 107.

7. See Max Whyte, "'The Uses and Abuses of Nietzsche in the Third Reich: Alfred Baeumler's 'Heroic Realism,'" *Journal of Contemporary History* 43, no. 2 (2008): 171–94.

8. Heidegger, *Ponderings II–VI: Black Notebooks 1931–1938*, 132–33.

9. Nietzsche's Overman or *Übermensch* is a concept that first appears in *Thus Spoke Zarathustra*. Such a man is able to overcome nature and the human condition and become the creator of his own values. The Overman is characterized

by a manliness of spirit, and his ability to surpass the human condition, has been appropriated by proponents of eugenics who see him as a step up in the evolutionary chain.

10. As I will go on to discuss, according to Heidegger, any possible understanding of *beyng* gets concealed by culture, as an organization of lived experience. Such concealing happens as a "parrying of thrusts of being," an evading of the rare instances in history when an appropriation of beyng is possible. See Heidegger, *Ponderings VII–XI: Black Notebooks 1938–1939*, 3.

11. Friedrich Nietzsche, *Ecce Homo*, ed. Oscar Levy, trans. Anthony M. Ludovici and Paul V. Cohn (Project Gutenberg Ebook, 2016), 111.

12. Fredrik Appel, "The Übermensch's Consort: Nietzsche and the 'Eternal Feminine,'" *History of Political Thought* 18, no. 3 (1997): 521.

13. Sarah Kofman, "The Psychologist of the Eternal Feminine (Why I Write Such Good Books, 5)," *Yale French Studies* 87, "Another Look, Another Woman: Retranslations of French Feminism" (1995): 181.

14. As noted in chapter 1, in *OHF*, Heidegger analyzes Dasein via a hermeneutics of facticity. In such an analysis, he is interested in the "how" of Dasein's formation and not the "what" of Dasein's predetermined predicates. Heidegger moves away from a definition of Dasein that characterizes it in terms of dialectical relations (that is, man vs. woman) for dialectic turns the "how" of facticity (as an historical process) into an objective "what" (a stasis).

15. Heidegger, *Ponderings VII–XI: Black Notebooks 1938–1939*, 1.

16. Heidegger, *Ponderings VII–XI: Black Notebooks 1938–1939*, 3.

17. Heidegger, *Ponderings VII–XI: Black Notebooks 1938–1939*, 3.

18. Filippo Tommaso Marinetti, "The Futurist Manifesto," 1909, https://www.societyforasianart.org/sites/default/files/manifesto_futurista.pdf.

19. Martin Heidegger, GA 40. *Einführung in die Metaphysik* (1935), ed. Petra Jaeger, 1983; *Introduction to Metaphysics*, trans. Gregory Fried and Richard Polt, 2nd ed. (New Haven, CT: Yale University Press, 2014), 198.

20. Gregory Fried read an initial draft of this chapter and provided this insight.

21. Heidegger, *Ponderings VII–XI: Black Notebooks 1938–1939*, 12.

22. See G. W. F. Hegel, *Phenomenology of Spirit*, trans. A. V. Miller (Oxford, UK: Oxford University Press, 1977). According to Hegel, history is a dialectical movement, comprised of a series of revolutions. During different stages of history, "world historical figures," select people like Napoleon, are called forth via a cunning of reason (the rational design of the world) by what Hegel calls the "Absolute."

23. Heidegger, *Ponderings VII–XI: Black Notebooks 1938–1939*, 12.

24. Heidegger, *Ponderings II–VI: Black Notebooks 1931–1938*, 17.

25. Martin Heidegger, GA 96. *Überlegungen XII–XV (Schwarze Hefte 1939–1941)*, ed. Peter Trawny, 2014; *Ponderings XII–XV: Black Notebooks 1939–1941*, trans. Richard Rojcewicz (Bloomington: Indiana University Press, 2017), 149.

26. See footnote 2.

27. Friedrich Nietzsche, *Ecce Homo*, 110.

28. Clifford R. Lovin, "Blut Und Boden: The Ideological Basis of the Nazi Agricultural Program," *Journal of the History of* Ideas 28, no. 2 (1967): 281.

29. Farías states, "[Heidegger] spoke against another concern: the German's desire to shift the political center to the northeast. And since this displacement brought power to the large cities (especially Berlin), Heidegger fought to prove that spiritual and political impetus was not simply in the provinces but was actually found in the countryside," Victor Farías, *Heidegger and Nazism* (Philadelphia, PA: Temple University Press, 1989), 173.

30. Heidegger, *Ponderings II–VI: Black Notebooks 1931–1938*, 29.

31. Heidegger, *Ponderings II–VI: Black Notebooks 1931–1938*, 107.

32. Heidegger, "Origin of the Work of Art," 159–60.

33. Heidegger, "Origin of the Work of Art," 159.

34. Philippe Lacoue-Labarthe, *Heidegger, Art and Politics: The Fiction of the Political*, trans. Chris Turner (Oxford, UK: Basil Blackwell, 1990), 62.

35. Lacoue-Labarthe, *Heidegger, Art and Politics: The Fiction*, 62.

36. Martin Heidegger, *Der Ursprung des Kunstwerkes*, ed. H. G. Gadamer (Stuttgart, Germany: P. Reclam, 1960); "The Origin of the Work of Art," trans. Albert Hofstadter in David Farrell Krell ed., *Basic Writings* (San Francisco, CA: Harper Collins, 1993), 166.

37. Heidegger, "The Origin of the Work of Art," 193.

38. Heidegger, *Ponderings VII–XI: Black Notebooks 1938–1939*, 3.

39. Farías, *Heidegger and Nazism*, 240.

40. Farías, *Heidegger and Nazism*, 173.

41. Farías, *Heidegger and Nazism*, 174–75.

42. Friedrich Nietzsche, *Thus Spoke Zarathustra* ed. Adrian de Caro and Robert Pippin (Cambridge, UK: Cambridge University Press, 2006), 50.

43. A parallel could also be made between the old peasant woman and Diotima, a woman through whom Socrates learns the truth of love in *The Symposium*.

44. Farías, *Heidegger and Nazism*, 174.

45. Martin Heidegger, GA 12. *Unterwegs zur Sprache* (1950–1959). Ed. Friedrich-Wilhelm von Herrmann, 1985; "Language in the Poem A Discussion on Georg Trakl's Poetic Work," *On the Way to Language*, trans. Peter D. Hertz and Joan Stambaugh (New York: Harper & Row, 1971), 167.

46. Refer to citation 23 for Farías's full quote on Heidegger's argument to place the spiritual and political impetus of Germany in the South, in the countryside. Farías, *Heidegger and Nazism*, 173. In *Thus Spoke Zarathustra*, Nietzsche consistently speaks of Zarathustra's "down going" or "going down." Such a "down going" toward the earth is in opposition to a looking above via religious doctrine.

47. Heidegger, "Language in the Poem," 163.

48. Heidegger, "Language in the Poem," 170.

49. Heidegger, "Language in the Poem," 186.

50. Heidegger, "Language in the Poem," 191.

51. Heidegger, "Language in the Poem," 179. "Of the spirit" is not a language of metaphysics in that spirit is not diametrically opposed to materiality or flesh. It is not a question of the suprasensuous (spirit) in an ethereal realm versus a sensuous (materiality) on earth.

52. Heidegger, "Language in the Poem," 179.

53. Heidegger, "Language in the Poem," 170.

54. Heidegger, "Language in the Poem," 170.

55. Heidegger, "Language in the Poem," 171.

56. Heidegger, "Language in the Poem," 170.

57. Heidegger, "Language in the Poem," 195.

58. Martin Heidegger, GA 9. *Wegmarken* (1919–1961), ed. Friedrich-Wilhelm von Herrmann, 1976, 1996 (rev. ed.); "On the Essence of Ground," in *Pathmarks*. Ed. William McNeill (Cambridge, UK: Cambridge University Press, 1998), 123.

59. Rodrigo Therezo, "From Neutral Dasein to a Gentle Twofold: Sexual Difference in Heidegger and Derrida," *Philosophy Today* 63, no. 2 (2019): 501.

60. Therezo, "From Neutral Dasein to a Gentle Twofold," 502.

61. Therezo, "From Neutral Dasein to a Gentle Twofold," 502.

62. Rosemary Radford Ruether, *New Woman, New Earth: Sexist Ideologies and Human Liberation* (New York: Seabury Press, 1975), 194–95. Quoted from Michael Zimmerman, *Heidegger's Confrontation with Modernity: Technology, Politics, Art* (Bloomington: Indiana University Press, 1990), 269.

63. Heidegger states, "Flesh-*spirit* [. . .] to be in them, a *how* as a "what," objective heavenly, the *what* as the how of a history coming to an end. Explanation of facticity: of the unredeemed, and being redeemed: [. . .] [sons of God] (Rom. 8:14). Death-life, sin-righteousness, slavery-sonship [. . .]. 'History of salvation' unclear!" Heidegger, *Ontology—The Hermeneutics of Facticity*, 86.

64. Heidegger, *Ontology—The Hermeneutics of Facticity*, 35.

65. Ian Alexander Moore, *Dialogue on the Threshold: Heidegger and Trakl* (Albany: SUNY Press, 2023), 171–77.

66. Charu Gupta, "Politics of Gender: Women in Nazi Germany," *Economic and Political Weekly* 26, no. 17 (1991): 40–48.

67. As discussed in chapter 1, Heidegger rejects Judeo-Christian interpretations of sexual difference. This difference can be described by St. Augustine as one where man is created for the contemplative life and woman is created for procreative purpose (even though they are equal in the eyes of God). That is, woman was created to give Adam descendants. This type of sexual difference (old decaying Geschlecht) is what Heidegger rebukes when he highlights that a new beginning of "one generation" is not founded on biological ties.

68. Heidegger, "Language in the Poem," 185.

69. Heidegger, "Language in the Poem," 185.

70. Heidegger, "Language in the Poem," 119.

71. Jacques Derrida, *Geschlecht III: Sex, Race, Nation, Humanity*, trans. Katie Chenoweth and Rodrigo Therezo (Chicago, IL: University of Chicago Press, 2020), 90.

72. Luce Irigaray, *L'oubli de l'air chez Heidegger* (Paris: Éditions de Minuit, 1983), 109.

73. Patricia Huntington, *Ecstatic Subjects, Utopia, and Recognition: Kristeva, Heidegger, Irigaray* (New York: SUNY Press, 1998), 48.

74. Jennifer Anna Gosetti, "Feminine Figures in Heidegger's Theory of Poetic Language," *Feminist Interpretations of Martin Heidegger*, ed. Nancy J. Holland and Patricia Huntington (University Park: Pennsylvania State University Press, 2001), 199–200.

75. Gosetti, "Feminine Figures in Heidegger's Theory," 198.

76. Heidegger, "Language in the Poem," 169.

77. Luce Irigaray, *Speculum of the Other Woman*, trans. Gillian C. Gill (Ithaca, NY: Cornell University Press, 1985), 133–34.

78. Irigaray, *Speculum of the Other Woman*, 137.

79. Irigaray, *Speculum of the Other Woman*, 246.

80. Irigaray, *Speculum of the Other Woman*, 197.

81. Heidegger, "Language in the Poem," 169.

82. Heidegger, "Language in the Poem," 193.

83. Heidegger, "Language in the Poem," 163.

84. Heidegger, "Language in the Poem," 188.

85. Heidegger, "Language in the Poem," 188.

86. In Plato's *Symposium*, Socrates defines love, as explained to him by Diotima. In this speech, he describes two ways of propagating the eternal, through reproduction of the body and reproduction of the mind. The former is deemed an inferior type of procreation, while the intellectual legacies of Homer and Hesiod, who Plato mentions have statues erected in their honor, are of a higher cast. Plato, *Symposium*, trans. Alexander Nehamas and Paul Woodruff (Indianapolis, IN: Hackett, 1989).

87. See Victoria I. Burke, "The Substance of Ethical Recognition: Hegel's Antigone and the Irreplaceability of the Brother," *New German Critique* 40, no. 1 (2013): 1–27.

88. Heidegger, "Language in the Poem," 184.

89. Heidegger, "Language in the Poem," 184.

90. Thanks to Shane Ewegen for alerting me to this passage in the 1943 Heraclitus lecture. See Martin Heidegger, *Heraclitus: The Inception of Occidental Thinking and Logic: Heraclitus's Doctrine of the Logos*, trans. Julia Goesser Assaiante and Shane Ewegen (London: Bloomsbury Academic, 2018).

91. Heidegger states, "To be sure, the sculptor uses stone just as the mason uses it, in his own way. But he does not use it up. That happens in a certain way only where the work miscarries." Heidegger, "The Origin of the Work of Art," 173. I spoke to Anne O'Byrne about the sexual tension inherent in the artwork, and she asked Alan Kim about the proper translation of "miscarry." Kim noted that the

English translation of "miscarry" may be overstepping in suggesting a miscarriage in the sense of birth, as the original states, "Das gilt in gewisser Weise nur dort, wo das Werk mißlingt."

92. Shane Montgomery Ewegen, "Gestures of the Feminine,'" *Journal of Speculative Philosophy* 30, no. 4, 2016, 487.

93. Jean Graybeal, Language and "The Feminine," in *Nietzsche and Heidegger* (Bloomington: Indiana University Press, 1990). Graybeal borrows Kristeva's distinction between the semiotic and the symbolic. According to Kristeva, the human subject is always in a process of becoming, always caught between the semiotic (unnamable excess of signification) and the symbolic (signification).

94. Shane Montgomery Ewegen, "Gestures of the Feminine," 494.

95. Heidegger, "Language in the Poem," 166–67.

96. A *phusical* way of birthing is birth by way of *poiēsis*, a bringing forth in contrast to challenging forth via techniques of domination. Heidegger's reading of Trakl seems to suggest there is nothing wrong with the breeding of a "people" as "one generation." This generation can come forth and negate the "old decaying generation" insofar as it is not done by way of scientific racism.

97. Rodrigo Therezo, "Heidegger's National-Humanism: Reading Derrida's Geschlecht III," *Research in Phenomenology* 48 (2018): 1–28.

98. Therezo, "Heidegger's National-Humanism," 27.

99. Gupta, "Politics of Gender," *Economic and Political Weekly*, 40.

100. Gosetti, "Feminine Figures in Heidegger's Theory," 203.

101. Gosetti, "Feminine Figures in Heidegger's Theory," 211.

102. William McNeill, "Buried Treasure: Greeting and the Temporality of Remembrance in Heidegger's Lectures on '*Andenken*,'" *Heidegger Circle Conference Proceedings*, 2010, 272.

103. McNeill, "Buried Treasure: Greeting," 271.

104. On page 1 of *Ponderings II*, Heidegger states, "Philosophizing proceeds out of these questions upward into unity." He goes on to say, "Only someone German can in an originarily new way poetize being and say being." Heidegger, *Ponderings II–VI: Black Notebooks 1931–1938*, 21.

Chapter 6

1. Martin Heidegger, GA 95. *Überlegungen VII–XI (Schwarze Hefte 1938–1939)*, ed. Peter Trawny, 2014; *Ponderings VII–XI: Black Notebooks 1938–1939*, trans. Richard Rojcewicz (Bloomington: Indiana University Press, 2017), 75.

2. GA 29/30. *Die Grundbegriffe der Metaphysik. Welt—Endlichkeit—Einsamkeit* (1929–30), ed. Friedrich-Wilhelm von Herrmann, 1983; *The Fundamental Concepts of Metaphysics: World, Finitude, Solitude*, trans. William McNeill and Nicholas Walker (Bloomington: Indiana University Press, 1995), 177.

3. As noted in chapter 1, "cases of Dasein," is a term borrowed from John Haugeland. This term indicates my mineness (*Jemeinigkeit*) that is also part of a larger shared community. See John Haugeland, Dasein *Disclosed: John Haugeland's Heidegger*, ed. Joseph Rouse (Cambridge, MA: Harvard University Press, 2013).

4. Martin Heidegger, *Vorträge* und Aufsätze (Pfullingen, Germany: Günther Neske Verlag, 1954), 145–62; "Building Dwelling Thinking," trans. Albert Hofstadter in *Basic Writings*, ed. David Farrell Krell (San Francisco, CA: Harper Collins, 1993), 349.

5. Heidegger, "Building Dwelling Thinking," 349.

6. Martin Heidegger, GA 94. *Überlegungen II–VI (Schwarze Hefte 1931–1938)*, ed. Peter Trawny, 2014; *Ponderings II–VI: Black Notebooks 1931–1938*, trans. Richard Rojcewicz (Bloomington: Indiana University Press, 2016), 29.

7. Anne O'Byrne, "Generational Being," *Logics of Genocide* ed. Anne O'Byrne and Martin Shuster (Abingdon: Routledge, 2022), 95–111.

8. Anne O'Byrne, "Generational Being," 95–111.

9. Martin Heidegger, GA 79. *Bremer und Freiburger Vorträge* (1949, 1957), ed. Petra Jaeger, 1994; "The Thing," *Bremen and Freiburg Lectures: Insight into That Which Is and Basic Principles of Thinking* trans. Andrew Mitchell (Bloomington: Indiana University Press, 2012), 24–45.

10. Heidegger, "Building Dwelling Thinking," 362.

11. Gregory Fried, *Heidegger's Polemos: From Being to Politics* (New Haven, CT and London: Yale University Press, 2000), 16.

12. Fried, *Heidegger's Polemos: From Being to Politics*, 18.

13. Ortega, *In-Between: Latina Feminist Phenomenology, Multiplicity, and the Self*, 53.

14. See Gloria Anzaldúa, "Chapter 4: La herencia de Coatlicue/The Coatlicue State," *Borderlands/La Frontera: The New Mestiza* (San Francisco, CA: Aunt Lute, 1987), 41–51.

15. Ortega, *In-Between: Latina Feminist Phenomenology, Multiplicity, and the Self*, 59.

16. Jennifer Gammage, "Not-Being-at-Ease: Ortega on Heidegger's *Unheimlichkeit* and Anzaldúa's Coatlicue State," *Philosophy Today* 65, no. 2 (Spring 2021): 441–48.

17. Heidegger, *The Metaphysical Foundations of Logic*, 18–21.

18. Ortega, *In-Between: Latina Feminist Phenomenology, Multiplicity, and the Self*, 58.

19. Martin Heidegger, GA 12. *Unterwegs zur Sprache* (1950–1959), ed. Friedrich-Wilhelm von Herrmann, 1985; "Language in the Poem a Discussion on Georg Trakl's Poetic Work," *On the Way to Language*, trans. Peter D. Hertz and Joan Stambaugh (New York: Harper & Row, 1971), 195.

20. Heidegger, *The Metaphysical Foundations of Logic*, 137.

21. Heidegger, *The Metaphysical Foundations of Logic*, 137.
22. Martin Heidegger, GA 2. *Sein und Zeit* (1927), ed. Friedrich Wilhelm von Herrmann, 1977; *Being and Time*, trans. John Macquarrie and Edward Robinson (Oxford, UK: Blackwell, 1962), 68.
23. Ortega, *In-Between: Latina Feminist Phenomenology, Multiplicity, and the Self*, 64–65.
24. As stated in chapter 6, "*The essence of the Germans:* That they may be chained to the *struggle* over their essence, for only inasmuch as they take up this struggle are they the people they alone can be. Suitable for this struggle is only that which, with unwavering confidence in its essential pride, is able to suffer the highest question—worthiness of what is most question—*worthy* (beyng)." See Martin Heidegger, GA 95. *Überlegungen VII–XI (Schwarze Hefte 1938–1939)*, ed. Peter Trawny, 2014; *Ponderings VII–XI: Black Notebooks 1938–1939*, trans. Richard Rojcewicz (Bloomington: Indiana University Press, 2017), 1.
25. Jessica S. Elkayam, "Invitations to Multiplicity: Revisiting Travel in Response to Marianna Ortega's *In Between*," *Philosophy Today* 65, no. 2 (Spring 2021): 433–40.
26. Harding's standpoint epistemology was previously discussed in the introduction.
27. María Lugones, *Pilgrimages/Peregrinajes: Theorizing Coalition against Multiple Oppressions* (New York: Rowman & Littlefield, 2003).
28. María Lugones, "Playfulness, 'World'-Travelling, and Loving Perception," *Hypatia* 2, no. 4 (Summer 1987): 3–19.
29. G. Sue Kasun, "Chicana Feminism as a Bridge: The Struggle of a White Woman Seeking an Alternative to the Eclipsing Embodiment of Whiteness," *Journal of Curriculum Theorizing* 32 (2018): 116.
30. Heidegger, "Building Dwelling Thinking," 347.
31. Heidegger, "Building Dwelling Thinking," 357.
32. Martin Heidegger, GA 7. *Vorträge und Aufsätze* (1936–1953), ed. Friedrich-Wilhelm von Herrmann, 2000; "The Question Concerning Technology," trans. William Lovitt in David Farrell Krell, ed., *Basic Writings* (San Francisco, CA: Harper Collins, 1993), 317.
33. Heidegger, "Building Dwelling Thinking," 361.
34. Marin Heidegger, "The Anaximander Fragment," *Early Greek Thinking*, trans. David F. Krell and Frank A. Capuzzi (New York: Harper & Row, 1975), 57.
35. Heidegger, "The Anaximander Fragment," 56.
36. Heidegger, "The Anaximander Fragment," 57.
37. Heidegger, "The Anaximander Fragment," 21.
38. Heidegger, "Building Dwelling Thinking," 357.
39. Heidegger, *The Metaphysical Foundations of Logic*, 136–37.
40. Heidegger, "Building Dwelling Thinking," 363.
41. Andrea Pitts, *Nos/Otras: Gloria E. Anzaldúa, Multiplicitous Agency, and Resistance* (Albany: SUNY Press, 2021), 127.

42. See Erique Zhang, "The Radical Act of Invisibility on Trans Day of Visibility," *Washington Post*, March 21, 2022, https://www.washingtonpost.com/lifestyle/2022/03/31/trans-day-visibility-erique-zhang/.

43. Ephraim Das Janssen, *Phenomenal Gender: What Transgender Experience Discloses* (Bloomington: Indiana University Press, 2017), 5.

44. Janssen, *Phenomenal Gender*, 5.

45. Perry Zurn, *How We Make Each Other: Trans Poetics in and at the Edge of the University* (Durham, NC: Duke University Press, 2025). Zurn presented portions of this work at the 2022 *philo*SOPHIA meeting at George Mason University. After attending his talk, which I found very thought-provoking, I reached out and Zurn sent me sections of his work, including "Trans Poetics" and "Dust." Because the book is not yet published, I do not have exact page numbers when quoting his text. I will, however, indicate whether they come from the section on "Trans Poetics" or "Dust." I would like to thank Zurn for sharing his work with me.

46. Heidegger, *Ponderings VII–XI: Black Notebooks 1938–1939*, 244.

47. Ian Thomson, "Rethinking education after Heidegger: Teaching learning as ontological response-ability," *Educational Philosophy and Theory* 48, no. 8 (2016): 853.

48. Thomson, "Rethinking Education after Heidegger: Teaching Learning as Ontological Response-Ability," 846.

49. Ian Thomson, "Heidegger on Ontological Education, or: How We Become What We Are," *Inquiry* 44 (2001): 243–68.

50. Zurn, "Trans Poetics," *How We Make Each Other*.

51. Zurn breaks down poetics to poiēsis in chapter 1 "Pivoting," under the section "Trans Poetics." Heidegger discusses poiēsis in "The Question Concerning Technology."

52. Zurn, "Trans Poetics," *How We Make Each Other*.

53. Patricia Huntington, *Ecstatic Subjects, Utopia, and Recognition: Kristeva, Heidegger, Irigaray* (Albany: SUNY Press, 1998), 41.

54. Zurn, "Trans Poetics," *How We Make Each Other*.

55. Zurn, "Trans Poetics," *How We Make Each Other*.

56. Zurn, "Trans Poetics," *How We Make Each Other*.

57. Zurn, "Trans Poetics," *How We Make Each Other*.

58. Adam Knowles, "93. Gathering (Sammeln, Sammlung)," *The Cambridge Heidegger Lexicon*, ed. Mark A. Wrathall (Cambridge, UK: Cambridge University Press, 2021), 349–51.

59. Rebecca A. Longtin, "Heidegger and the Poetics of Time," *Gatherings: The Heidegger Circle Annual* 7 (2017): 137.

60. Heidegger, *Being and Time*, 173.

61. See Heidegger, *Being and Time*, 70–74.

62. Andrew Royle, "Heidegger's Ways of Being," *Philosophy Now* (2018), https://philosophynow.org/issues/125/Heideggers_Ways_of_Being.

63. David R. Cerbone, "Heidegger and Dasein's 'Bodily Nature': What Is the Hidden Problematic," *International Journal of Philosophical Studies* 8, no. 2 (2000): 221.
64. See Heidegger, Being and Time, 158–59.
65. Perry Zurn, "Dust," *How We Make Each Other*.
66. Perry Zurn, "Dust," *How We Make Each Other*.
67. Perry Zurn, "Dust," *How We Make Each Other*.
68. Perry Zurn, "Dust," *How We Make Each Other*.
69. Perry Zurn, "Dust," *How We Make Each Other*.

Bibliography

Agacinski, Sylviane. *Corps en Miettes*. Paris: Flammarion, 2013.
———. "Deux mères = un père?" *Le Monde*, February 3, 2013.
———. "Heidegger, une pensée brûlante." *Cinéma Étoile Saint-Germain-des-Prés*, December 8, 2013.
———. *Politique des sexes*. Paris: Éditions du Seuil, 2001.
Ahmed, Sara. *Queer Phenomenology: Orientations, Objects, Others*. Durham, NC and London: Duke University Press, 2006.
Aho, Kevin A. *Heidegger's Neglect of the Body*. Albany: SUNY Press, 2009.
———. *Existential Medicine: Essays on Health and Illness*. Lantham, MD: Rowman & Littlefield, 2018.
———. "Gender and Time: Revisiting the Question of Dasein's Neutrality." *Epoché* 12, no. 1 (Fall 2007): 137–55.
Anders, Günther. "Pseudo-concreteness of Heidegger's Philosophy." *Philosophy and Phenomenological Research* 8, no. 3 (1948): 337–71.
Anzaldúa, Gloria. *Borderlands/La Frontera: The New Mestiza*. San Francisco, CA: Aunt Lute, 1987.
Appel, Fredrik, "The Übermensch's Consort: Nietzsche and the 'Eternal Feminine.'" *History of Political Thought* 18, no. 3 (1997): 512–30.
Arendt, Hannah. *The Human Condition*. Chicago, IL: University of Chicago Press, 1998.
Askay, Richard R. "Heidegger, the Body, and the French Philosophers." *Continental Philosophy Review* 32 (1999): 29–35.
Barad, Karen. "Posthumanist Performativity: Toward an Understanding of How Matter Comes to Matter." *Signs: Journal of Women in Society and Culture* 28, no. 3 (2003): 801–31.
Bartky, Sandra Lee. *Femininity and Domination: Studies in the Phenomenology of Oppression*. New York and London: Routledge, 1990.
BBC News. "Hungary to Provide Free Fertility Treatment to Boost Population." January 10, 2020. Last accessed April 24, 2022, https://www.bbc.com/news/world-europe-51061499.
Beauvoir, Simone de. *The Second Sex*. New York: Random House, 1991.

Beistegui, Miguel de. *The New Heidegger*. London: Continuum, 2005.
Belu, Dana S. *Heidegger, Reproductive Technology, and the Motherless Age*. Cham, Switzerland: Palgrave Macmillan, 2017.
———. "Nature and Technology in Modern Childbirth: A Phenomenological Interpretation." *Techné* 16 (2012): 3–15.
Belu, Dana S., and Andrew Feenberg, "Heidegger's Aporetic Ontology of Technology." *Inquiry: An Interdisciplinary Journal of Philosophy* 53, no. 1 (2010): 1–19.
Bernasconi, Robert. "Who Invented the Concept of Race," in *Theories of Race and Racism: A Reader*, 2nd ed. Milton Park, UK: Taylor & Francis, 2020.
Bettcher, Talia Mae. "Full-Frontal Morality: The Naked Truth about Gender." *Hypatia* 27, no. 2 (2012): 319–37.
———. "'When Tables Speak': On the Existence of Trans Philosophy." *Daily Nous* (2018). http://dailynous.com/2018/05/30/tables-speak-existence-trans-philosophy-guest-talia-mae-bettcher/.
Beury, Manon. "En couple aves une femme trans, je suis exclue de la 'PMA pour toutes.'" *Libération*, August 4, 2020; last accessed April 19, 2021, https://www.liberation.fr/debats/2020/08/04/en-couple-avec-une-femme-trans-je-suis-exclue-de-la-pma-pour-toutes_1795938/.
Bigwood, Carol. *Earth Muse: Feminism, Nature, and Art*. Philadelphia, PA: Temple University Press, 1993.
Brison, Susan J. *Aftermath Violence and the Remaking of a Self*. Princeton, NJ: Princeton University Press, 2022, xi–xii.
Brunet, Laurence. "Procréations médicalement assistées et catégories 'ethno-raciales': l'enjeu de la ressemblance." *Les catégories ethno-raciales à l'ère des biotechnologies*. Paris: Société de législation compare, 2011, 135–54.
Buchanan, Brett. *Onto-Ethologies: The Animal Environments of Uexkull, Heidegger, Merleau-Ponty, and Deleuze*. Albany: SUNY Press, 2008.
Burke, Megan. "Cis Sense and the Habit of Gender Assignment." *Journal of Speculative Philosophy* 36, no. 2 (2022): 206–18.
Burke, Victoria I. "The Substance of Ethical Recognition: Hegel's Antigone and the Irreplaceability of the Brother." *New German Critique* 40, no. 1 (2013): 1–27.
Butler, Judith. *Frames of War: When Is Life Grievable?* London: Verso Books, 2009.
———. *Gender Trouble*. New York and London: Routledge, 1990.
Caputo, John D. *Hermeneutics: Facts and Interpretation in the Age of Information*. London: Penguin, 2018.
———. *Radical Hermeneutics: Repetition, Deconstruction, and the Hermeneutic Project*. Bloomington: Indiana University Press, 1987.
Carel, Havi. *Phenomenology of Illness*. Oxford, UK: Oxford University Press, 2017.
Cassirer, Ernst, and Martin Heidegger. *Débat sur la kantisme et la philosophie: (Davos, mars 1929) et Autres textes de 1929–1931*. Paris: Beauchesne, 1972.
Cavarero, Adriana. *In Spite of Plato: A Feminist Rewriting of Ancient Philosophy*, trans. Serena Anderlini-D'Onofrio and Aine O'Healy. Cambridge, UK: Polity Press, 1995.

———. *Relating Narratives: Storytelling and Selfhood*, trans. Paul Kottman. New York: Routledge, 2000.
Cerbone, David R. "Heidegger and Dasein's 'Bodily Nature': What Is the Hidden Problematic?" *International Journal of Philosophical Studies* 8, no. 2 (2000): 209–30.
Chanter, Tina. "The Problematic Normatives Assumptions of Heidegger's Ontology," *Feminist Interpretations of Martin Heidegger*, ed. Nancy J. Holland and Patricia Huntington. University Park, PA: Penn State University Press, 2001, 73–108.
Claxton, Susanne Dawn. *Heidegger's Gods: An Ecofeminist Perspective*. London and New York: Rowman & Littlefield International, 2017.
Cleage, Pearl. *Mad at Miles: A Blackwoman's Guide to Truth*. Detroit, MI: Cleage Group, 1990.
Collins, Patricia Hill *Black Feminist Thought: Knowledge, Consciousness, and the Politics of Empowerment*. Abingdon, UK: Routledge, 1990.
Crapanzano, Vincent. *Hermes' Dilemma and Hamlet's Desire: On the Epistemology of Interpretation*. Cambridge, MA: Harvard University Press, 1992.
Crenshaw, Kimberlé. "The Urgency of Intersectionality," TEDWomen, San Francisco, CA, 2016, 18 min., 50 sec., https://www.ted.com/talks/kimberle_crenshaw_the_urgency_of_intersectionality?subtitle=en.
Currah, Paisley. *Sex Is as Sex Does: Governing Transgender Identity*. New York: NYU Press, 2022.
Darwin, Charles. *The Descent of Man, and Selection in Relation to Sex*. Westminster, UK: Penguin, 2004.
Dembroff, Robin. "Cisgender Commonsense and Philosophy's Transgender Trouble." *TSQ: Transgender Studies Quarterly* 7, no. 3 (2020): 399–406.
Derrida, Jacques. "*Geschlecht: différence sexuelle, différence ontologique.*" *Cahier de l'Herne*, ed. Michel Haar (1983): 419–30. Translated as "*Geschlect: Sexual Difference, Ontological Difference.*" *Research in Phenomenology* 13, no. 1 (1983): 65–83.
———. *Geschlecht III: Sex, Race, Nation, Humanity*, trans. Katie Chenoweth and Rodrigo Therezo. Chicago, IL: University of Chicago Press, 2020.
———. *Marges de la philosophie*. Paris: Éditions de minuit, 1972. Translated as *Margins of Philosophy*, trans. Alan Bass. Chicago, IL: University of Chicago Press, 1972.
Dorléac, Laurence Bertrand, and Jérôme Neutres. "Argo," *Artistes et Robots*. Grand Palais, Galeries nationals, April 5–July 9, 2018, 106.
Drouillard, Jill. "Heidegger on Being a Sexed or Gendered Human Being," *Gatherings: The Heidegger Circle Annual*, no. 12 (2022): 162–65.
———. "Problem: What Is Woman? The Hermeneutics of Sex/Gender Facticity," *Heidegger, Dasein, and Gender: Thinking the Unthought*, ed. Trish Glazebrook and Susanne Dawn Claxton (Lanham, MD: Rowman & Littlefield, 2024).
———. "Queering *Gestell*: Thinking Outside Butler's Frames and Inside Belu's Reproductive Enframing." *Journal of Speculative Philosophy*. SPEP issue, 36, no. 3 (2022): 194–205.

———. "The Rhetoric of Sexual Difference in French Reproductive Politics." *Culture and Dialogue* 2, no. 9 (2021): 225–42.

Duggan, Lisa. *The New Homonormativity: The Sexual Politics of Neoliberalism.* Durham, NC and London: Duke University Press, 2002.

Elkayam, Jessica S. "Invitations to Multiplicity: Revisiting Travel in Response to Marianna Ortega's *In Between*." *Philosophy Today* 65, no. 2 (Spring 2021): 433–40.

Epstein, Rachel. "Space Invaders: Queer and Trans Bodies in Fertility Clinics." *Sexualities* 21, no. 7 (2018): 1039–58.

Ewegen, Shane Montgomery. "Gestures of the Feminine in Heidegger's 'Die Sprache.'" *Journal of Speculative Philosophy* 30, no. 4 (2016): 486–98.

Farías, Victor. *Heidegger and Nazism.* Philadelphia, PA: Temple University Press, 1989.

Fausto-Sterling, Anne. "The Five Sexes: Why Male and Female Are Not Enough." *The Sciences* 33 (1993): 20–24.

Fernandez, Anthony Vincent. "Embodiment and Objectification in Illness and Healthcare: Taking Phenomenology from Theory to Practice." *Journal of Clinical Nursing* 29, no. 21–22 (2020): 4403–12.

Ferrell, Robyn. *Copula: Sexual Technologies, Reproductive Powers.* Albany: SUNY Press, 2006.

Fielding, Helen. "Questioning Nature: Irigaray, Heidegger, and the Potentiality of Matter." *Continental Philosophy Review* 36, no. 1 (2003): 1–26.

Foucault, Michel. *The History of Sexuality Vol. I: An Introduction.* New York: Vintage, 1990.

Freeman, Lauren. "Reconsidering Relational Autonomy: A Feminist Approach to Selfhood and the Other in the Thinking of Martin Heidegger," *Inquiry* 54, no. 4 (2011): 361–83.

Fried, Gregory. *Heidegger's Polemos: From Being to Politics.* New Haven, CT and London: Yale University Press, 2000.

———. *Towards a Polemical Ethics: Between Heidegger and Plato.* Lantham, MD: Rowman & Littlefield, 2021.

Gammage, Jennifer. "Not-Being-at-Ease: Ortega on Heidegger's *Unheimlichkeit* and Anzaldúa's Coatlicue State." *Philosophy Today* 65, no. 2 (Spring 2021): 441–48.

Garfinkel, Harold. *Studies in Ethnomethodology.* Englewood Cliffs, NJ: Prentice Hall, 1967.

Gavrell, Sara. "Obstetrics' Security Blanket: The Case of Continuous Electronic Fetal Monitoring in Healthy Births." *APA Women in Philosophy Blog*, July 14, 2021.

———. *Heidegger on Science.* Albany: SUNY Press, 2012.

Gill-Peterson, Jules. *Histories of the Transgender Child.* Minneapolis: University of Minnesota Press, 2018.

Glazebrook, Trish. "Heidegger and Ecofeminism," in *Feminist Interpretations of Martin Heidegger*, ed. Nancy J. Holland and Patricia Huntington. University Park, PA: Penn State University Press, 2001, 221–51.

———. *Heidegger on Science*. Albany: SUNY Press, 2012.
Goffe, Tao Leigh. "Stolen Life, Stolen Time: Black Temporality, Speculation, and Racial Capital," *South Atlantic Quarterly* 121, no. 1 (2022): 109–30.
Gosetti, Jennifer Anna. "Feminine Figures in Heidegger's Theory of Poetic Language," *Feminist Interpretations of Martin Heidegger*, ed. Nancy J. Holland and Patricia Huntington. University Park, PA: Penn State University Press, 2001, 196–218.
Grau, Marion. "Putting Hermes Back into Hermeneutics," in *Refiguring Theological Hermeneutics: Hermes, Trickster, Fool*. New York: Palgrave Macmillan, 2014.
Graybeal, Jean. *Language and "The Feminine" in Nietzsche and Heidegger*. Bloomington: Indiana University Press, 1990.
Grey, Kimberly. "From *A Mother Is an Intellectual Thing*." *Adroit Journal* 30 (2019), https://theadroitjournal.org/issue-thirty/kimberly-grey-prose/.
Grosz, Elizabeth. *Becoming Undone: Darwinian Reflections on Life, Politics, and Art*. Durham, NC: Duke University Press, 2011.
Grumet, Madeleine R. *Bitter Milk: Women and Teaching*. Amherst: University of Massachusetts Press, 1988.
Guenther, Lisa. "Being-from-Others: Reading Heidegger after Cavarero," *Hypatia* 23, no. 1 (2008), 99–118.
Guignon, Charles. "Authenticity," *Philosophy Compass* 3, no. 2 (2008): 277–90.
Halberstam, Jack. *In a Queer Time and Place: Transgender Bodies, Subcultural Lives*. New York: NYU Press, 2005.
Hale, Jacob. "Suggested Rules for Non-Transsexuals Writing about Transsexuals, Transsexuality, Transsexualism, or Trans__." (1997); last updated November 18, 2009, https://sandystone.com/hale.rules.html.
Haraway, Donna. "Situated Knowledges: The Science Question in Feminism and the Privilege of Partial Perspective," *Feminist Studies* 14, no. 3 (1988), 575–99.
Harding, Sandra. "Introduction: Is There a Feminist Method." in *Feminism and Methodology*, ed. Sandra Harding. Bloomington: Indiana University Press, 1988.
———. "Rethinking Standpoint Epistemology: What Is Strong Objectivity?" in *Feminist Epistemologies*, ed. L. Alcoff and E. Potter. New York: Routledge, 1993.
Hatab, Lawrence. *Ethics and Finitude*, Lanham, MD: Rowman & Littlefield, 2000.
Haugeland, John. *Dasein Disclosed: John Haugeland's Heidegger*, ed. Joseph Rouse. Cambridge, MA: Harvard University Press, 2013.
Hay, Carol. "Girlfriend, Mother, Professor," in *The Stone, New York Times Opinionator*, January 25, 2016.
Hegel, G. W. F. *Phenomenology of Spirit*, trans. A. V. Miller. Oxford, UK: Oxford University Press, 1977.
Heidegger, Martin. "The Anaximander Fragment," *Early Greek Thinking*, trans. David F. Krell and Frank A. Capuzzi. New York: Harper & Row, 1975.
———. "Brief über den Humanismus," *Wegmarken*. Frankfurt am Main, Germany: Vittorio Klostermann Verlag, 1967, 145–94. "Letter on Humanism," in *Basic*

Writings, ed. David Farrell Krell. San Francisco, CA: Harper Collins, 1993, 217–65.

———. *Der Ursprung des Kunstwerkes*, ed. H. G. Gadamer (Stuttgart, Germany: P. Reclam, 1960). "The Origin of the Work of Art," trans. Albert Hofstadter, in David Farrell Krell ed., *Basic Writings*. San Francisco, CA: Harper Collins, 1993, 143–203.

———. GA 2. *Sein und Zeit* (1927), ed. Friedrich Wilhelm von Herrmann, 1977. *Being and Time*, trans. John Macquarrie and Edward Robinson. Oxford, UK: Blackwell, 1962.

———. GA 7. *Vorträge und Aufsätze* (1936–1953), ed. Friedrich-Wilhelm von Herrmann, 2000. "The Question Concerning Technology," ed. David Farrell Krell, trans. William Lovitt, *Basic Writings*. San Francisco, CA: Harper Collins, 1993.

———. GA 9. *Wegmarken* (1919–1961), ed. Friedrich-Wilhelm von Herrmann, 1976, 1996 (rev. ed.). "On the Essence of Ground," in *Pathmarks*, ed. William McNeill. Cambridge, UK: Cambridge University Press, 1998, 97–135.

———. GA 12. *Unterwegs zur Sprache* (1950–1959), ed. Friedrich-Wilhelm von Herrmann, 1985. *On the Way to Language*, trans. Peter D. Hertz. San Francisco, CA: Harper & Row, 1982.

———. GA 18. *Grundbegriffe der aristotelischen Philosophie* (1924), ed. Mark Michalski. 2002. *Basic Concepts of Aristotelian Philosophy*, trans. Robert D. Metcalf and Mark Basil Tanzer. Bloomington: Indiana University Press, 2009, 4.

———. GA 26. *Metaphysische Anfangsgründe der Logik im Ausgang von Leibniz* (1928), ed. Klaus Held, 1978, 1990 (2nd rev. ed.), 2007 (3d rev. ed.). *The Metaphysical Foundations of Logic*, trans. Michael Heim. Bloomington: Indiana University Press, 1984.

———. GA 29/30. *Die Grundbegriffe der Metaphysik. Welt—Endlichkeit—Einsamkeit* (1929–30), ed. Friedrich-Wilhelm von Herrmann, 1983. *The Fundamental Concepts of Metaphysics: World, Finitude, Solitude*, trans. William McNeill and Nicholas Walker. Bloomington: Indiana University Press, 1995.

———. GA 40. *Einführung in die Metaphysik* (1935), ed. Petra Jaeger, 1983. *Introduction to Metaphysics*, 2nd ed., trans. Gregory Fried and Richard Polt. New Haven, CT: Yale University Press, 2014, 198.

———. GA 51. *Grundbegriffe Basic Concepts* (1941), ed. Petra Jaeger, trans. Gary E. Aylesworth.1981, 1991 (rev. ed.). Bloomington and Indianapolis: Indiana University Press, 1993.

———. GA 63. *Ontologie. Hermeneutik der Faktizität* (1923), ed. Käte Bröcker-Oltmanns, 1988. *Ontology—The Hermeneutics of Facticity*, trans. John Van Buren. Bloomington: Indiana University Press, 1999.

———. GA 65. *Beiträge zur Philosophie (Vom Ereignis)* (1936–1938), ed. Friedrich-Wilhelm von Herrmann, 1989, 1994 (rev. ed.). *Contributions to Philosophy (Of the Event)*, trans. Richard Rojcewicz and Daniela Vallega-Neu. Bloomington: Indiana University Press, 2012.

---. GA 79. *Bremer und Freiburger Vorträge* (1949, 1957). ed. Petra Jaeger, 1994. "The Thing," *Bremen and Freiburg Lectures: Insight into That which Is and Basic Principles of Thinking*, trans. Andrew Mitchell. Bloomington: Indiana University Press, 2012.

---. GA 89. *Zollikoner Seminare* (1959–1969), ed. Peter Trawny, 2017. *Zollikon Seminars: Protocols—Conversations—Letters*, trans. Franz Mayr and Richard Askay. Evanston, IL: Northwestern University Press, 2001.

---. GA 94. *Überlegungen II–VI (Schwarze Hefte 1931–1938)*, ed. Peter Trawny, 2014. *Ponderings II–VI Black Notebooks 1931–1938*, trans. Richard Rojcewicz. Bloomington and Indianapolis: Indianapolis University Press, 2016.

---. GA 95. *Überlegungen VII–XI (Schwarze Hefte 1938–1939)*, ed. Peter Trawny, 2014. *Ponderings VII–XI: Black Notebooks 1938–1939*, trans. Richard Rojcewicz. Bloomington: Indiana University Press, 2017.

---. GA 96. *Überlegungen XII–XV (Schwarze Hefte 1939–1941)*, ed. Peter Trawny, 2014. *Ponderings XII–XV: Black Notebooks 1939–1941*, trans. Richard Rojcewicz. Bloomington: Indiana University Press, 2017.

---. *Heraclitus: The Inception of Occidental Thinking and Logic: Heraclitus's Doctrine of the Logos*, trans. Julia Goesser Assaiante and Shane Ewegen. London: Bloomsbury Academic, 2018.

---. N1. *Nietzsche*, vol. 1: *The Will to Power as Art*, ed. and trans. Joan Stambaugh, David Farrell Krell, and Frank A. Capuzzi. San Francisco, CA: Harper, 1991.

---. N3. *Nietzsche*, vol. 3: *The Will to Power as Knowledge and Metaphysics*, ed. and trans. Joan Stambaugh, David Farrell Krell, and Frank A. Capuzzi. San Francisco, CA: Harper, 1991.

---. "Nur noch ein Gott kann uns retten," *Der Spiegel* 30 (May 1976): 193–219, trans. by W. Richardson as "Only a God Can Save Us," in *Heidegger: The Man and the Thinker*, ed. T. Sheehan. London and New York: Routledge, 2017, 45–67.

---. *Vorträge* und Aufsätze (Pfullingen, Germany: Günther Neske Verlag, 1954), 145–162. "Building Dwelling Thinking," trans. Albert Hofstadter in *Basic Writings*, ed. David Farrell Krell (San Francisco, CA: Harper Collins, 1993).

---. "The Way to Language," trans. Peter Hertz (revised by David Farrell Krell), *Basic Writings*, ed. David Farrell Krell. San Francisco, CA: Harper Collins, 1993, 397–426.

---. *Zur Sache des Denken*. Tübingen: Max Niemeyer Verlag (1969): 61–80. "The End of Philosophy and the Task of Thinking," ed. David Farrell Krell, trans. Joan Stambaugh, *Basic Writings*. San Francisco, CA: Harper Collins, 1993, 431–49.

hooks, bell. *Teaching to Transgress: Education as the Practice of Freedom*. New York and London: Routledge, 1994.

Huntington, Patricia. *Ecstatic Subjects, Utopia, and Recognition: Kristeva, Heidegger, Irigaray*. Albany: SUNY Press, 1998.

Irigaray, Luce. *L'oubli de l'air chez Martin Heidegger*. Paris: Éditions de minuit, 1983. Translated as *The Forgetting of Air in Martin Heidegger*, trans. Mary Beth Mader. Austin: University of Texas Press, 1999.

———. *Speculum. De l'autre femme*. Paris: Éditions de minuit, 1974. Translated as *Speculum of the Other Woman*, trans. Gillian C. Gill. Ithaca, NY: Cornell University Press, 1985.

International Fertility Law Group, "Why Is There a Shortage of Black Egg Donors and Black Sperm Donors?" March 12, 2021, last accessed, April 14, 2022, https://www.iflg.net/black-egg-donor-sperm-donor-shortage/.

Jacob, François. *The Possible and the Actual*. New York: Pantheon, 1982.

Janssen, Ephraim Das. *Phenomenal Gender: What Transgender Experience Discloses*. Bloomington: Indiana University Press, 2017.

Kafer, Alison. *Feminist, Queer, Crip*. Bloomington: Indiana University Press, 2013.

Kasun, G. Sue. "Chicana Feminism as a Bridge: The Struggle of a White Woman Seeking an Alternative to the Eclipsing Embodiment of Whiteness," *Journal of Curriculum Theorizing* 32 (2018): 115–33.

Käufer, Stephan. "Jaspers, Limit-Situations, and the Methodological Function of Authenticity," *Heidegger, Authenticity and the Self: Themes from Division Two of Being and Time*, ed. Denis McManus. London and New York: Routledge, 2015, 95–115.

Kisiel, Theodore. "Heidegger's *Gesamtausgabe:* An International Scandal of Scholarship," *Philosophy Today* 39, no. 1 (1995): 3–15.

Knowles, Adam. "93. Gathering (Sammeln, Sammlung)," *The Cambridge Heidegger Lexicon*, ed. Mark A. Wrathall, Cambridge, UK: Cambridge University Press, 2021, 349–51.

Kofman, Sara. "The Psychologist of the Eternal Feminine (Why I Write Such Good Books, 5)," *Yale French* Studies 87, Another Look, Another Woman: Retranslations of French Feminism (1995): 173–89.

Kristeva, Julia. *Revolution in Poetic Language*, trans. Margaret Waller. New York: Columbia University Press, 1984.

Lacoue-Labarthe, Philippe. *Heidegger, Art and Politics: The Fiction of the Political*, trans. Chris Turner. Oxford, UK: Basil Blackwell, 1990.

Longtin, Rebecca A. "Heidegger and the Poetics of Time," *Gatherings: The Heidegger Circle Annual* 7 (2017): 124–41.

Lovin, Clifford R. "Blut Und Boden: The Ideological Basis of the Nazi Agricultural Program," *Journal of the History of* Ideas 28, no. 2 (1967): 279–88.

Lugones, María. *Pilgrimages/Peregrinajes: Theorizing Coalition Against Multiple Oppressions*. New York: Rowman & Littlefield, 2003.

———. "Playfulness, 'World'-Travelling, and Loving Perception," *Hypatia* 2, no. 4 (Summer 1987): 3–19.

MacAvoy, Leslie. "The Heideggerian Bias toward Death: A Critique of the Role of Being-towards-Death in the Disclosure of Human Finitude," *Metaphilosophy* 27 (1996): 63–77.

MacKinnon, Catherine. "Points Against Postmodernism," *Chicago-Kent Law Review* 75, no. 3 (2000).
Manif pour tous, "Qui sommes-nous?" https://www.lamanifpourtous.fr/qui-sommes-nous/le-mouvement, last accessed August 15, 2023.
Marinetti, Filippo Tommaso. "The Futurist Manifesto," 1909. https://www.societyforasianart.org/sites/default/files/manifesto_futurista.pdf.
Markotic, Lorraine. "Paternity, Enframing, and a New Revealing: O'Brien's Philosophy of Reproduction and Heidegger's Critique of Technology," *Hypatia* 31, no. 1 (2016): 123–24.
Martin, Emily. "The Egg and the Sperm: How Science Has Constructed a Romance Based on Stereotypical Male-Female Roles," *Signs* 16, no. 3 (1991): 485–501.
Massey, Heath. *The Origin of Time: Heidegger and Bergson*. Albany: SUNY Press, 2015.
McNeill, William. "Buried Treasure: Greeting and the Temporality of Remembrance in Heidegger's Lectures on '*Andenken*,'" Heidegger Circle Conference Proceedings, 2010.
Mercier, Michel. *Colette au Temps de Claudine*. Paris: Livre de Poche, 2004.
Mitchell, Andrew J. *The Fourfold: Reading the Late Heidegger*. Evanston, IL: Northwestern University Press, 2015.
Moore, Ian Alexander. *Dialogue on the Threshold: Heidegger and Trakl*. Albany: SUNY Press, 2023, 171–77.
Napoleon Series Archive, "French Civil Code," trans. George Spence. London: William Benning, 1827. https://www.napoleonseries.org/research/government/code/book1/c_title05.html, last accessed August 15, 2023.
NCHS Data Brief, No. 387, October 2020. https://www.cdc.gov/nchs/data/databriefs/db387-H.pdf.
Nelson, Eric Sean. "Heidegger and the Questionability of the Ethical," *Studia Phenomenologica* VIII (2008): 411–35.
Nelson, Maggie. *The Argonauts*. Minneapolis, MN: Graywolf Press, 2015.
Nietzsche, Friedrich. *Ecce Homo*, ed. Oscar Levy, trans. Anthony M. Ludovici and Paul V. Cohn. Project Gutenberg Ebook, 2016.
———. *Thus Spoke Zarathustra*, ed. Adrian de Caro and Robert Pippin. Cambridge, UK: Cambridge University Press, 2006.
O'Byrne, Anne. "Generational Being," *Logics of Genocide*, ed. Anne O'Byrne and Martin Shuster, Abingdon, UK: Routledge, 2022, 95–111.
———. *Natality and Finitude*. Bloomington: Indiana University Press, 2010.
Olafson, Frederick. *Heidegger and the Ground of Ethics*. Cambridge, UK: Cambridge University Press, 1998.
Orr, Deborah. "Thinking Through the Body: An Introduction to *Beliefs, Bodies, and Being*," *Belief, Bodies, and Being: Feminist Reflections on Embodiment*, ed. Deborah Orr, Linda López McAllister, Eileen Kahl, and Kathleen Earle. Lanham, MD: Rowman & Littlefield, 2006, 1–10.
Ortega, Marianna. *In-Between: Latina Feminist Phenomenology, Multiplicity, and the Self*. Albany: SUNY Press, 2016.

Pelluchon, Corine. *Nourishment: Philosophy of the Political Body*, trans. Justin E. H. Smith. London & New York: Bloomsbury, 2019.
Perreau, Bruno. *Queer Theory: The French Response*. Stanford, CA: Stanford University Press, 2016.
Pitts, Andrea. *Nos/Otras: Gloria E. Anzaldúa, Multiplicitous Agency, and Resistance*. Albany: SUNY Press, 2021.
Plato. *Republic*, trans. Paul Shorey, book V, section I in *The Collected Dialogues*, ed. Edith Hamilton and Huntington Cairns. Princeton, NJ: Princeton University Press, 2005.
———. *Symposium*, trans. Alexander Nehamas and Paul Woodruff. Indianapolis, IN: Hackett, 1989.
Puar, Jasbir K. "Homonationalism as Assemblage: Viral Travels, Affective Sexualities," *Jindal Global Law Review* 4, no. 2 (2003): 23–43.
Puwar, Nirmal. *Space Invaders: Race, Gender, and Bodies Out of Place*. London: Bloomsbury, 2004.
Quijano, Aníbal. "Qué tal Raza!" Paper prepared for the Conference of Coloniality Working Group, at SUNY-Binghamton, 2000.
Rawlinson, Mary. *Just Life: Bioethics and the Future of Sexual Difference*. New York: Columbia University Press, 2016.
Roberts, Dorothy. *Killing the Black Body: Race, Reproduction, and the Meaning of Liberty*. New York: Vintage, 1999.
Rodemeyer, Lanei. "Applying Time to Feminist Philosophy of the Body," in *Belief, Bodies, and Being: Feminist Reflections on Embodiment*, ed. Deborah Orr, Linda López McAllister, Eileen Kahl, and Kathleen Earle. Lanham, MD: Rowman & Littlefield, 2006, 197–207.
———. "*Dasein* Gets Pregnant," *Philosophy Today* 42 (1998): 76–84.
Royle, Andrew. "Heidegger's Ways of Being," *Philosophy Now* (2018). https://philosophynow.org/issues/125/Heideggers_Ways_of_Being.
Rubin, Gayle. "The Traffic in Women: Notes on the 'Political Economy' of Sex." *Toward an Anthropology of Women*, ed. Rayna R. Reiter. New York: Monthly Review Press, 1975, 157–210.
Ruether, Rosemary Radford. *New Woman, New Earth: Sexist Ideologies and Human Liberation*. New York: Seabury Press, 1975.
Russell, Camisha A. *The Assisted Reproduction of Race*. Bloomington: Indiana University Press, 2018.
Ryding, Elsa Lena, Klaas Wijma, and Barbro Wijma, "Experiences of Emergency Cesarean Section: A Phenomenological Study of 53 Women," *Birth* 25, no. 4 (1998): 246–51.
Saint Augustin. "La Trinité, Livre XII, 10," trans. Sophie Dupuy-Trudelle. *Philosophie, Catéchèse, Polémique, Œuvres III*, published under the direction of Lucien Jerphagnon. Paris: Gallimard, 2002.

Schalow, Frank. *The Incarnality of Being: The Earth, Animals, and the Body in Heidegger's Thought*. Albany: SUNY Press, 2006.
Schmidt, Ben. "Gendered Language in Teaching Reviews: Interactive Chart," https://benschmidt.org/profGender.
Scott, Joan W. *The Politics of the Veil*. Princeton, NJ: Princeton University Press, 2007.
Scuro, Jennifer. *The Pregnancy [does-not-equal] Childbearing Project: A Phenomenology of Miscarriage*. Lanham, MD: Rowman & Littlefield, 2017.
Seely, Stephen. "Does Life Have (a) Sex? Thinking Ontology and Sexual Difference with Irigaray and Simondon in *Feminist Philosophies of Life*. Montreal, QC and Kingston, ON: McGill-Queen's University Press, 2016.
Shapiro, Meyer. "The Still Life as a Personal Object: A note on Heidegger and van Gogh," *The Bloomsbury Anthology of Aesthetics*. New York: Bloomsbury, 2012, 403–7.
Simondon, Gilbert. *L'individuation à la lumiere des notions de forme et d'information*. Grenoble, France: Jérôme Millon, 2017.
Singer, Benjamin T. "From the Medical Gaze to Sublime Mutations: The Ethics of (Re)Viewing Non-Normative Body Images." *The Transgender Studies Reader*, ed. Susan Stryker and Stephen Whittle. New York: Routledge, 2006, 601–20.
Spivak, Gayatri. "Can the Subaltern Speak?," in *Marxism and the Interpretation of Culture*, ed. Cary Nelson and Lawrence Grossberg. London: Macmillan, 1988.
Stoler, Ann Laura. *Race and the Education of Desire: Foucault's History of Sexuality and the Colonial Order of Things*. Durham, NC: Duke University Press, 1995.
Stone, Alison. *Being Born: Birth and Philosophy*. Oxford, UK, Oxford University Press, 2019.
Svenaeus, Fredrik. *Phenomenological Bioethics: Medical Technologies, Human Suffering, and the Meaning of Being Alive*. New York: Routledge, 2017.
Theoi Project, 2000–2019, https://www.theoi.com/Olympios/HermesMyths3.html#Fostering, last accessed October 15, 2020.
Therezo, Rodrigo. "From Neutral Dasin to a Gentle Twofold: Sexual Difference in Heidegger and Derrida." *Philosophy Today* 63, no. 2 (2019): 491–511.
———. "Heidegger's National-Humanism: Reading Derrida's Geschlecht III." *Research in Phenomenology* 48 (2018): 1–28.
Thomson, Ian. "Heidegger on Ontological Education, or: How We Become What We Are," *Inquiry* (2001): 243–68.
———. "Rethinking Education after Heidegger: Teaching Learning as Ontological Response-ability." *Educational Philosophy and Theory* 48, no. 8 (2016): 846–61.
Tuana, Nancy. "The Weaker Seed: The Sexist Bias of Reproductive Theory." *Hypatia* 3, no. 1 (1988): 35–59.
Vallega-Neu, Daniela. *The Bodily Dimension in Thinking*. Albany: SUNY Press, 2005.
Warnes, Mathias. "Heidegger and the Festival of Being: From the Bridal Festival to the Round Dance." PhD diss., University of British Columbia, 2012.

Watson, Lori. "The Woman Question." *Transgender Studies Quarterly* 3, no. 1–2 (2016): 246–53.

Winnubst, Shannon. *Queering Freedom*. Bloomington: Indiana University Press, 2006.

Wolin, Richard. *Heidegger in Ruins: Between Philosophy and Ideology*. New Haven, CT: Yale University Press, 2023.

Wooten, Sara Carrigan. "Whispers in the Halls: Exploring the Mother/Teacher in Madeleine Grumet's *Bitter Milk: Women and Teaching*," *Journal of Curriculum Theorizing* 27, no. 3 (2011).

Wynter, Sylvia. "Unsettling the Coloniality of Being/Power/Truth/Freedom: Towards the Human, after Man, Its Overrepresentation—an Argument." *New Centennial Review* 3, no. 3 (2003): 257–337.

Whyte, Max. "The Uses and Abuses of Nietzsche in the Third Reich: Alfred Baeumler's 'Heroic Realism.'" *Journal of Contemporary History* 43, no. 2 (2008): 171–94.

Young, Iris Marion. *On Female Body Experience: "Throwing Like a Girl" and Other Essays*. Oxford, UK: Oxford University Press, 2005.

———. "Pregnant Embodiment: Subjectivity and Alienation." *Journal of Medicine and Philosophy* 9 (1984), 45–62.

Zhang, Erique. "The Radical Act of Invisibility on Trans Day of Visibility." *Washington Post*, March 21, 2022. https://www.washingtonpost.com/lifestyle/2022/03/31/trans-day-visibility-erique-zhang/.

Ziarek, Ewa. "Toward a Radical Female Imaginary: Temporality and Embodiment in Irigaray's Ethics." *Diacritics* 28, no. 1 (1998): 59–75.

Zimmerman, Michael E. *Heidegger's Confrontation with Modernity: Technology, Politics, Art*. Bloomington: Indiana University Press, 1990.

———. "Ontical Craving versus Ontological Desire." *From Phenomenology to Thought, Errancy, and Desire*, ed. Babette Babich. Dordrecht, the Netherlands: Springer, 1995, 501–23.

Zurn, Perry. *How We Make Each Other: Trans Poetics in and at the Edge of the University*. Durham, NC: Duke University Press, forthcoming.

Index

Adorno, Theodor, 108, 122
Aesthetic(s), 5, 108, 122
Affective labor, 89
Affective state (*see also* attunement, mood, *Stimmung*), 18–19, 29, 34–35, 47, 84, 86, 92, 100–101, 105–105, 126–127, 130–134, 136, 141, 143, 149, 159
   c.f. *Befindlichkeit*, state-of-mind, 34
Agacinski, Sylviane, 61–62, 164
Agency, 8, 81, 93, 138
Ahmed, Sara, 63
Aho, Kevin, 14, 17, 44–45
Alētheia (*see also* revealing/concealing), 10, 64, 68, 72, 110, 129, 150
Anaximander's fragment, 135–139
"Andenken," 121–122, 142
Anders, Gunter, 9
Animal, 44, 51–54, 92, 120, 126 160
Anxiety, 18–19, 29, 34, 39, 130
Antigone, 114–116, 118, 121
Anti-immigration discourse, 79
Anzaldúa, Gloria, 18, 123, 125, 129–132, 135–139, 142
Apeiron, 17, 125, 135–139, 145
Appel, Fredrick, 102
Appresentation, 26–27
Apollonius Rhodius, 86
Arendt, Hannah, 7, 44, 157

Aristotle, 15, 72, 128, 136, 149
Artwork, 54–55, 67, 81–82, 107–109, 122, 128, 174
Assisted reproductive technology (ART), 17, 35, 59–82, 120
Attunement (*see also* affective state, mood, *Stimmung*), 18–19, 29, 34–35, 47, 84, 86, 92, 100–101, 105–105, 126–127, 130–134, 136, 141, 143, 149, 159
   c.f. *Befindlichkeit*, state-of-mind, 34
Auerbach, Berthold, 106
Augenblick (*see also* moment of vision), 13, 18, 29–30, 32, 33–35, 38–39, 47, 131–132
Augustine, St., 43–44, 85
Authentic enactment, 42, 58
Authentic care, 18, 31, 37–38, 42, 44, 48, 52, 58, 91–94, 128, 131, 144, 159
Authentic temporality, 4, 17–18, 23, 26, 28–39, 44, 48, 131
Autonomy, 24, 87, 94
Average everydayness, 47, 131

Baeumler, Alfred, 101–103
Baer, Karl Ernst von, 53
Bartky, Sandra Lee, 34
Beauvoir, Simone de, 3, 85, 147, 157

Befindlichkeit (*see also* state-of-mind), 34 c.f. *see* affective state, attunement, mood, *Stimmung*, 18–19, 29, 34–35, 47, 84, 86, 92, 100–101, 105–105, 126–127, 130–134, 136, 141, 143, 149, 159

Being and Time (GA 2), 1, 3, 11, 19, 30, 48, 52, 127–128, 131

Being-between-worlds, 133

Being-in-the-world, 5, 23, 38, 47, 53, 70–71, 92, 94, 130, 165

Being-in-worlds, 130–133

Being guilty, 44

Being-toward-birth (*see also* natality), 14, 34, 84, 94

Being-toward-death, 3, 18, 29–30, 34, 39

Being-with/Being-with-others (see also *Mitsein*), 4, 16, 27, 50–51, 94, 130, 133

Belu, Dana S., 14, 15, 24–25, 33–38, 59, 64–67, 81, 154

Bergson, Henri, 51, 52, 56

Bestand (*see also* standing reserve), 23, 33, 61, 65, 71–72, 84–91, 69, 154, 164

Beyng, 100–108, 112, 114, 120, 126–127, 130, 133–134, 149, 169

Beury, Manon, 60

Bigwood, Carol, 15, 157

Binary logic, 112, 119, 122, 126

Bioethics legislation, 17, 59–63, 67–68, 75–76, 79

Biology, 11, 49–56, 58, 69, 101, 105

Birthing, 4, 15, 23–39, 118, 120, 175

Birthing (authentic), 23, 26, 33–39, 92, 159

Black Notebooks (GA 94/95/96), 1, 6, 7, 14, 45, 62, 99–123, 125–127, 138, 142

Blood and soil, 100–101, 105–109, 121, 126

Bodiliness (*see also* embodiment), 1, 32, 46, 55–57, 132, 144

Body knowledge, 4, 24, 26, 87, 95

Bodying forth (see also *Leiben*), 57, 91–94

Bodyreading, 83–95

Borderlands, 129, 130, 135, 139, 140

Both/and, 54–56

Brandom, Robert, 45

Breeding, 3, 59, 69–74, 82, 100, 104, 105, 118, 120, 170, 175

Bridge, 17, 125, 135–138, 145, 146

Bringing forth, 33, 54, 72–72, 120, 136, 175

Brison, Susan, 19

Brunet, Laurence, 76

Buchanan, Brett, 53, 160

"Building Dwelling Thinking" (BDT), 14, 17, 113, 126–128, 136–138

Burke, Megan, 17

Butler, Judith, 1, 2, 13, 50, 59–64

Buytendjk, F. J. J., 53

Calculative thinking (*see also* enframing, *Gestell*, *Machenschaft*, machinational thinking, positionality, technological thinking), 3, 4, 10–11, 23–25, 33, 35–36, 38, 59–82, 89–90, 104–105, 120, 134, 137, 140, 148, 169

Call of conscience, 39

Caesarean birth, 26, 34–35

Caputo, John, 84

Carceral solutions, 75

Care (as authentic), 18, 31, 37–38, 42, 44, 48, 52, 58, 91–94, 128, 131, 144, 159

Care (as nurturing and as ontological structure), 83–95

Care (as ontological structure, see also *Sorge*), 18, 37, 42, 44–50, 52, 58, 63, 128, 131–132, 144, 159
Carel, Havi, 14
Carnal procreation, 60, 63, 65, 120
Cases of Dasein (per Haugeland), 3, 45, 93–94, 126, 133
Cassirer, Ernst, 57
Cavarero, Adriana, 15, 155
Cerbone, David, 144
Challenge forth, 25, 36–37, 71–73, 90, 104, 140
Chanter, Tina, 70, 158
Childbirth (the act of, *see also* labor), 14, 23–39, 64–65, 85, 119, 154
Circumspective concern, 18, 47, 53, 73, 158
Cisgender, 16–17, 145
Cis sense, 17
Cixous, Hélène, 8
Claxton, Susanne Dawn, 41
Cleage, Pearl, 6–7
Clearing, 45, 52, 120
Clock time, 15, 18, 23–39
Coatlicue (*see also* not-being-at-ease), 19, 130–132
Collective identities, 13, 125, 136
Collins, Patricia Hill, 10
Conocimiento, 135
Contributions to Philosophy (GA 65), 19, 153
Crenshaw, Kimberlé, 77
Currah, Paisley, 2

Darwin, Charles, 51–54, 74, 99, 170
Dasein, 3–5, 14–18, 24–33, 38, 41–58, 70–71, 74, 93–94, 100, 103–104, 107, 112, 115, 120, 126–134, 138, 143–144, 148, 159, 160
Dasein (laboring), 14, 23–39, 154

Das Man (*see also* the they), 2, 17–18, 28–29, 31, 45, 130–132
Davos debate, 57
Decolonial, 80, 139
Deleuze, Gilles, 8
Dembroff, Robin, 17
Derrida, Jacques, 8, 9, 41, 49, 50, 55, 57, 58, 112, 115, 120
Descartes, Réné (Cartesian), 9, 46, 56, 71
Dialectic/Dialectical, 8, 43, 45, 74, 83, 112–114, 117, 127, 132
Dilthey, Wilhelm, 142
Dionysus, 86–87
Diotima, 85, 118, 152, 174
Discourse, 60, 68–81, 102, 104–109, 114
Discourse (anti-immigration), 79–80
Discourse (pronatalist), 104–109
Discourse (racial), 68–81
Dispersion (see also *Zerstreutheit*), 48, 55–58, 131–133, 138, 157
Docile body, 36
Dreyfus, Hubert, 45
Driesch, Hans, 53
Duggan, Lisa, 63
Dwell/Dwelling, 12, 14, 17, 18, 19, 51, 54, 89, 106, 113, 118, 121, 125, 126, 128, 129, 132–134, 136–140, 142, 145

Earth/world, 54, 114–115
Ecstatic moment/opening, 18, 26, 28–31, 34, 38, 86–87, 92, 111, 119, 131
Education (*see also* pedagogy), 4, 36, 83–95, 139–143
Education (banking systems of), 84–85, 91
Egg donation, 76–77
Ek-stasis (*see also* ecstatic moment/opening), 18, 26, 28–31, 34, 38, 86–87, 92, 119, 131

Elkayam, Jessica, 134
Embodiment, 1, 32, 46, 55–57, 132, 144
Empathic/Empathy, 4, 32, 34–36, 84
Enframing (*see also* calculative thinking, *Gestell*, *Machenschaft*, machinational thinking, positionality, technological thinking), 3, 4, 10–11, 23–25, 33, 35–36, 38, 59–82, 89–90, 104–105, 120, 134, 137, 140, 148, 169
Environment (see also *Umwelt*), 46–48, 51–53, 57, 70–71, 85–86, 88, 92, 128, 131, 133, 144, 158, 163
Epigenetic development, 53
Epistēmē, 73
Epstein, Rachel, 67
Essence (of finitude), 52, 54
Essence (of Germans), 8, 100, 103–108, 114, 141
Essence (of language), 81
Essence (of technology), 64, 66, 68–69, 71, 80–82, 89, 139
Essence (potency of the), 49, 54, 138
Eternal feminine, 99–106
Ethics, 4, 5, 8, 38, 134, 148, 149, 160
Eugenics, 73, 76, 80, 101, 104, 118, 126, 171
Evolution (Darwin), 42, 51–56, 58, 71, 73
Ewegen, Shane, 119
Existential analytic, 5, 41, 44, 52, 112

Facticity, 2, 3, 13, 19, 30, 41–58, 71, 100, 125, 155, 171, 173
False consciousness, 37
Farías, Victor, 6, 108–109, 122, 172
Faye, Emmanuel, 6, 108, 122
Filiation (French context), 59–64, 78, 166

Female temporality, 16
Feminine (as eternal feminine), 99–106
Feminine, the (in language), 4, 14, 110, 113–122, 125, 157–158
Feminine-democratic, 101
Feminist pedagogy, 83–95
Ferrell, Robyn, 67
Fertility, 61, 65–67, 76–77, 84, 161
Fichte, Johann Gottlieb, 120
Finitude, 14–15, 29–30, 34, 52, 54, 84
Fluidity (of sex/gender), 4–5, 12–14, 41–58, 113, 133, 143–146
Foucault, Michel, 8, 68, 81
Four causes (of Aristotle), 72, 128, 136
Fourfold, 128, 136–137, 142, 145
Framework of orientation (see also *repère*), 62–68
Framing (per Butler), 60–65, 68, 75
France (reproductive policy), 59–66, 68, 75–80
Freedom (reproductive), 3, 35, 59–82
Freedom for ground, 18, 30, 39, 46, 49, 52, 54, 56, 132
Freeman, Lauren, 94
Freire, Paulo, 89
Fried, Gregory, 8, 103–104, 113, 128–129
Frye, Marilyn, 135
Fundamental Concepts of Metaphysics: World, Finitude, Solitude, The (GA 29/30), 51–53

Gammage, Jennifer, 131
Gathering (as *Sammeln*, *Sammlung*), 72, 92, 114, 128, 136–137, 142, 145
Genderqueer, 55, 77
Generation (as "one"), 15, 100, 104, 111–123, 126–129, 132

Generation (as passing down), 30, 85–86, 90, 94, 111–123, 126–129
Generation (linked to sexual difference), 42, 43, 50, 54, 56, 60, 62, 85, 111–123
Genesis, 12, 41, 42, 44, 112
Genocide, 126–127, 136
Genos, 42, 126–127, 136
Gentle twofoldness, 15, 50, 104, 111–114, 127, 132
Germanien, 116
Geschlecht, 5, 15, 41, 45, 50, 111–114, 120, 122, 132, 141
Geschlecht (old decaying and new homecoming), 112, 114, 120, 122
Gestell (calculative thinking, enframing, *Machenschaft,* machinational thinking, positionality, technological thinking), 3, 4, 10–11, 23–25, 33, 35–36, 38, 59–82, 89–90, 104–105, 120, 134, 137, 140, 148, 169
Gestell (paradox of), 66
Gewalt, 104
"Ghostly Twilight," 116–117
Gigantic, 126
Glazebrook, Trish, 11, 45, 49–50
Glissant, Édouard, 142
God/gods, 5, 11, 41, 43–44, 73–74, 84, 86, 87, 99, 102, 112, 115, 117
Goebbels, Joseph, 108
Goffe, Tao Leigh, 16
Gosetti, Jennifer Anna, 116, 121
Graybeal, Jean, 119
Greeting, 117, 121–122
Grey, Kimberly, 99
Grosz, Elizabeth, 56
Ground, the/grounding of meaning, 2, 5, 7, 12, 13, 14, 18, 47–49, 51, 52, 54, 56, 58, 73–74, 82, 112–113, 115, 127, 129, 132, 146, 153
Groundlessness, 44, 141–142
Grumet, Madeleine, 83–95
Guattari, Félix, 8
Guenther, Lisa, 15
Guignon, Charles, 45
Guilt, 34–35, 44
Gupta, Charu, 114

Halberstam, Jack, 16
Hale, Jacob, 17
Haraway, Donna, 11
Harding, Sandra, 10, 12, 14, 134, 150
Haugeland, John, 23, 31, 45, 94
Hay, Carol, 89
Health-care system, 38
Hegel, Georg Wilhelm Friedrich, 104, 115, 118
Herida abierta, 132
Hermeneutic(s), 5, 41–58, 71, 84–86, 94, 100, 110, 135
Hermeneutics (of sex/gender facticity), 41–58
Hermes, 84–88
Heroic realism, 101
Heteronormative framework, 2, 63–64, 65–66, 68
Historical awareness, 2, 6, 23, 47, 52
Historical contingency, 1, 4, 9, 13, 67, 92, 113, 131
Historical destiny, 14, 16, 115, 125, 127, 129, 138, 140, 142
Historicity (of beyng and the eternal feminine), 100–105
Hölderlin, Friedrich, 54, 116, 121, 142
Homecoming, 111–112, 114, 118–119, 121–122, 126
Homonationalism, 77–80
Homonormativity, 64

How (as distinguished from whatness), 44–45, 48, 55, 133
Humboldt, Wilhelm von, 88–89
Huntington, Patricia, 8, 116
Husserl, Edmund, 11, 27, 32, 151

Identity/identity politics, 1, 3–4, 7–10, 13–14, 17, 56, 66, 68, 77–80, 107, 109, 113, 127, 135–136, 142, 145–146
Immanence, 14, 85
Immigration, 79–80
Inauthentic care, 18, 37, 44, 48, 92, 128, 159
Inauthentic time, 18, 26, 28, 44
In-between/In-betweenness, 125, 130, 132–133, 135–139, 143–146
Indigenous, 106
Infinitude, 30, 34
Informed consent, 35
Intersubjectivity, 9, 13–17, 24–28, 33, 35, 129
Introduction to Metaphysics (GA 40), 103–104, 120
Irigaray, Luce, 15, 16, 110, 116–117, 157
Islam, 80
Islamo-gauchisme, 80
Israel, 78
IVF, 35, 60, 64–67, 76, 79

Jacob, François, 54
Janssen, Das Ephraim, 50, 138, 139
Jemeinigkeit (*see also* mineness), 27, 45, 49, 93–94, 133, 176
Jouissance, 119
Judeo-Christian origin stories, 4–5, 12, 42–43, 45, 49, 73, 100, 112

Kafer, Allison, 16
Kasun, G. Sue, 135
Käufer, Stephan, 93

Kinship, 72, 75–76, 111, 118
Kisiel, Theodore, 6
Knowles, Adam, 108, 122
Kofman, Sarah, 1022
Körper, 11–12, 26, 32, 42, 47, 56–58, 9
Krell, David, 54
Kristeva, Julia, 8, 119

Lacan, Jacques, 32
Labor (the act of, *see also* childbirth), 14, 23–39, 64–65, 85, 119, 154
Lacoue-Labarthe, Philippe, 108, 122
Laïcité (*see also* secular politics), 61–62, 66
Lamaze, 36–37
La mère qui jouit, 119
Language (ambiguity of), 9, 19, 110, 120, 125
Language (as revelatory), 81–82, 87, 109, 119, 136, 138, 142
Language (capacity for), 52
Language (feminine), 4, 14, 110, 113–122, 125, 157–158
Language (intelligible intersubjectivity), 25, 47, 50, 88–89, 91–92
Language (phallocentric), 16, 115
Latina feminist scholarship, 14, 123, 125, 129–139
Latour, Bruno, 76
Leaping-ahead, 37, 92–93, 159
Leaping-in, 37, 92–93, 159
Lebensphilosophie, 42, 51
Legal gender recognition, 2–3, 60
Leib, 11–12, 26, 32, 42, 47, 56–58, 91–92
Leiben (*see also* bodying forth), 57, 91–94
Leiblichkeit, 58
Lesbian couples (access to ART), 59–64
Liminal space, 138–139, 144–146

Lineage, 50, 100, 113
Lived temporality (of birth), 23–39
Longtin, Rebecca A., 142
Lovin, Clifford, 106
Lugones, Maria, 94, 123, 125, 129–130, 135

Machenschaft (*see also* calculative thinking, enframing, *Gestell*, machinational thinking, positionality, technological thinking), 3, 4, 10–11, 23–25, 33, 35–36, 38, 59–82, 89–90, 104–105, 120, 134, 137, 140, 148, 169
Machinational thinking (*see also* calculative thinking, enframing, *Gestell*, *Machenschaft*, positionality, technological thinking), 3, 4, 10–11, 23–25, 33, 35–36, 38, 59–82, 89–90, 104–105, 120, 134, 137, 140, 148, 169
MacAvoy, Leslie, 15, 30
Manif pour tous, 59, 78, 166
Manliness/masculinist ethos, 8, 101, 116
Marianne (as symbol of France), 79
Markotic, Lorraine, 72
Massey, Heath, 51
Materialist (feminist), 12, 56
Maternal (phenomenology/ontology), 23–39
Maternal (feminine language), 4, 14, 110, 113–122, 125, 157–158
McNeill, William, 121
Medicaid, 17, 24, 37–38, 154
Medical community, 4, 15, 24–26, 31–33, 39
Medicalized birth, 33–39
Medical gaze, 31
Medical infertility, 61, 66, 77
Medical optimization, 36, 64

Meditative thinking, 100, 104–105, 110, 120, 134, 138, 139, 141
Merleau-Ponty, Maurice, 88
Mestiza/Mestizaje, 130–131
Metaphysical Foundations of Logic, The (GA 26, Marburg lecture), 5, 41, 46–56, 100, 111–112, 127
Metaphysical neutrality, 46–56
Metaphysics (of presence), 10, 19, 110, 115, 118, 120
Meyer, Conrad Ferdinand, 106
Midwife, 37–38
Mimesis, 89, 91
Mineness (see also *Jemeinigkeit*), 27, 45, 49, 93–94, 133, 176
Mitchell, Andrew, 81
Mitsein, 4, 16, 27, 50–51, 94, 130, 133
Mood (*see also* affective state, attunement, *Stimmung*), 18–19, 29, 34–35, 47, 84, 86, 92, 100–101, 105–105, 126–127, 130–134, 136, 141, 143, 149, 159
  c.f. *Befindlichkeit*, state-of-mind, 34
Moore, Ian Alexander, 113–114
Moment of vision (see also *Augenblick*), 13, 18, 29–30, 32, 33–35, 38–39, 47, 131–132
Moraga, Cherry, 135
Mother, 15, 31–38, 54, 60–64, 75, 85–89, 99, 100, 105–110, 119–121, 126
Mother's blood, 99–100, 105–109, 120–121, 126
Multiplication, 55, 132–133
Multiplicitous self, 129–135
Multiplicity, 55, 133, 157
Muslim women, 79

Napoleonic code, 78
Natality (*see also* being-toward-birth), 14, 34, 84, 94

National identity (and race), 74, 77–80, 141
Nationalism (France), 60–62, 77–80
Nationalism/National Socialism (Germany), 1, 4, 8, 14, 69, 99–123, 141
Natural childbirth, 33–38
Neoliberalism, 61
Neutral Dasein/Neutral temporal structure (*see also* sex/gender neutrality), 5, 18, 42–58, 63, 92, 107, 111–112, 128, 131–139
New beginning, 109–123, 126, 129
Nietzsche, Friedrich, 70, 87, 101–102, 104–106, 109–110, 114, 120, 122
Nonbinary, 55, 154
Nonnus, 86
Not-being-at-ease (see also *Coatlicue*), 19, 130–132
Nothingness, 13, 18, 29–30, 39

O'Byrne, Anne, 15, 30, 94, 126–127, 136
"On the Essence of Ground" (OEG), 47–48, 54, 112
Ontic concern, 3, 45, 49, 52, 55, 57, 69, 70–71, 75, 134–135, 147
Ontological difference, 1–4, 8–9, 12, 15–16, 41–58, 74–75, 104, 112, 119–120, 137, 147
Ontological holism, 90
Ontology—The Hermeneutic of Facticity (GA 63, Freiburg lecture), 1, 5, 14, 16, 41–46, 49, 100, 112–113, 120
Onto-somatic denial, 9, 85
Orban, Viktor, 79–80
Orientation (queer modes of), 59–64
Origin stories of birth, 9, 12, 42–43, 45, 49, 58, 73, 100, 112
Originary temporality, 17–19

"Origin of the Work of Art" (OWA), 54, 66–67, 107–108, 119–120, 128
Orr, Deborah, 15
Ortega, Mariana, 18, 123, 125, 129–135, 142
Ousia, 72, 135, 137, 147
Overman (see also *Übermensch*), 101–102, 170
Owned choices, 13–14, 18, 25, 28–29, 42, 48, 117, 130–131

Pageau-St-Hilaire, Antoine, 38
Partial enframing, 59–82
Peasant woman, 5–6, 99–100, 105–111, 117–118, 121–122, 126, 139
Pedagogy (*see also* education), 4, 36, 83–95, 139–143
Pelluchon, Corine, 24
Peras, 136–137, 140, 145
Perreau, Bruno, 78
Phallicized whiteness, 67
Phenomenology (of labor), 23–39
Phenomenology (queer), 59–82
Phronesis, 8
Physis, 37, 72–73, 135–137
Pinkwashing, 78
Pitts, Andrea, 138
Plato, 15, 72–73, 85, 111–112, 116–118
PMA pour toutes, 59–62, 77
Poetic work (Trakl), 14, 54, 100, 104, 109–123, 125, 127, 129, 132
Poetics (trans), 14, 19, 123, 125, 138–146
Poetry (danger of ambiguity), 19, 110, 125
Poiēsis, 33–39, 66, 72–73, 16
Poiēsis of birth (*see also* unenframed birth), 33–39, 66, 136, 140, 142
Polemos, 8, 13, 126–129, 150

Politico-poetic, 15, 100, 125
Polt, Richard, 103–104
Population, 74, 79
Positionality (*see also* calculative thinking, enframing, *Gestell*, *Machenschaft*, machinational thinking, technological thinking), 3, 4, 10–11, 23–25, 33, 35–36, 38, 59–82, 89–90, 104–105, 120, 134, 137, 140, 148, 169
Potency of the essence, 49, 54, 138
Potentiality for being, 13, 18, 52, 93, 127, 159
Present-at-hand, 28, 143, 158, 164
Primitive Dasein, 48
Primordial time, 18, 24–34, 44, 49
Primordial time (during labor), 24–34
Procreative freedom, 3, 63
Productivity, 70, 90
Pronatalist discourse, 104–109
Proper cast, 111, 114, 122
Properly queer, 77–79
Projection (as thrown), 17–18, 29–30, 44, 47–49, 71, 155
Puar, Jasbir, 77–80
Public time, 26–31
Purwal, Nirmal, 67

Queer phenomenology, 59–82
"Question Concerning Technology, The" (QCT), 7, 66, 68–69, 89–90, 150
Quijano, Aníbal, 74

Race, 4, 9, 25, 36, 50, 59–60, 68–82, 100, 105–106, 111, 114, 120, 141
Race (as technology), 4, 59, 68–82
Racial breeding, 68–82, 104–105, 118, 120
Racial categories, 76–77
Racial discourse, 68–81

Rawlinson, Mary, 15
Ready-to-hand, 63, 70, 143–144, 158
Remembrance, 109, 121–122, 112
Repère (*see also* framework of orientation), 62–68
Reproductive difference, 11–12, 55–56
Reproductive enframing, 23–39, 59–82, 162
Reproductive freedom, 3, 35, 59–82
Reproductive technology, 3, 15, 17, 24–25, 33–39, 59–82
Resistance, 7, 68, 81–82, 112, 132, 138, 144–146
Resoluteness (*see also* owned choices), 13–14, 18, 25, 28–29, 42, 48, 117, 130–131
Response-ability, 140–142
Revealing/concealing (*see also* alētheia), 10, 64, 68, 72, 110, 129, 150
Rhetoric, 14, 61–62, 77–79, 105, 110, 121
Rift, 115–116, 119–120
Roberts, Dorothy, 75
Rodemeyer, Lanei, 14, 26–28, 30, 33–35
Rootedness, 14, 125–127, 134–136, 143
Roots (blood and soil), 14, 100–101, 105–109, 121, 125–127, 134–136
Rosenberg, Alfred, 121
Royle, Andrew, 143–144
Rubin, Gayle, 2, 15
Ruddick, Sara, 36
Ruether, Rosemary Radford, 112
Russell, Camisha, 68–69, 74–77, 80–82

Sagen, 32, 34, 81, 92, 94, 125
Same-sex marriage, 59, 62, 78, 161
Saving power, 66, 81
Scientism (representational thinking), 11, 16

Schmidt, Ben, 89
Scott, Joan W., 79
Secular politics (see also *laïcité*), 61–62, 66
"Seven-Song of Death," 110
Seely, Stephen, 56
Seinkönnen (see also potentiality for being), 13, 18, 52, 93, 127, 159
Sexual difference, 1, 3–5, 9, 12, 15–16, 41–58, 60–63, 74–75, 78, 104, 112–120, 132
Sex/gender classification 3
Sex/gender facticity (hermeneutics of), 41–58
Sex/gender neutrality (see also neutral Dasein/neutral temporal structure), 5, 18, 42–58, 63, 92, 107, 111–112, 128, 131–139
Sexual selection, 51–54
Shapiro, Meyer, 5–6
Shared time, 24–33
Shame, 34–35
Simondon, Gibert, 56
Singer, T. Benjamin, 64
Site (as manifestation of being), 12, 54, 103, 110, 128, 130, 132–137
Situated knowledges, 10, 47, 134, 138, 145
Solicitude, 18, 37, 47–48, 73, 92–93, 128, 159
Sorge (see also care), 18, 37, 42, 44–50, 52, 58, 63, 128, 131–132, 144, 159
Space invaders, 67
Spatiality, 26, 35, 57, 92
Species being, 44, 51–54, 100, 112
Sperm donation, 60, 63–64, 76–77, 79
Spivak, Gayatri, 10
Standing reserve (see also *Bestand*), 23, 33, 61, 65, 71–72, 84–91, 69, 154, 164

Standpoint epistemology (feminist), 10–14, 16, 150
State-of-mind (see also *Befindlichkeit*), 34
c.f. see affective state, attunement, mood, *Stimmung*, 18–19, 29, 34–35, 47, 84, 86, 92, 100–101, 105–105, 126–127, 130–134, 136, 141, 143, 149, 159
Sterilization, 3, 75
Stimmung (see also affective state, attunement, mood), 18–19, 29, 34–35, 47, 84, 86, 92, 100–101, 105–105, 126–127, 130–134, 136, 141, 143, 149, 159
c.f. *Befindlichkeit*, state-of-mind, 34
Stoler, Ann Laura, 74
Stone, Allison, 15, 30
Strife (earth/world), 114, 128
Strong objectivity, 10, 12, 134
Surrogacy, 61, 64–65, 75, 161
Survival writing, 142
Svenaeus, Fredrik, 14
Symposium, the, 15, 72, 85, 118
Syncopated temporality, 30

Tactical polyvalence of discourse, 68, 81
Taubira Act, 78
Technē, 65–66, 73, 136
Technology, 3, 4, 6, 15, 17, 19, 24–25, 31, 33, 35–38, 59–82, 87, 89, 113, 136, 150
Technology (reproductive), 3, 15, 17, 24–25, 33–39, 59–82
Technological thinking (see also calculative thinking, enframing, *Gestell*, *Machenschaft*, machinational thinking, positionality), 3, 4, 10–11, 23–25, 33, 35–36, 38, 59–82, 89–90, 104–105, 120, 134, 137, 140, 148, 169

Temporal awareness, 2, 6, 23–39, 47, 52
Temporal awareness (during labor/childbirth), 23–39
Temporality, 4, 15–19, 23–39, 44–51, 54, 131
Temporality (authentic), 4, 17–18, 23, 26, 28–39, 44, 48, 131
Temporality (female), 16
Temporality (originary), 17–19
Temporospatial fracturing, 24, 33
They, the (see also *Das Man*), 2, 17–18, 28–29, 31, 45, 130–132
Therezo, Rodrigo, 112, 120
Thomson, Iain, 90, 140
Thrownness, 17, 28–30, 44, 71, 155, 159
  c.f. projection (as thrown), 17–18, 29–30, 44, 47–49, 71, 155
Thrusts of being, 103–104, 106, 108, 120
Time (as clock time), 15, 18, 23–39
Time (as public time), 26–31
Time (as shared time), 24–33
Time reckoning, 23–39, 42
Time reckoning (during labor/childbirth), 23–39
Trakl, Georg, 14, 54, 100, 104, 109, 110–123, 125, 127, 129, 132
Transcendence, 14, 46–49, 52–58, 115, 131–132
Trans bodies and bioethics legislation, 17, 59–68, 78
Trans bodies (hypervisibility of), 3, 138, 145
Transgender sublime, 64
Trans poetics, 14, 17, 19, 123, 125, 138–146
Trawny, Peter, 108, 122
Twofoldness (of the sexes), 15, 50, 104, 111–114, 127, 132

Übermensch (*see also* Overman), 101–102, 170
Uexküll, Jacob von, 53
Umwelt (*see also* environment), 46–48, 51–53, 57, 70–71, 85–86, 88, 92, 128, 131, 133, 144, 158, 163
Unenframed birth (see also *poiēsis* of birth), 33–39, 66, 136, 140, 142
Ursprung, 54
Utility (education), 89–91, 139–143
Utility (language), 81
Utility (future use), 11, 23, 38, 64, 69–72, 81, 89–91, 104, 139–143

Vitalism, 52–53

Warnes, Mathias, 87
Warren, Karen, 15
Water birth, 26, 36–38
Weiss, Helene, 50
Whatness (of existence), 42, 45, 48, 54, 58
White feminism, 75
Will to power, 70–71, 104–105
Winnubst, Shannon, 67
Wolin, Richard, 6, 108, 122
Woman question, the, 1–7, 14, 59, 77, 113
Wooten, Carrigan, 87
Work of conscience, 36–37
World-forming, 42, 45–49, 52, 57–58, 115, 126, 128–135, 138, 146, 158
Worldlessness, 126–127
World time, 18
World-traveling, 129–138
Wynter, Sylvia, 73–74

Young, Iris Marion, 14, 30

Zeigen, 32, 34, 81, 92, 94, 125

Zerstreutheit (*see also* dispersion), 48, 55–58, 131–133, 138, 157
Ziarek, Ewa, 16

Zimmerman, Michael, 52, 115
Zollikon Seminars, 1, 11, 32, 57
Zurn, Perry, 14, 17, 19, 123, 125, 138–146

www.ingramcontent.com/pod-product-compliance
Lightning Source LLC
Chambersburg PA
CBHW021841220426
43663CB00005B/344

www.ingramcontent.com/pod-product-compliance
Lightning Source LLC
Chambersburg PA
CBHW051809230426
43672CB00012B/2665